# PLAY WITH YOUR HEARTS

# PLAY WITH YOUR HEARTS

The Broughton Caps 1970 Championship Season

**David Riggs**

MCKINNON
PRESS
Durham, NC

MCKINNON PRESS
2704 Bexley Avenue
Durham, NC 27707
(919) 943-6501

Special discounts are available on bulk orders of this book. To inquire, please contact David Riggs at davidlriggs@gmail.com.

*This book is dedicated to EVERY player on the
1970 Broughton State Championship Football Team.*

# Table of Contents

# INTRODUCTION

I suppose that when you get older, you may think, "What will I be remembered for?" When you're young, these thoughts never cross your mind as the hour glass of life has just started and there is only a small pile that's accumulated. But when you're older, you begin to see more at the bottom of the glass and much less at the top. So – "What will people remember about me?" Maybe that really doesn't matter to anyone, but for those who witnessed it and for those who were directly involved, the season of 1970 for the Broughton Caps is one many will never forget.

When I was a younger kid, the Broughton Caps were huge. They had stars, they won big games and they played in one of the shrines of football in Raleigh. Let's see. There was speedy Al Godwin who later played at the University of Kentucky. Lee Coleman was an All-American defensive lineman, and Sonny Leach was a sure handed end. They both played and sometimes starred at the University of Tennessee. Then there was Bill Bradford who quarterbacked the Caps and later had a distinguished career at UNC as a defensive end. He was the captain of the Tar Heels that year as well. But what was so cool about all these "heroes" of ours, is that they played on Friday nights at Riddick Stadium where on Saturdays, the host N.C. State Wolfpack battled on the collegiate level. I will never forget going to the NCSU vs. UNC game with Jim Lumsden. We must have been all of 10 or 12 years old, didn't have a ticket or any money for that matter, but our parents dropped us off at Riddick to our assurances that we would get into the game and be just fine. We did get in the game as a last minute fan had to leave and gave two tickets to two forlorn boys sitting on a wall with their heads down in disappointment. That day Jim and I not only got in the stadium to watch the game, we saw Roman Gabriel and company, chased extra point attempts at the field house and begged for chin straps after the game from the players. We even got some. The point is, these were our idols and we dreamed to be in their place one day. The college thing was a gas but the high school games were the ones we felt a part of. After all, we knew these guys and sometimes we played on their teams, albeit as the youngest and lowest on the totem pole as a team member.

Back in 1965, the Country Club Hills Bulldogs were State runners up in midget football. No easy task when there was the "Little Orangemen of Gastonia" in your way. But some of those kids did play for Broughton, and by God, we knew them! We played with them and everything. That's what we wanted to become. Because these guys would go on to Broughton, wear the purple and gold and play in Riddick against the best teams that eastern North Carolina had to offer.

Wilson Fike and Durham High were the bests, I recall, but Goldsboro, Winston-Salem, Greensboro, Wilmington New Hanover, New Bern and almost any Fayetteville team could be dangerous during any year. I will never forget the Broughton team playing Durham High. It must have been about 1968 or so and Durham had quarterback Brad Evans (who later played both football and basketball at Duke) leading their team. I don't know, but I think they may have lost once, maybe not, and Broughton had a stud team that had lost once at the most. It was played at Durham County Stadium and all us kids went. These were our stars from Raleigh, and we just knew they were the best. Durham won the game on a spectacular play from Evans, so what can you say? How about all the guys we had coming back? Surely we'd get them next year. And frankly, I don't recall if we did or not, but that was one heck of a game, and Broughton had another great year after that. I know they were at least 8-2 and I think they lost one of their last games in the playoffs and it was an upset at that for them to get beat that year.

Such were the memories of many young boys as we grew through our adolescence in Raleigh. I know I am not alone in my memories because these were high school kids we idolized and their feats were legendary to us. Maybe one day, we could play for Broughton and share in that glory. What a dream.

But times change, and back in the late sixty's and early seventies, it was no different. Raleigh was growing and new schools were needed. In 1969, Raleigh Sanderson was opened and much of the promise of Broughton football went with it. The team, a good one, was split. Half of the stars went to Sanderson and half stayed at Broughton. Most people thought it to be the end of the powerful Broughton Caps. They had been split and all talent dispersed.  How could they ever regain the past prominence and respect they once had throughout the state? Other towns were much smaller, and school expansion was years to come. Wilson Fike began to rule. Someone named Carlester Crumpler came along and no one had ever seen anything like him.  At about 6' 3" and 225 lbs. with speed to burn, he was the State Champion at the 115 high hurdles and ran on all the sprint teams as well. Wilmington had good teams as did Goldsboro, Rocky Mount and a lot of others. Surely Broughton and all of Raleigh had lost importance and impact on the high school football scene east of Winston-Salem.

When my group was growing up during the midget football ranks, we always had a very good team. We were always small but gutsy and once in a while had enough talent to be a true threat. Midget football is for the very young. I think you had to weigh under 120 lbs. and could be no older than 13. Eighth grade had to be the last year of eligibility. My team was Country Club Hills and for a while we were very good. As time went by and the younger kids (us) became the older kids, we still had our moments in the sun. Then one year, yes, one Saturday morning, along came Pepsi Cola. Man, these guys had hair on their legs and everything. I swear Doug Murray was shaving. They had tall guys, big guys, fast guys and big reputations. I would read in the paper about games where Jim Bass would score 5 touchdowns and they would beat a team by 40 points or more when we may have beat that same team by 10. And most of those games Bass never played in the 4th quarter. Needless to say, it was a massacre. Just ask Rick Hunter. He had Doug Murray in front of him all morning and that was a mess. Even their younger guys were tough. I don't think Larry Otto could have been more than 11 and he scared us to death. He was everywhere. But times change and foes become teammates and bonds grow between young friends.

At Daniels Jr. High, we got most of the Pepsi group and the Country Club Hills group as well. Nobody beat us. Most of the time it wasn't even close. Martin Jr. High had a big team with a lot of good players (many of which had already become good friends) and Daniels beat them up good, 28-0. I know you Martin guys remember. It was a Saturday morning and we played at Devereux Meadow. Little did we know at the time, that would be the home field for most of us through our high school years.

At the time, Carter Finley Stadium had just been built and the old Riddick Stadium was needed for space. The former home of the Broughton Caps (and many a kid's dream) became a parking lot.

Melding Two Classes

The junior class in 1970 may have been a "lucky" class. As "seniors" in Jr. High, Daniels was 7-0 and Martin was the next best team. When we all went to high school, practically all of Daniels and a lot of Martin went to Broughton, with some of Martin having to go to Sanderson HS. But basically we had the nucleus of 2 pretty good football teams from which to build on once we started high school. Even though the Varsity "stole" Jim Bass from us, our JV team at Broughton was undefeated, and that felt like everything was continuing as it should for us. This feeling even stemmed back prior to Jr. High football. Pepsi and Country Club Hills (sorry, Dr. Pepper) were usually the best teams in Midget football and that's where most of the players of that class came from. So there was a deep-seated experience of winning that seemed to bind us all.

Although a lot of the same can be said of the senior class of 1971, it just wasn't quite the same. They were good guys from winning teams, it just seemed like the underclassmen always had it a little better and were just a little more successful. The senior class inherited the end of the declining structure called "Broughton Football" their junior year. The coaches were a shell of what Broughton was used to in the Clyde Walker days. Though they remained a good team for a year or so after Walker, with the advent of Sanderson and the coaching retirements, etc., it seemed that a general decline was inevitable. The news media would later pick up on this near the end of the 1969 season.

Don't get me wrong, they were not losers by any means. In fact, as sophomores, we were scared to death of them. Occasionally the JV would scrimmage the Varsity. Now they had our best player in Bass already up with them (they really needed his help too), so we could say it wasn't a fair fight. But regardless, they could murder us at will on the field. When you look back on it, that year the Varsity got a lot of help from their junior class. It just was a hard time for them to live up to the past. It had been that way since 1968 when Sanderson opened and Broughton was split. We, as a school, never seemed to get over the hump. That year the Varsity went 3-7 and won their last 2 games to do it. But every game was close except for one game against Wilson Fike.

When the 1970 season started, change was definitely in the air. We had a whole new set of coaches and they were YOUNG!!! It sometimes felt like our older brothers were now our coaches. Robbie Evans may as well have been. He was a former Cap star who went on to star at NC State. Many of us knew him personally and he was one of those we had idolized as kids. Having that new staff may have well been the single most binding thing for both players and coaches alike. Broughton desperately needed a change and here they were. I think we all believed we could win. We could change Broughton and recreate the atmosphere that had been missing. We may not have really spent any time actually thinking that, but it sounds good, and in the back of our minds I really think the thought was there.

These coaches were unlike anything most of us could ever remember. When it was time to do drills, they did them better than us. When Coach Riggs would call for neck isos (done standing, you bent forward with your helmet on until it rested on the ground, then you twisted to look left then right), he would be right there doing it with us with no helmet. We'd run in place and hit the ground on command, get up and start running again with Riggs and Evans doing it right along with us. Then you'd have to crab walk several yards, summersault and get up running. Yes, they'd do that too. Now if the coaches can do it, we damn well better be able to. This was definitely a new gig now and nobody but us knew it. It was almost like a bunch of really good midget league players had finally come back together and it was our time to show what we could do.

*- David Turner, Quarterback, 1970 Broughton Caps*

David Turner

The Culture of the Times, 1970

What a year for the Caps. Football season came after our age group's own "summer of love," sort of, meaning when the "hippie" movement made it so deep into the culture that it hit us in this school in Raleigh. Said another way, it was when the long hair appeared as it had never before. It wasn't just the hair, it was a tidal wave of attitude that changed everything. It was far more important than any fad in history, and its impact on high school-age students was greater than anything except Pearl Harbor.

It was like someone hit the reset button, and everyone for a moment was on the same plane socially. This is inconceivable today at Broughton where the cliques form in elementary school and are as hard as concrete by the time the kids get to high school. Unfortunately, some traditions get swept away, and something else occurred; those who were on top before resisted for a time, but it was a tide and it swept all before it. An example of one casualty was the Cavaliers, one of the eight or so social clubs - gangs -which had been around since the early fifties (Pistol Pete Maravich was a Cavalier, as opposed to a Casual, an Elite or an Esquire) and were a symbol of the old regimes. These "gangs" were really important before—now they sort of dissipated without any organized effort or movement. Why bother being in a social club? Everyone was in the Age of Aquarius and we had the Beatles, the Stones, Led Zeppelin and Mothers of the Hutch. Everything was new again, and somehow a social club to highlight and indicate one's social superiority (amongst 18-year olds) seemed kind of unnecessary.

And for those of us who loved football, we finally had a coach, in fact a whole new set of coaches, men who were very good coaches, and also young men with a clue about what we were like, and what we had gone through before, and who understood that though Broughton had been losing for years, it wasn't because we had bad athletes. I will never forget David Riggs taking a look at me, Shaner, Doug Murray, and a few others of the longer-haired set and saying the most brilliant thing that anyone ever said in my presence, "I don't give a darn what your hair looks like, so long as you are giving me 100% effort at all times." SAY WHAT?

It is hard today to convey just how revolutionary this was at the time. Our parents were still watching the "bad" Jesse Helms on TV each and every night saying that we all were threats to the American Way. It was the single most brilliant decision in a tactical situation I ever saw made and FROM THAT MOMENT the ball was rolling, which culminated in the State 4A Championship. We went at the pre-training period like madmen – meeting voluntarily on hot summer afternoons to run sprints and to lift weights. When practices finally began, hallelujah! It was fun again! I remember pulling my VW beetle, which had an 8-track and a big speaker system, down by the door to the locker room alongside the gym every day, and putting the speakers in the dressing rooms to pump in Crosby, Stills & Nash and to pump up the team for practice. It was awesome, baby!

*- Jim Lumsden, Senior Linebacker, 1970 Broughton Caps*

Jim Lumsden

"It is amazing what can be accomplished when no one cares who gets the credit."

As I, David Riggs, have gotten closer to the "three scores and ten" years of my life on this earth, I reflect about the key influences in my life. I have been very blessed and fortunate to have coached football in six different decades. I have been privileged to have been born into a family and a country that gave me freedom to succeed in anything I wanted to. I have known many people who have been a great influence on my life as well as others.

My dad was an influential family medical doctor who, along with my mother and siblings, encouraged and supported me in all that I did as a child. I was fortunate to have played football under some wonderful and innovative coaches such as Earle Broome (high school), Bill Dooley, Bill Hickman, and Ace Parker (college). I have met and learned a lot from other coaches such as Moyer Smith, Grant Teaff, Ken Sparks, Tony

Dungy, Homer Rice, and Dean Smith. I was lucky over the years to have coached against and with many coaches on the high school level who I learned from like Bill Shirley, Bobby Poss, Ken Browning, Bob Jamieson, and Russell Blunt, I was able to work with many exceptional assistant coaches, too numerous to name here, who helped me and influenced me to be a better coach and person. I have learned a lot from many players who I played with in high school and college, and I have continued to glean from players who I have been privileged to coach over the years at seven different high schools across North Carolina. Also I have been influenced and continue to be shaped by Jesus and his teachings that have helped me become all that is good in my life.

I have played football and have been associated with many games, programs, places, and organizations that have to do with football and athletics. I played in the "Big House" at Michigan, the Ohio State Buckeye stadium, Air Force Academy, Notre Dame, and other college stadiums across this great country. I was fortunate to have coached in the N.C. East-West All Star game, the N.C. Shrine game, and I have been part of coaching staffs that have won several conference championships since I began coaching in 1968.

Out of all of these people, coaches, programs, and associations, the one thing people still want to talk about is the 1970 North Carolina 4-A State Football Champions. In fact, there have been many famous and hard-working coaches across the state of North Carolina who were better coaches than me who have never won a State Championship. I wish I could say that it was my football wisdom, intelligence, innovative skills, and football knowledge that have made me well-known in the area of football. However, that is not the case. Many people know David Riggs because of his association with the 1970 Broughton Caps football team.

I think it was Maya Angelou who said that there is no greater agony than bearing an untold story inside of you. Stephen King said, "Some stories cry out in such loud voices that you write them to shut them up." This book is one of those stories for me. It is about more than just a football team that won a championship and esteemed their coaches. It is about people and families and community that exemplified life, values, goals, and dreams and were successful.

I am writing this book in honor of the young men from Raleigh

Broughton High School who participated and were part of the 1970 North Carolina State High School Football Championship. This was a different time and place than 2016. I began coaching in 1968 as a graduate assistant at the University of North Carolina in Chapel Hill under Coach Bill Dooley. Many people have asked me how football has changed between 1968 and 2016 and what are the biggest changes in coaching athletes in that time. I hope this book will also help answer some of those questions.

At its core, **football is still running, blocking, catching, and tackling – playing with heart and hustle.**

I am writing this story as well because my experiences with this team have helped make me a better person and a better high school coach. I used so many things I learned from this particular football team in my entire coaching career and life. I hope that every individual who reads this book may be inspired in some small way by the principles or stories shared.

Also, this book is for all the thousands of high school coaches who have made a difference in young kids' lives over the years. I would say that 90% of high school coaches are great people and try to make a difference in people's lives. They put in many hours of hard work and sacrifices while they are coaching. They often get criticized by parents, students, fans, sports writers and the public because of plays they call, games they lose, and the way their players perform. But they persevere, trying not to allow criticism to plague them because they are coaching for the kids and the love of the game of football. So I hope this will be encouraging in some way for coaches and all who read it.

There is no doubt that winning football games is important, and that seems to be the major emphasis in any competitive sport. However, I feel that what is really learned from football and most sports are "life lessons" along with establishing personal relationships with others. I can honestly say that the primary thing that means more to me and is most prominent in my mind after coaching for more than 30 years is the relationships developed with coaches, players, managers, trainers, parents, and administrations. This is not to say that the competitiveness and winning are not important, but what I remember most as I reflect over my coaching career is relationships. Developing true relationships is one of the keys to life, and I hope to share some of the relationships that characterized this football team.

To cite one player, one coach, without recognizing the entire team would be an injustice. So many people gave of themselves to make this team successful. So often a coach makes a difference in players' lives, but in this case all the players on this Caps team made the difference in the coaches' and fans' lives at Broughton High School and in the Raleigh community.

# PROLOGUE

It was a beautiful and sunny Thanksgiving Saturday fall afternoon at Carter-Finley Stadium in Raleigh, North Carolina. There was a slight breeze and a great day for high school football.

It was halftime of the 1970 4-A North Carolina State High School Football Championship game between the Broughton Caps and the Olympic Trojans. We were ahead 7-0 with only 24 minutes to go in the game of our life. As the coaches ended up their group sessions with the team and any change of strategy for the second half, the team was getting ready to go out to try to finish the season with a victory and win the State Championship.

As we gathered near the exit door, one of our players, Larry Height said, "We can't let up and lose this ball game!" Out of instinct, I rushed to him and grabbed him by his shoulder pads and lifted him up off the floor against the wall, and with tears in my eyes, I hollered, "Do not use that word LOSE! You have all worked too hard and too long for us to lose this ball game! No losing, just win – let's go!!"

What happened? Who were these 15, 16, 17, 18 year-old boys who had given so much time to each other and to this team? What were some of the down times, the up times, the struggles and hurdles that came along with this unforgettable journey of coaches, players, managers, trainers, parents, and community? Was there one key to the turnaround in this championship season? Was it luck, skill, leadership or all three?

What did the individuals who participated in this "dream season" of football learn from it? What does it teach us about life? What do they remember and where are they now? Let me tell you the story.

# CHAPTER 1
My Football Background

"Discipline yourself and others will not have to."
- John Wooden

Broughton High School

So much of my life has been involved in football. It is a great team sport. I would say football is the greatest team sport there is. It cannot be about one player or a couple of players. It is about the whole team.

I have known this ever since growing up in Drexel and Morganton in the western part of the state of North Carolina, where I played all sports including football. As a young kid, I played a lot of sandlot football and learned a lot of "life lessons." Even though we were not organized as a team. I would gather with my childhood friends and we would play every Saturday in the fall all day long. We were our own referees, coaches, cheerleaders, and rule makers. It was here where I learned to be tough, assertive, and competitive. We often would play with older boys in the neighborhood, and it was not a place for wimps. I learned about perseverance, toughness, pride, unselfishness, relationships, and myself. I am afraid today that many young people often miss out on how to be leaders, how to work out problems, and how to get along with others, because they are always being organized into teams and told how to play the game, told when they score, told when they commit fouls, and how they should treat each other. They can learn how to do a lot of this by playing together without an "outsider" telling them.

After moving to Morganton, N. C. in the fifth grade, I played all sports at Morganton High School. My very best friends were the guys who I played sports with. We grew up together in this small town and did everything together. It was on the football field where we learned a lot about ourselves.

I was awarded a full athletic scholarship to play football at UNC in Chapel Hill in 1964. I was fortunate to be able to get an education and also play a game I loved. Even though the college game was much more sophisticated and complex, it was still a game, and I loved it. I became a starter at running back my sophomore year at Carolina. During those years at Carolina, in addition to playing against Michigan in Ann Arbor, Ohio State under Coach Woody Hayes, and Notre Dame under Ara Parsegian, I was able to get an education, travel to places I had never been, and meet people I would never have had the chance to meet if it was not for football.

The spring of 1967 brought a new head football coach to Carolina. He was Bill Dooley from Mississippi State University. He had played at the University of Georgia and was a young 33 year-old assistant coach when he was hired by Carolina.

Football began changing in Chapel Hill with the arrival of Coach

Dooley and his assistant coaches. He was a very discipline-oriented coach. I remember the first meeting we had with him in a Carmichael Auditorium classroom. He walked in and told us in January of 1967 that there were a lot of lazy football players on our team and that was going to change. He told us we would have to work hard and decide if we really wanted to play football at Carolina. That was fine with me because I wanted to be part of a winning program, and I was confident Coach Dooley was going to make us a winner.

We went through a difficult and trying spring practice. It was a very strict and high-disciplined spring practice on and off the field. It became mandatory that we get up and eat breakfast and go to all classes. Our attendance would be checked daily, and if we missed any of these, we would be up running at 6 a.m. the next morning. We were held accountable for everything we were part of, from our education to football practice to our behavior off the field.

I learned more about discipline than I did about football that spring. My nature was to do what I was told and to do it the best I could possibly do. I had learned a lot of that from my dad as he had held me responsible and accountable for chores and responsibilities he gave me when I was growing up.

Zemaitis, Coach Dooley and Me

# CHAPTER 2
## Decision to Attend Graduate School and Coach Football

"Intelligence plus character - that is the true goal of education."
- Dr.. Martin Luther King Jr.

As I was finishing up my college education with a major in history during the spring of 1968, I did not know what I wanted to do for a living. I had been involved in Fellowship of Christian Athletes all through my college years. It had influenced me as a person and introduced me to the Bible and to Jesus and his teachings. The only other interest I had at that time was football. Coach Moyer Smith, one of the Carolina coaches, suggested to me that I should look into graduate work in education and talk to Coach Dooley about being a graduate assistant football coach. This way I could get a Masters Degree in teaching history and get some experience in coaching on the college level. I talked to coach Dooley about this, and he offered me a position on the football staff as a graduate assistant.

I began taking graduate classes in education in the summer of 1968 and planned to student teach during the 1968-69 academic year. This program would also include coaching the freshman football team in the fall of 1968. I was excited about having this position even though it would mean many hours of studying, writing papers, attending morning classes, as well as being a full-time assistant football coach. I did not know what I was getting into, but I had no clue what I wanted to do professionally, so I accepted the position.

I lived in the dorm in the fall of 1968 and was responsible for the freshmen halls, curfews, discipline, breaking down films for varsity coaches, coaching the freshmen offensive backs and scouting high school seniors for recruiting for next season. Coach Moyer Smith was the Head Freshmen coach and he was helpful in teaching me many things about football and college coaching.

I was around a lot of the varsity coaches on a daily basis in meetings, meals, and on the field. It was a little strange for me in some ways having just played for them the previous season.

The coaches were very good to me and taught me a lot. I was included in all areas of coaching, and I was a little intimidated by being included in staff meetings, position meetings, coaches dressing and locker room, etc. where I was accepted as part of the "official" staff. Most, if not all, of these coaches began the same way I did as a graduate assistant on a college staff. To change clothes, play handball, talk football, eat meals, with the same coaches who were coaching and hollering at me the previous year was quite shocking and  a bit intimidating. However, as time went on, I felt less and less awkward and uncomfortable.

One of the areas I did not like very much was the recruiting aspect of college football. I was going to class, coaching, and then leaving on Friday afternoons to go see high school football games and recruit kids that I was just a few years older than. The travel was also tough because I would rarely get back to Chapel Hill before midnight on Friday and then had to get up early Saturday mornings to pick up recruits at the airport and to entertain them and their parents before the football game that afternoon. On Saturday nights after the games, I would go out to eat with a recruit and his family and take him out afterwards to parties on campus. When the games were away from Chapel Hill, I would usually leave on Friday afternoons and recruit the Washington, D.C. area and see high school games on Friday night, Saturday afternoons and nights, and then return early Sunday mornings to Chapel Hill.

I enjoyed seeing a lot of things work behind the scenes in coaching. UNC football supporters and alumni would often show up during the week to visit the football offices. Mr. Bob Osterneck, who was from Lumberton, N.C., would show up several mornings during the week with all kinds of doughnuts and pastries for the staff. Other people may bring coaches new shoes, sweaters, and other items of clothing to wear. Many of these people would stay around for practices and talk to coaches and players. They felt like they were part of building the football program and were proud to be associated with Tarheel football.

In all the staff meetings and plans for practices, I never heard my fellow coaches degrading players other than they may say that "so and so" is not making it and will probably not help the football team. I do not remember any coach saying anything about "running players off" or forcing players to leave the program. This surprised me because I had felt like they had abused some people my senior year. There had been some writing about this in the newspapers in the summer, and some former players even accused some of the assistant coaches of abusing and mistreating them in practice. I, as a coach on staff, never saw or heard anything like this during the two years I was on staff as a graduate assistant at UNC. Of course, I was primarily working with the freshmen football players.

Remember this was at the end of the 1960's, and a lot happened during this decade that changed America. The United States had gotten heavily involved in the Vietnam War. There were the assassinations of John F. Kennedy, Martin Luther King Jr., Malcolm X, and Robert F. Kennedy. There was Woodstock, the introduction of drugs to the white middle class, "being free from authority," the Civil Rights movement, and many changes were taking place in American society. Even though I was living in the middle of all of this, most of it went over my head because I was interested in playing football and getting a degree and moving on with my life. I did not give much thought to all that had happened in the '60's because I was only interested in myself.

I remember going to class during the mornings working on my MAT degree in education and then spending the rest of my time coaching and working on football. Time was not something I had a lot of for myself, but I enjoyed it all.

Dr. Jerry Unks and Dr. Blackburn were two professors in the MAT program who were very helpful and challenging to me in graduate school. I began to see a lot of prejudices in society that I had never thought about that much. For the first time in my life, I began to think for myself outside of sports. Studying and reading about Black History and taking some Black History classes opened up my mind to many things that had gone on in our country and my life. Having been brought up in a segregated society, I had had very little knowledge about the things that had happened to black people in America, much less in other countries. I never gave it much thought since I was so involved in "me and my athletics."

Growing up as a child, I was very fortunate to have had Elizabeth Jenkins (Biba to me) in my life. Biba was 16 years old when she began to work for our family looking after the Riggs children. She had a loving influence on my life as well as my sisters and brother. Biba was a young black mother who had a lot of compassion for all people, and she seemed to always be happy and content. She also stood up for herself, but was sensitive to other peoples' feelings.

Biba was my only contact with black people until I became a teenager and started playing cards and occasionally sneaking to play golf on back holes with the black caddies at Mimosa Hills golf club. She exhibited integrity and discipline in her life and passed that on to me. I remember one time, when I was about 8 years old, the boys in the neighborhood were playing ball in our backyard in Drexel. We were choosing teams and we always used the phrase "Any miny minny mo, catch a nigger by the toe, if he hollers let him go, any miny minny mo." That is how we chose teams back then.

Biba came over and asked, "David, what did you say?"

I repeated the phrase. She asked me what a nigger was. I told her I did not know, and I didn't. I was just repeating the phrase. She said, "Why not say rabbit instead of nigger?"

From then on that is what I did. I just substituted "rabbit" for "nigger." In her own quiet way, she taught me to be careful of words I use. I never forgot that lesson.

Another learning experience in our lives was one summer we were on our way to Cherry Grove beach as a family to spend a week vacation. Biba would always go with us and stayed in the maid's room at the cottage we were renting for the week. We stopped at a place in South Carolina to eat lunch and we went in to order our food. The owner said we could order, but Biba would have to go in the back to eat. My dad said, "Well, if you don't let her eat with us then we are not eating." We all got up and left.

During my two years of graduate school, as I was reading about the mistreatment of blacks in America, I began to seriously take it into my brain and heart and see how unfair the discrimination had been over the years and in the 1960's. I wondered how I could have been so ignorant about all of this. Yet, if there is no education about these things, what else can one expect? It was like "out of sight, out of mind." I began to have a yearning and desire to help disadvantaged people, especially black people. I had no idea where this would take me, but I was open to God guiding me.

As I began my graduate assistant coaching at UNC, I also began my student teaching at Guy B. Phillips Junior High School. In 1968, the Chapel Hill city schools were being integrated for the first time in history.

I taught a young black girl in the 8th grade, and I visited her along with several students in their home in Chapel Hill. It was the first time I had visited a black student and her parents in their home, and she told me later I was the first white teacher to come to her home. She later became a professor in the Afro-American Department at UNC. Her name was Charlene Register. In April of 2013, I was able to have lunch with her in Chapel Hill. We visited a couple hours and talked a lot about her time in junior high school. I also went by to see her mother, who is 89 and lives in the same house Charlene grew up in. I had a wonderful visit, and she remembered me coming by as Charlene's teacher over 40 years ago.

As I think back about my student teaching days, I remember I had a lot of confidence due to being prepared well by my graduate MAT professors. I also felt like I knew what students wanted in a teacher because we, as graduate students, talked a lot about what students wanted and needed from teachers. I always remember that my favorite teachers were the ones who listened and maintained good discipline in the classroom. If not, very little learning ever took place. I wore a tie (which I hated and still do today) and tried to look and act professional as I began my teaching career at Guy B. Phillips Junior High School. I did my student teaching under Mrs. Abernathy, who was a superb teacher and mentor. I was able to observe how she interacted with the students. She was firm, but gentle at the same time. She really cared about the students learning and getting along with others. I was not sure if I wanted to teach for the rest of my life, but I did enjoy seeing kids learn and grow.

I did learn by the end of the year of student teaching that I did not want to stay with the Junior High School age group. I thought I would prefer working with high school students. I loved the interaction with students and getting to know them. I had always enjoyed history and social studies, so I knew I would enjoy teaching it to other people. One of the best ways I remember learning in school was asking questions and discussing different topics, so I was interested in leading any classroom in learning and discussion.

In June of 1969, Marie, actually my 5th grade girlfriend, and I were married. I had decided to finish my Masters in Education and be a graduate assistant coach again the following fall of 1969. We were both in graduate school getting our education paid for and had very little money. I had not thought a lot about how we would make a living when we got out of school. I know I had talked to Moyer Smith and Academic Advisor Bill Cobey who shared a lot of ideas on coaching and teaching in high school based on their experiences doing that before they came back to join the football staff at UNC. Moyer suggested after I finished my Masters in the fall of 1969 that I start looking around for high school jobs or stay on at UNC with Coach Dooley and stay in college coaching. As I look back at those choices, they were major decisions that would direct my life for the future. I did not worry about it because we did have trust in God that He would work it out for us.

# CHAPTER 3
Accepting the Broughton Job and the Advancement School

"A good teacher or coach must not only understand others, but himself or herself as well."
- John Wooden

Principals Bill Blackburn, Joel Long, Richard Jewell

Coaching freshmen football, recruiting, and sitting in on coaches' meetings taught me an enormous amount of football and exposed me to many Carolina people, all of which has helped me over the years and given me a lot of friends. However, I also began to see that football on the college level was too much of a business for me, and I began to think about teaching and coaching on the high school level.

After the 1969 football season was over and Coach Dooley and his staff began to make some positive changes at UNC, I was still thinking about high school. I went to the NCAA Coaches clinic in Washington, D.C. with the UNC coaching staff. All through the 1960's, Coach Clyde Walker was a famous high school coach from Raleigh Broughton, an esteemed school with a very rich football tradition, and Coach Dooley had persuaded him to leave high school coaching and work at Carolina beginning in 1968.

One morning at the clinic, Coach Walker asked me if I would be interested in high school coaching. He said that the Broughton High School head football coaching position was open, and he wanted to know if I would be willing to consider the job. I told him I definitely would. I had already been thinking about what I might do in the future.

My days as a graduate assistant coach at UNC had been more than full. It was a treat for all of us coaches to start almost each morning having coffee with donuts brought to us by "alumni supporters." When I worked as a graduate assistant at UNC, we would usually meet as a staff, break up into specific position meetings, and then our Freshmen staff would meet. Then we would eat lunch at the training table, and go back and watch some film before getting dressed for practice. However, there was very little time to get to be around the players off the field, and I know, as a player myself, I had wanted to feel closer to my coaches.

I will never forget that one of the main things I learned from Coach Bobby Collins was asking players to your home for visits. After my senior year playing at Carolina, Coach Collins asked me and a couple other seniors to eat dinner one evening at his home in Chapel Hill. I remember visiting and eating with his family and thoroughly enjoying it all. I asked myself, boy, this is neat, but why in the world did you not do this sooner? I thought how great this would have been if he had asked me over to do this while I was playing for him during the football season. I truly believe it would have made us closer as player and coach.

That experience stayed with me for years. When and if I began a high school coaching career, I resolved to be more involved with my players and really try to get to know them, a tall order with a team of at least 50-70 young men. Being personal with players cannot help but build closer relationships. Since football was a game, and I knew it was a good teacher of life, high school coaching and teaching interested me more at this time in my life than the idea of working my way up the ladder in the college ranks. So I immediately felt intrigued by the possibility of the Broughton High School coaching position.

When I returned from the NCAA clinic in Washington, D.C., Marie and I discussed at length the Broughton position. I set up an interview with Joel Long, the assistant principal and athletic director at Broughton. Joel had attended East Carolina Teachers College in the 1950's where he played baseball. After graduating from East Carolina, he took a teaching and coaching job in Cary, N.C. (population 4,000 at that time compared to over 100,000 today) for two years and then in 1959, he joined Clyde Walker at Broughton as an assistant coach. Broughton won the state championship in 1963. After coaching a few years, Joel was appointed the Athletic Director and Assistant Principal at Broughton. Following the 1967 season, Coach Walker went to UNC to be Coach Bill Dooley's head recruiter.

There had been some problems at Broughton after Coach Walker had departed to UNC. Coach Stutts, who was appointed the head coach at Broughton after Coach Walker left, became upset about student assignments in the Raleigh school system. Several football players and athletes were being re-assigned from Broughton to Sanderson High School, which was opening in 1968. There were only four high schools in Raleigh at the time (Enloe, Ligon, Broughton, and Sanderson). Coach Stutts felt like it was unfair and spoke against the school board members who were making the decisions about student assignments. He decided to resign from coaching football at Broughton.

Coach Buddy Stewart was named the interim head football coach in 1969. Sanderson did not open up until the second semester of the 1968-69 school year, so the Sanderson and Broughton student bodies were both in school on the Broughton campus. The football teams shared the gym, practice fields, and even used the front lawn of the Broughton campus for football practice. The varsity team won only 3 games that year. Because of the controversy concerning student assignments, Sanderson opening up, and the football team only winning 3 games the previous year, a decision was made to hire a new football coach.

Broughton's Principal John Norton, who had been principal for about three or four years, and was leaving to return to  his home area of Mocksville, asked Joel Long to be in charge of hiring a completely new football coaching staff. When I had my first official interview for the Broughton job, it was with Carroll King, the Raleigh School system athletic director. I discussed briefly the problems that had occurred the previous year. I was concerned that the coaches who had been at Broughton would have some animosity towards me, and I did not know if they would still be there on staff when I began my job. Most of them decided to leave Broughton and continue coaching and teaching at other schools.

I met with Joel Long and Broughton's great basketball coach, Ed Mclean, and a few other people in early February of 1970. Joel and Ed showed me around and it was like a small college campus except they did not have a football stadium. Over the years, they had played their home games at Riddick Stadium, N.C. State's football stadium, located on the NCSU campus. In 1968, Carter Stadium was built for the N.C. State football program, and Riddick Stadium was no longer available for use. When Broughton lost the use of Riddick, Devereux Meadow was to become their "new" home stadium. About a mile away from Broughton, it had been built years before for a local semi-pro baseball team and was to be converted to football field for the fall 1970 football season. As people travel on Downtown Boulevard today, they would never know that what is now the Raleigh Sanitary Department parking lot had once been an exciting place for high school football.

I do not remember a lot about the interview with Joel, so I recently asked him what he remembers about that time and why he ended up hiring me and the other coaches. He explained that what he remembers most is that my philosophy was a lot like Clyde Walker's in that I wanted to keep football simple so that every player would go full speed. I believed in 1970 and I believe today that football is about running, blocking, tackling, and playing with your heart and desire. Joel and Coach Walker and I believe that you can play your best when you understand the game, and the confusion comes when a player does not know his responsibility. I think that is true in anything you do. A person must understand the basic and elementary aspects of anything he or she does in order to perform the best they can. This is true about athletics, religion, politics, and any profession.

What was also important to me then and what was always important to me was my desire to influence the boys I would coach to be upstanding players, students, and citizens in all areas of their lives. I felt that Jesus' teachings contain the best principles of life, and I hoped to share those by the way I loved and cared and lived my life.

I realized my knowledge of football was not the best compared to most coaches since I only had about two years of coaching at Carolina, but I had been involved in football as a participant from my days of sandlot football in Drexel and Morganton all the way through college. I did not know a lot about X's and O's, but I also was aware that it took more than a great amount of knowledge to be a winner on the field. In fact, I have always believed that a coach cannot teach his students/players but so much. As a coach, I always wanted my players to understand their responsibilities so that they could be their best. A lot of coaches have taught and coached a lot of football, but do their players take it all in? Players are going to do what "they know and understand," not all that their coach knows and understands. I remember spending time with Coach Tony Dungy at a Fellowship of Christian Athletes Conference in Black Mountain, N.C. when he was coaching at Tampa Bay, and he told me they had only three stunts and three coverages on their defensive teams, and these were National Football Players. Keeping things simple so often is the wise thing in coaching.

There are some little league teams who try to run college plays, schemes and techniques. I still believe from Pop Warner players to NFL players, the game is still about running, blocking, tackling, and heart. Certainly defensive and offensive schemes, scouting the opponents, motivational techniques, and all kinds of new innovations make up today's game of football, but usually the team who wins is the one who can tackle and block better and who keeps turnovers to a minimum.

So in 1970, due to the reassignment of some players and a few years of disunity of the coaching staff, Broughton High School had decided to build a new staff altogether, to begin afresh with new and young and enthusiastic coaches. Actually the 1969 Broughton football program had had a good junior varsity team the year before, but the varsity had not done very well for a couple years. After Joel talked to me on a couple occasions and after I visited with Mr. Norton about teaching and coaching on the high school level, they both decided I would be a good match for Broughton. In March I accepted the job as history teacher and head football coach, though I could not start until I could get there in the summer.

Robbie Evans, who I had known through Fellowship of Christian Athletes in college, and John Thomas from Appalachian State were two men hired as assistants at Broughton. I did not have any say in hiring any of the assistant coaches. Joel Long was the one who did all the interviews and put the football coaching staff together by the late spring of that year. He did tell me that I could talk to each one of them, and if I did not want them to be part of staff then that would be okay. I was fresh out of UNC graduate school and did not know anyone in coaching on the high school level. I rightly trusted Joel after visiting with him that he knew more than me about hiring the right assistant coaches. Indeed I was inexperienced and naïve as I look back at this in my life. There were 5 of us on the entire football staff: me and assistants Robbie Evans, John Thomas, Mac Caldwell, Mike Kral. How fortunate I was to be 24 (one of the youngest ever head high school football coaches) and have a coaching position at a school like Broughton in Raleigh. At the time, I didn't realize how lucky I was and how prominent the Broughton job was. All I wanted to do was teach and coach kids. Marie and I tremendously were excited about moving on to this next stage of our lives. She had majored in special education in graduate school and got a job teaching educable handicapped kids at the old all-black Washington Elementary School in southeast Raleigh that would begin in the fall of 1970. So here we were, 24 years old, launching out together with both of us working in education in Raleigh. It was scary, but exciting.

In late January of 1970 a few months before this great adventure began, we had moved to Winston-Salem, N.C. to teach at the N.C. Advancement School, an experimental school working with $6^{th}$ and $7^{th}$ grade boys who were labeled "underachievers." We had graduated from graduate school in December and had accepted these jobs because we needed to work and make some money to live on until we hopefully knew what the next step was. Feeling we were going to be there for only about five months, we rented a small furnished house from one of the teachers at the Advancement School, and off we had gone to teach at this unique school. We arrived in Marie's 1960 yellow Volkswagen and my 1967 Camaro, jam-packed with almost everything we owned minus furniture.

Let me tell you briefly how this school and teaching experience influenced me for the Broughton job I was taking a few months later. The Advancement School had been created to work with underachieving boys, who were basically from poor families in North Carolina. They would come and stay in dormitories for two weeks, and every other weekend they would go home and stay with their families. I was to teach P.E. with Coach Price, and Marie headed up the testing department of the school. It was a super learning experience for us and very enjoyable. It was one of my first experiences with poverty and poor black families. We became very close to some of the boys like Ken Rogers (who went on and played football at UNC), Pee Wee, Ralph Milligan and many others. I learned, once again, how lucky I had been in growing up with all the things I had, and coming from the family I had compared to so many of these young boys.

On the third day of this new job, I had an experience that has influenced me as much as any early experience I ever had. The N. C. Advancement School's aim was to encourage these underachieving boys and to identify ways to help them learn and to be better people. There was a new philosophy of education that was sweeping the nation and North Carolina. As I remember, a lot of the philosophy was centered on the education philosophy of Dr. B. F. Skinner. The head of the Advancement School talked to me as I entered my first real job away from athletics. He explained that the philosophy of the school allowed students freedom to do and behave as they desired. If they wanted to get up and leave class, then allow them to do so and do not go after them. If they called you names, ignore it and try to get them to understand to be kind to each other. Teachers were told that you should not touch any of the kids or discipline them in any way and allow the kids to work out their own problems and differences with others. So, needless to say, this was entirely new to me and called for me to behave in a different way than what I was used to. Being a coach, I felt like you had to have discipline in order to learn. Kids needed to learn to behave correctly and show respect to people, and this included having good manners. So, even though the philosophy of the school was not exactly what I agreed with, I was looking forward to learning from and teaching in this environment.

One of the first duties I had was to supervise the cafeteria and the lunch lines during the first lunch period. On this day, I was standing in the middle of the cafeteria and visiting with the different students as they walked by.

All of a sudden, one of the boys came running up to me and said, "Mister, Randy broke in line ahead of us and he is causing problems."

Now, remember this is my first job and only the second week since school had started. Thinking about the philosophy of the school and remembering that I should allow students to work things out themselves without me interfering, I told him to go back and work things out with Randy. After about three minutes, there was a lot of hollering and loud noise coming from a group near the serving line. I walked over and asked what was happening. Several boys said that Randy broke in line ahead of everyone and was not cooperating. I (thinking about the philosophy of the school) said, "Randy, is this true?"

He said "Yes, and nobody is going to move me either."

I said, "Well, why don't you guys come on around Randy, and Randy will wait in line until it is his turn."

Randy began to holler and curse, using language that I do not think many teenagers had used, much less a sixth grader. There were women serving the boys in the cafeteria line, and the language was very vulgar. I grabbed Randy with one of my hands and told him to wait and let others go by him. He began to swing his fists and continue cursing at the top of his voice. Wow, was this embarrassing for everyone, especially for me being on my first job and knowing the philosophy of the school.

I grabbed Randy and put him on the floor and threw his jacket on him and told him to get out of the cafeteria. He got up still hollering and cursing and now crying very loud. As he marched out of the cafeteria, he hit the glass window in the door with his fist and broke the glass, causing even more of a scene. Finally, after things calmed down in the cafeteria, I thought, *What should I do about all of this?* What a scene I had been in the middle of on my second week of my first job!

After 15 or 20 minutes, I decided to go find Randy and make sure he was okay. I finally found him outside near a big oak tree where he was sitting and crying by himself. I decided to sit down next to him and make sure he was okay. I asked him if he was hurt and if he was okay. He finally muttered that he was okay. After sitting with him for about ten minutes, I finally asked him what in the world had caused that outburst. Remember that the students had gone home for the weekend and returned Sunday evening, and this incident occurred on Monday morning during lunch.

Randy said that when he got home Friday night he learned that his father was missing in action in Vietnam. During the night on Friday, his home caught on fire and there was a lot of smoke damage. He, his mother, and two brothers had to move out and stay with different people in the neighborhood that night. The next morning, his young four-year old brother was staying down the street and was riding his tricycle in the driveway when he was hit by a car accidentally driven by the father who lived in the home where he was staying. His brother had to be taken to the hospital and checked out by doctors on Saturday. Randy came back to school on Sunday, and the incident in the cafeteria occurred on Monday. I felt so bad for Randy as I sat with him under the tree. He told me he was angry and he was looking for a fight and did not care who it was with.

I thought to myself, well just because your dad is missing in action and is probably dead, and your house caught on fire, and your brother was hit by an automobile, you just cannot go around beating up on and bullying other people to get your way. Even though that thought was true, I did not say that to him. Things worked out okay, and Randy eventually continued his classes that day. However, I was the one who really learned a lesson that has helped me to this day. What this taught me was that you never know what is going on with people and some problems they may have. In fact, I learned that all of us have problems, but some are worse than others. I learned that there is usually a reason behind all behavior, and what I needed to do is try to understand people even though I may not agree with their behavior. Most people appreciate others listening and trying to understand them. You see, I am not sure how I would act if I found out that someone dear to me was missing or killed, and my house had burned, and a friend or family member had been hit in an automobile accident and was in the hospital. Would you? I do believe that even in the midst of having problems like Randy had, one still needs to try to have some control of their life, but this would be very difficult for me, much less a sixth grade boy away from home. Since that experience, I have tried to do my best to understand students, players, and people who are acting in a way that is not accepted by society. Again, I may not agree with someone's behavior, but I can try to listen and understand them. This has helped me in working with parents of players I have coached over the years as well as people in general.

Marie and I enjoyed teaching at the Advancement School, and I believe it helped prepare us for things we would face at Broughton and at Washington Elementary. After accepting the head coaching job at Broughton that spring, I made several trips to Raleigh to start meeting with my future players and to meet some of the faculty. I brought back with me a number of the game films from the previous year and got to work studying and analyzing and thinking. Frankly, I was impressed with the players who were coming back for the fall of 1970 and would be my first team as head coach. I had no idea what an extraordinary football season that was going to be for Marie and me, those players, Broughton, and the city of Raleigh. I also had no idea how this 1970 football season would influence my life in athletics, coaching, and spiritually. I did know I was thrilled at the opportunity and began working hard to put a plan and philosophy together.

We remained in Winston-Salem until the end of the semester in early June of 1970 when we headed to Raleigh to begin this new phase of our lives. I do not remember how I felt God was working in our lives, but I do remember praying a lot and asking God for His wisdom and guidance. I really wanted to be a good witness for Him in my coaching and teaching. I knew a coach could really impact boys under him because I had been influenced by my high school and college coaches. Due to the influence of Jesus in my life through the Fellowship of Christian Athletes, I tried to walk daily with God. I did not have very much knowledge about the Bible and had a lot of questions about it and God, but I did have faith and trust in an all-knowing and creative God. I did depend on Him and turned to Him for wisdom and knowledge and guidance. It was a very baby-like faith, but it was true and real for me.

When we moved, Marie and I did not have a lot, just basic furniture and belongings a young couple would have. I used my whole life insurance policy to put about $2000 down for the house we bought for $24,000 that was located about ten miles outside of Raleigh. It is still there today and is only a half-mile from the soccer center on Perry Creek Road. We bought it through a realtor who told us it had been one of two houses that had been built as part of a residential neighborhood that had flopped a few years earlier. He said that it would remain isolated and there would be no other houses nearby. The week after we moved in, Marie and I woke up to the sounds of buzz saws and trucks clearing the land right around us. We were not happy. Today, it is known as Bentley Woods Subdivision and more than 10,000 people live there.

As we drove into Raleigh, I was greeted by a policeman who pulled me over for speeding in a 35 mph zone. Great welcome. We moved into our new home with a lot of anxious anticipation of what was ahead for us, but we were also filled with enthusiasm and eagerness.

As we got situated in our new home, I was finally able to devote myself to Broughton football. I met the newly BHS hired principal from Virginia, Dr. Richard Jewell, who had completed his doctoral work in education at Duke University. I also began to get familiar with Broughton High School and the physical plant itself. I continued to talk to Joel Long, who was a great encourager to me, but really I was on my own. I am an introvert in general (thank goodness I married Marie, who is definitely an extrovert), and there were times I thought, "What in the world am I doing here?" However, I knew that one had to work hard to be successful, which I learned growing up in Morganton, continued at UNC, and knew it would be true at Broughton. One lesson in life I learned from all of this was once you make a decision, get on with it. My dad used to say, "If you are thrown into the lake, you either sink or swim." I decided to swim.

Weight lifting was not very important in many high school football programs at this time, but Broughton had a summer weight program that had been started by Coach Ray Durham, an assistant coach for Broughton in 1969 before he moved on to other coaching positions. We began our official workouts on August 15 even though my assistants and

I worked some with the special positions early that summer. The North Carolina High School Athletic Association had changed a few rules where you could have six days of conditioning before official practice began.

I was impressed by the student involvement at Broughton. We had our own sports information person, Tom Wagoner. He and his student helpers had a preseason football brochure they produced, which included information on every coach and player for the upcoming year along with years of history about the Broughton Capitals football program. I was young and knew only so much football, but I was excited and enthusiastic about the prospects of this 1970 football team.

I developed a lot of my football plans based on what I had learned from Moyer Smith and Coach Dooley in my two years of coaching experience at Carolina and on my experience as a player. I learned a lot of football in the back rooms of Kenan Stadium. As I have already stated, I felt strongly that the simpler a coach could keep it, the better off the team would be. But I also had grown to realize and know by experience that one of the most important things in coaching is relationships, how you treat players, and how you can make each player feel like they are part of something larger than himself.

I never forgot the good feeling I had when UNC Coach Bobby Collins and his wife had senior players who played in the backfield for him over to their house for supper the spring I completed my eligibility. It was so good to see the coach somewhere other than on the field with a whistle in his mouth hollering and coaching.

One of the things I was determined to do was to try to visit the prospective players in their own homes before the season began. I did not get around to all of them, but I do remember visiting a lot of them all over Raleigh. I would get my Raleigh map out and find addresses of players and take off to find them and try to meet their parents and families. A GPS would have been helpful, because many a night and day I would get lost and have nothing to show for my efforts. However, there were many more pluses than minuses when I pulled up at a player's home and got to meet him and his parents. I was almost always warmly received, and I remember some of those visits to this day. In fact, I have been by some of their homes almost 45 years later and remember them like yesterday. I honestly think this was the beginning of making a close team. I continued to visit prospects at new coaching jobs over the years at most of the schools I headed up from Broughton, Cary, Athens, Sanderson, McDowell, Fuquay Varina, and Holly Springs. I was never able to visit every player, but it was very meaningful for me to get to visit many of them and meet with their parents and see what kind of families they came from. I still feel that high school coaches can make a difference in kids' lives, and it all begins with establishing relationships. Only the person himself or herself can change himself or herself, but I think a coach can get them started on, challenge them to be on or reinforce that they are on the right path. A major role I played in kids' lives was that I tried to support the values and the teachings of parents of boys who played for me; I tried to live my life as a good role model, and I did it by trying to follow Jesus' teachings. This was on my mind and was my main motivation even back in the summer of 1970 when I was just beginning in the coaching world.

I did a lot of thinking, planning, and praying about the upcoming responsibility I had been given as the head football coach at Needham Broughton High School. It never entered my mind that I would not be successful. In fact, I honestly did not think much about success in coaching in regards to a winning or championship season. I was thinking only about getting organized and giving my players a healthy and memorable experience.

Football, for me, had been such a character and life-building experience, and it really had contributed to my developing from a boy to a man. Discipline, perseverance, work ethic, and enjoying what you do were principles I learned from participating in football in high school and college. I hoped that I could help my football players to have these same experiences along with helping them to contribute to making a better society.

## CHAPTER 4
The Coaching Staff and the Pre-Season

"In football as in life, the little things make a big difference."
- Phillip Fulmer

It seems like yesterday that I walked into Needham Broughton High School auditorium with my wife Marie and Mr. Joel Long to meet with the football prospects for the first time in the spring of 1970 in Raleigh, North Carolina. Marie and I had driven from Winston-Salem to Raleigh since we were still teaching at the N.C. Advancement School. The Broughton High School building was massive in my eyes. It looked like a tremendous castle in Europe. Remember, I came from a high school that graduated about 105 students. Graduating classes at NBHS numbered about 500.

There was a lot of history of and pride in Broughton. It was named after Mr. Needham B. Broughton who was a Raleigh businessman and politician who contributed much to the public schools in the area. It served as the neighborhood school for most of the upper class white families in Raleigh. I was not aware of it at the time I took the job, but it was probably one of the four best high schools in the state of North Carolina. In 2010, when I was thinking about writing this book, I walked down the hallways where I taught and coached, and a special feeling of the "spirit of Broughton" jumped out of the mortar of the walls into my heart once again. Even though a lot of things had physically changed and the addition of the science annex and other wings, it still had a "special feel."

On that day back in 1970, I still remember I had a light blue shirt on and the tie I had worn to my wedding reception. I remember being nervous and excited as I walked in front of these young men, some not more than six years younger than I was at that time. I was a 24 year-old former UNC football player and graduate assistant coach, meeting with these high school teenagers who were interested in restoring and rebuilding a traditionally famous football program that had turned downward the last couple of years. The heart beneath my sport coat and tie was booming with anticipation, enthusiasm, and the challenge that was before me that day. It was my first "real" job in the world, and I was not fazed by it being at one of the most well-known high schools in North Carolina. I was too young and inexperienced at that time in my life to know what an opportunity I had been given. Yes, I was a little naïve. The players were spread out seated in the auditorium as Joel Long introduced me. I noticed that there were some who were sitting with each other and others sitting by themselves. Some looked like managers or trainers, but I did not see very many boys that afternoon who were big and burly football types. But what did I know?

I do not remember a lot that I said that beautiful spring afternoon in 1970, but I know I expressed to them how lucky I was and they were to be part of the game of football. I remember talking about the importance of football and all we learn about life from the game. I also told them that God was very important to me. I hoped to treat all of them fairly, and that if we would work hard and come together as a team, that we could be successful. Several of the players remembered something I said that encouraged them in the auditorium that afternoon. I promised them that everyone would get a fair chance and no one had a starting position, but everyone starts with a clean slate and would need to earn a position on the team. Several guys asked what kind of rules we were going to have and if they could have facial hair and long hair as several of them already did. I told them that I really did not care what they looked like that much, but what I wanted were players who would work hard and play with their hearts. To many of them, starting all over with clean slates and not having to worry about a lot of rules interested them, as well as gave them some hope for themselves.

As a 24-year old, the only coaching experience I had was with Moyer Smith and the other UNC freshman coaches. However, there were other influences that helped me to form my coaching philosophy. I think back about my high school coach, Earl Broome, who was a tough coach and a hard-nosed disciplinarian. He did not compliment players very much, but when he did, you knew that you had done something above average and he made you feel like you were contributing to the team. It helped me realize that complimenting players was very important in making them better. I also think about my dad who was a tough-minded man, but he seemed to look on the good side of things instead of noticing and talking about the negative things in life. Coach Billy Hickman and Coach Ace Parker, who both coached me while I was playing at Carolina, were influential in forming the way I would coach. Neither of them were "hollerers" like so many coaches then and today. They talked in a calm voice and were teachers and instructors trying to get us to understand our playing responsibilities and how we fit in to the overall game of football. I believe these men made me a better player and challenged me as a player, and I wanted to do the same thing to the players I coached. Coach Dooley was serious about the game of football and was such a hard worker, and that certainly was passed on to me. Jesus' teaching about treating others the way I want to be treated certainly influenced me in how I wanted to treat individual players. All of these influences in my life were contributing factors in the kind of coach and teacher I became, and I am very thankful for all of them.

I was also hired to teach in the classroom and not just to be a football coach. I only had had one semester of teaching experience through the Master's program at UNC, and that was at Guy B. Phillips Jr. High School in Chapel Hill. With my undergraduate degree being in history, I was hired to teach three American History classes and two World History classes. That would mean teaching five out of seven classes with a planning period and a lunch period. I am so thankful for teachers like Roy Teel and Don Goodwin, who were so helpful to me with their assistance in teaching those classes. Roy, who would later become the principal of Broughton as well as several other schools, was a social studies teacher when I came to Broughton. Don, who was probably one of the very best history teachers in high school, taught just down the hall from me and was very helpful with his encouragement and history information he more than gladly shared with me. With this being my first teaching experience, teachers like Roy and Don taught me how important it is to help first year teachers at a school, which I've always tried to do at the schools where I have been fortunate to be employed.

It was a heavy load of class work for a first year teacher along with being the head football coach, but to be honest, I didn't think about it being "rough" because I was getting to coach football, and I did not have anything to compare it with. Also, that is just what you did. You were given an assignment and you did it without complaining or griping, and I know I was not the only high school coach and teacher who had a lot to do. At least I had a job.

I do not remember many specific details about the early coaching meetings or the summer practices we had in 1970, but I do remember loving it and the fact that we worked HARD. One of the first things I told the players was that they would be expected to run a mile in a specific time if they wanted to play at Broughton High School. The backs would need to run it under six minutes, and all linemen would need to run it under six and one-half minutes. If they did not make it in the time required, then they would have to keep trying until they succeeded. So we set a goal and expectation to begin with, and there would be more to follow.

I quickly learned that there was much more to coaching than teaching kids how to run, block, and tackle. I was thrown into a brand new situation for me where I learned that being head coach meant washing dirty uniforms, organizing the equipment to be used by over 100 players, checking the eligibility of all players, arranging travel plans for away games, and much more. All I knew was to start building a program and work hard, and that is what I did.

I certainly had a lot of help in the beginning thanks to assistant principal and athletic director Joel Long and Mr. Seth Jones, the chief custodian in charge of the two gyms, dressing facilities, and classrooms in the athletic area. Seth had been hired by Coach Walker a few years earlier to be the "equipment manager" for Broughton. He carried all the equipment, uniforms, and extras that the football team may need in his truck to the games. Seth taught me about washing uniforms and a lot about equipment repairs my first summer at Broughton. He was a great man and an encourager to me as a young high school coach. Seth left later that year to work full time with Johnson-Lambe Sporting Goods Store in downtown Raleigh on Salisbury Street. Mr. Johnson told me that Seth wanted a $.25 raise from the Raleigh City School System, but they would not give that to him. So, when Mr. Johnson heard about it he offered Seth a job at Johnson-Lambe for more money than he was being paid by the school system, and Seth took it. He was an extremely hard worker. There is one story about him that demonstrates his goal of getting things done ASAP. Mr. Johnson once said, "If you want that tree cut down outside, then be sure about it because the saw would be coming out within 5 minutes and you better not call him back and tell him not to do it because it would already be on the ground." My relationship continued with Seth even into the late '70's as I later moved on to other things. I hope I thanked him enough for all he did and all he meant to me in my first year getting started.

Gordon Blake, a student who had graduated from Broughton the year before I took the job, was a tremendous help in teaching me about the physical plant of Broughton and any detailed athletic statistic about Needham Broughton that I may want to know. Gordon took over as custodian at Broughton in charge of the gyms, dressing rooms, and surrounding area after Seth left. I remember also that Gordon was a topnotch fan for all Broughton Caps sports, and there was no more loyal fan for the Caps than Gordon Blake. He and I have remained in touch with each other and I consider him a good friend.

We began football practice on August 15th for high school teams. On the first day the boys showed up, we met in the bleachers of Holliday gym on Broughton campus before practice, and I remember being surprised by the number of players who were there. There were over 100. They were all dressed in t-shirts and shorts, and I could sense their excitement and their nervousness in anticipation for this first day of football practice. As I welcomed them, I was also excited and nervous. For the players who showed up for the first time, I explained about the mile run and times that linemen and backs were to finish. A lot of the boys had been working out during the summer, building up to the start of practice. After I answered a few questions, we headed toward the practice field to run the mile for time. From my personal experience, I knew it was a difficult run if the players had not been working out in the summer sun and heat because I had had to do it as a Carolina football player. I remember some of the players at UNC having a tough time with it. However, I really thought that a young man who had worked out in the summer could make a mile run in the time I had set for him. If a player did not make it in the required time, he would have to show up the next day before practice to run again. This went on for several days until if we determined a player would never be able to make the time, we had him to run sprints for so many days. There had to be some consequences for not meeting expectations.

It seems today we have lost the importance of setting high expectations for students and athletes. There are so many students and athletes who feel they are entitled to do what they want, regardless of the rules and expectations a coach and teacher may set for them. In many cases it is often the parents of these kids who feel their sons and daughters are entitled to playing time, having a certain position on a team, getting a certain grade or receiving a scholarship for college.

1st Row David Dupree, Preston Ruth, 2nd Row John Holding, David Turner

1st Row Jim Lumsden, Charles King, 2nd Row Macy Faulkner, Larry Height

We practiced two-a-days for about a week. We would begin about 7:00 in the morning and go until about 10:30 or 11:00 and then bring them back to practice about 4 o'clock and go for a couple more hours in the afternoon. Our coaching staff would get some lunch or bring our bag lunch and eat at the office. I remember not going home until late at night those first few years of my coaching career. I felt the harder you worked, the more successful one would be. There may have been some truth to that early on in my career, but I certainly learned that it was not always necessarily true. Experience taught me that it was not always how long you worked, but how smart you worked and how you used your assistant coaches.

As we prepared for the upcoming season, I knew that the kicking game was very important to a successful team. I had learned that from my playing and coaching days at UNC. Coach Dooley always emphasized that to us on game days as he read through the "rules of the kicking game" for about 20 minutes every Saturday. One of the first things I knew I had to do was find a good punter and kickoff person. I found out that we had several good kickers in John Holding, Gary Stainback, and Macy Falkner.

Another emphasis of my early coaching days was the necessity of being in shape and great condition to play the game of football. If you could not out-coach or out-play an opponent, you could definitely out-condition them. I had believed fully that you could win a few games a year if you were the better conditioned team, because when you get tired, you get lazy and careless. Being in shape and discipline were two important factors in winning any games, especially if the score was close. A lot of our practices early on were conditioning drills. We had stations that players would run through that would improve their foot speed, agility, strength, mental toughness and winning attitude. Again, a training and learning ground for me as a player in regards to this aspect of my coaching came from Coach Dooley at UNC. The first spring practice under Coach Dooley, we as players learned what commitment and hard work was in football. This can again be overdone and hurt kids if you do not treat them as individuals.

Thus, I decided to integrate that same attitude, work ethic, and discipline into my first high school football team, but I certainly wanted to include the idea of relationships and team concept. Truly caring about the individuals would take care of the team concept. I had a wonderful coaching staff who fit right into this philosophy.

1st row-Allan Parnell Gary Stainback Billy Starling Rick Eudy Phil Ficklin 2nd row-Vann Hinton Johnny Ford Doug Perry Wells Edmundson Bernard Williams Skip Hawkins

John Clarke, Jim Stoneham, Sam Beard

I learned early in my playing days how important all coaches are to a team. The assistant coaches are just as important as a head coach because they have daily contact with players. I certainly was lucky to have had Joel Long put together a super coaching staff for 1970. He had spent a lot of time going through applications and interviewing possible coaches. He had told me he wanted young, enthusiastic men who were going to be good, positive role models for high school players. He certainly selected some great ones and put it all together for us. Now, we had to pull the players and coaches together for the upcoming season. We only had five total coaches for our Varsity and Junior Varsity football teams in 1970. In 2016, some high school teams have ten or more coaches on their staffs. Things have changed.

Robbie Evans was going to be our offensive line coach at Broughton. He had played high school football at Needham Broughton in 1962-64 and was all conference in 1964 and had been part of some winning and championship teams under Coach Walker. Robbie was also co-captain of the 1964 team. He had won a scholarship to play ball at North Carolina

State under Earle Edwards and had been a top offensive lineman. The thing that impressed me so much about Robbie was his love for God and his involvement in the Fellowship of Christian Athletes along with his enthusiasm for the game of football. He and I had played against each other while I was at UNC and he was at N.C. State. We had met through a good friend, Johnny Clements, who was heading up the FCA chapter at N.C. State. He had majored in math at State and was hired as a math teacher at Broughton. We attended several Christian retreats together before we met officially as coaches at Broughton. Just like football and coaching, we both had a lot to learn about Christianity but it was exciting to me that we had those things in common in our background. After a couple years at Broughton, Robbie went to seminary in Virginia and was ordained as a Presbyterian minister in the early 1970's and has served God in that capacity in North Carolina and Virginia until now. In 2001, when I was coaching at McDowell High School, I went out on the field to meet the referees, and who was the head referee but Robbie. We talked with each other briefly and were able to catch up and visit the next morning. What a pleasant surprise for me to have Robbie as referee of our game over 30 years after we had coached together.

John Thomas was our defensive line coach. He played high school football at North Davidson High School and graduated from there in 1965. John had attended Appalachian State in Boone, N.C. in 1966 where he played football. He transferred to High Point College where he graduated with a BA degree in Physical Education. He was teaching elementary physical education and coaching at the junior high school in Wendell, N.C. in the Wake County School System before coming to Broughton. He was the coach behind our defensive unit of the 1970 State Championship team. There will be more about that later. From the beginning of our first coaches' meeting and first practice, I knew John loved the game and cared about the boys who were playing for us. John had a great football mind and proved this as time passed as he held several head coaching positions at different high schools across the state until he retired. John especially loved defense and studied the game and opponents in great detail. John is married to his wife Brenda, and they have celebrated over 40 years together.

Mac Caldwell was our head Junior Varsity football coach and coached

the linebackers and defensive ends on both varsity and JV teams. Mac
had come from the Carroll Junior High school program in the Raleigh
City School System. He also taught physical education. At 36, he was the
"old man" of our staff in 1970. Mac had been coaching in Raleigh for six
years. Before going to Carroll where he had been coaching for five years,
he had coached at Daniels Junior High for one year. Both of these
schools were feeder schools for Broughton. Mac had attended Christ
School in Asheville, N.C. and in 1952 attended Mars Hill College. He
then went to the University of North Carolina where he graduated in
1960 with a Masters in Physical Education. Mac coached in Fort Belvoir,
Virginia before coming to Raleigh. He was married to Suzie and had
three children and was very smart in handling people as well as coaching
sports. He was a very successful Broughton JV basketball coach as well
as being a key ingredient in our state championship team of 1970. He is
like so many thousands of high school assistant coaches who do not get
the credit they deserve. Mac did so many things behind the scenes like
helping wash uniforms, scouting the opponents for the next week, being
calm and cool in the heat of the action, following up with kids who had
problems off the field, and doing the "unsung hero" things that are done
around any successful program. I remember Mac being wise in handling
situations that could have been explosive on a high school athletic field.
In addition to being the Head Junior Varsity football coach for us, Mac
contributed a lot of wisdom and strategy to our varsity team throughout
the year.

Mike Kral was our backfield coach for the Junior Varsity football
team. Like most of us, he was young and inexperienced compared to so
many coaching staffs in the 1970's. Mike played a role for us in the fact
that he was the only one who had been at Broughton in the years before I
and the other coaches arrived. He was helpful in getting our coaches
some information about the athletic ability of some of the players coming
back in 1970. Mike had graduated from Oak Hill High School outside of
Morganton, N.C., where he played football and basketball. He then
attended Berea College in Kentucky for one year and transferred to
Appalachian State where he graduated with a BA in Social Studies and
Physical Education in 1964. Having been at Broughton the previous year,
Mike was not thrilled about a completely new staff coming to the school.

However, he certainly worked with us and helped us make the transition in 1970. Mike taught social studies and was assistant to the Junior Varsity football team, but also helped in our preparation for the Varsity games by scouting our opponents.

Coaches Caldwell, Evans, Kral, Riggs, Thomas

As a head football coach, I could not have been any luckier to have these men working with me at my first ever Head Football job on the high school level. One thing I learned early was one person cannot change a program. I think head football coaches or head coaches in general get far too much credit for winning. The assistants are such a key to building successful programs. I have been very fortunate in my coaching career in that I have been blessed in having good assistants at all the schools where I have been head coach. It is not easy to be an assistant coach sometimes, but I certainly tried to give them time off to be with their families, give them credit for what they did, and give them fewer responsibilities so they could coach. I knew and still know that no one goes into high school coaching for the money, but for the reason that they want to help young boys to become men. One major characteristic each of these men had, and I think it is one of the most important that anyone can give to a head coach, was loyalty.

One of the most important decisions we made early on was electing captains of our football team. I wanted to make sure that this team would be led by the players. As I visited with and got to know most of the players during the summer days, I sensed that many of them knew each other pretty well and had been through some rough times together. Having the players elect their leaders was one of the best things I did early on in my coaching career. Now a days so many coaches select their captains, but who else knows best but their teammates? It is a lot like calling plays. Today coaches have pages of play charts with what to do on third and short or second and long and feel like they have to call every play of the game. In so many ways the game has been taken out of the players' hands and put into the hands of a couple of coaches. I do not know which is best now, but I know in 1970 for a bunch of Broughton players, the best was to put it in the hands of players, including the quarterbacks and the captains.

The team elected Mark Shaner and Jimmy Durham as captains for their team. They were two completely different individuals, but were ideal for our team. Again, the players knew what they needed in leadership. Mark was a rough neck with long hair and beard and was a lineman (5' 9" 210 pounds.) He was a hitter and leader by actions as well as talking. Jimmy Durham, clean shaven and short hair, was a defensive back weighing about 165 pounds and was quiet on and off the football field. These two young men were chosen by their teammates to lead them through this season with a new coaching staff and a very difficult schedule.

Kent Kistler Doug Murray Jim Little George Lattimore Steve Brewbaker
2nd row-Dave Wooten Rick Hunter Paul Ussery  Randy Proctor Jim
Fitzgerald Horace Ayscue

1st row Jim Durham, Eric Handy  2nd row Bernard Kearney, Lindsey Knott, Dickie Thompson

In the first six days of conditioning drills, we would divide all the players up into three or four major stations, about 25-30 in each group, and send them through workouts. There was not a lot of football teaching that went on except some basic fundamentals like good football stances, quickness, running agilities and hustle all the time. (These basic fundamentals probably still win more football games today on the high school level than X's and O's.) One or two coaches would be at each station running the drills. The purpose of these first six days of practice was to get the players in good condition in order to make it through the football season. I also saw it as a time for our team to bond together since school had not started and we could focus on football.

STATION 1 – Boys would run agility drills, short 20 yard sprints, and would work on good stances, and do neck isometrics on the ground – not recommended today.

STATION 2 – One half of the players in this group would do 25 push-ups and sit ups while the other half were jumping benches or dummies 25 times and then they would flip flop back and forth until time was up.

STATION 3 – Players would be running the steps of the bleachers, then more agility drills, bear crawls, leg lifts, sit ups, and the like.

Each station would last for 15 minutes each without water breaks (unless a person <u>had</u> to have water). Managers did have water bottles at each station so players could get water as they began each station if they expressed a desire to. I am not sure why we did not schedule water breaks more often other than "that was the way you did it." When I played in high school, I remember drinking from mud puddles and putting lemons in my helmet as needing water was seen as a sign of weakness, which makes no sense. Obviously this would never happen today. It is interesting how things have changed in regards to first aid for players from then to now, and all of it is much better and safer. If we knew then what we know now, having official water breaks would have been part of our practice policy. The stations would last for a total of 45 minutes, which was constant movement and running. After the stations, we then would have a 10-15 minute water break to give them some rest. It was a difficult workout and certainly would not be done without water in this age of football. In 1970, I imagine most teams went through rigorous workouts like these.

I do not remember many boys quitting and/or complaining about the hard work. That is what set this bunch of guys above most teams because they were hungry to win football games. I was at the right place and right time as a coach. These guys from the beginning wanted to win and were determined to be successful.

During those summer workouts, it would not be unusual for our coaches to spend all day at the school. We would come in early, bring our lunches, and remain there working on personnel, practice schedules, and game planning. As we would practice, we would try to use our time wisely. Our typical practice schedule would be the following:

As soon as the players hit the field they would take one lap around the practice field, then they would circle up for calisthenics which would include jumping jacks, windmills, leg lifts, sit-ups, push-ups, neck isometrics, and more.

After calisthenics, we would have a specialty period where quarterbacks and receivers would work on the passing game, the linemen would work on fundamental blocking, and kickers and punters with the kick returners would work on their specialty. Every player would be part of one of these groups. These would last about 15 minutes daily.

After specialty period, we would have about 20 minutes of individual offense period when the backfield would work on fundamentals with me, the offensive linemen would go to Coach Evans and the tight ends and receivers would go with Coach Thomas. Then we would switch up to the defensive individual period where we would work for about 20-25 minutes in our three groups of defensive backs (Riggs), linebackers and ends (Evans), and defensive linemen (Thomas).

Then usually Coach Evans and I would take the offense for about 45 minutes and work on our offensive plans against the opponent's defense, which was run by coach Thomas using the third team as the opponent's defense. Then Coach Thomas and I would have the defense running our sets against Coach Evans and the third offensive team so we could prepare for the opponent's offense for that week for the next 45 minutes. All of our coaches would have watched and studied films of the opponent's offense and defense sets. Then after these ninety minutes of practice, Coach Thomas would take the defense and continue to prepare while Coach Evans and I would be fine-tuning our offense. This period would last about 20 minutes

The last 15 minutes of most practices before wind sprints were used for the kicking game as a team. The kicking game can be overlooked easily, but I had learned through playing and coaching for Coach Dooley that it was an important third of the game, and you cannot neglect it if you are going to be a winner.

Then we would line up and run 40 yard sprints for "fourth quarter drills." This would be about a three-hour practice. It was long and hard. The players persevered conscientiously and learned that conditioning and preparation were important. As the season progressed, I believe we knew what our opponents would be doing on offense and defense as well as we could know. Preparation was something that would help the underdog team a lot, and most of the games we played, we were underdogs. As we moved closer to the first ballgame, we let up some so the players' legs could recover. By this time in pre-season, we were ready to play against other people instead of practicing against ourselves! We were excited and ready for our first game coming up against Greensboro Grimsley.

1st row- Mark Shaner Murray Howell Ashleigh Spain Chris Morgan
2nd row- Dave Reynolds Gary Neal Jim Corter Grigg Mullen Jay Morgan

1st Row: Roland Massey, Jim Bass, 2nd Row: Willis Price, Charles Banks

"Correction does much, but encouragement does more."
- Johann Wolfgang von Goethe

## CHAPTER 5
Beginning the 1970 Football Season

"Well done is better than well said."
- Ben Franklin

Here I sit five decades later, and as I look over the pre-season team picture of the Needham Broughton 1970 Football Team taken in Holliday Gymnasium in August of 1970, I swell with pride as I gaze at each one of those guys' faces. What a motley crew. They are small, long-haired, innocent looking, and certainly do not look like a 4-A State Championship Football Team. The coaches look younger than some of the players, and it is a diverse group of kids who come from all different backgrounds and families. 1970 was some kind of year. Broughton High School was "integrated" at the time, but had fewer than 40 black students in a school of 2,200.

I guess it was a typical group of young men on any high school football team and that is what makes football such a great game. There was a very broad makeup on this team, but this team was different and special, as you will be able to tell as you read their story. This is not about me, or other coaches, or any special game or one defining moment or winning play, or any one individual who was "the player of the year." This is about what makes high school football such a great game. This story is about a team, about individuals who participate in something because they love it, and they understand that working together is superior to working individually. Who would have ever thought that this bunch of guys in this picture would become North Carolina State 4-A Champions in football? This is their story.

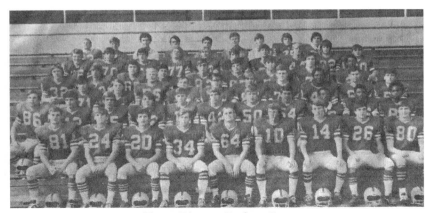

Team Picture Before Season

Our outlook for the 1970 football season was unknown in many ways. However, because of Broughton's past tradition, we could not be counted out of the Caps Division III Conference. The conference was made up of five other schools. Remember there were only four high schools in Raleigh in 1970, so a school would have to travel quite a few miles to play non-conference games in cities like Greensboro, Wilmington, Rocky Mount, and Wilson. The other high schools in the 4-A Conference with Broughton were Raleigh Enloe coached by George Thompson, Durham Hillside coached by Russell Blunt, Raleigh Sanderson coached by Jim Brown, Raleigh Ligon coached by Frank Roberts, and Durham Senior coached by Kelly Minyard. I knew very little about these teams and coaches as I entered this first year. I had known about Durham Senior High School and Broughton having played for state championships in earlier years, but I did not know the coaches.

The Raleigh coaches were very cordial and helpful to me as I came on board at Broughton. I heard years later that several coaches in the Raleigh School System, and especially at the Junior High Schools, were upset that I had been hired fresh out of graduate school when some of them had put in time for over ten years in the system. They did not feel that they were treated fairly in that I was given the job at Broughton before they were ever interviewed. I can understand their feelings and probably would have felt the same way. All the head coaches in our conference treated me fairly; Coach Thompson and Coach Brown were especially helpful to me in making the adjustment to high school coaching. They all made me feel welcome and glad I was there.

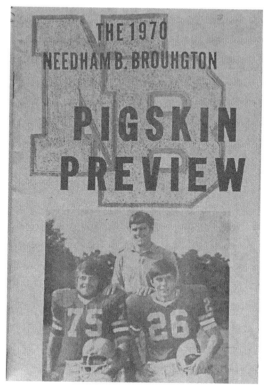

Pigskin Preview

The Pigskin Preview publication written by Tom Wagoner, a student and the sports information director at Broughton, stated the following:

*With a new staff of coaches and high enthusiasm, the 1970 Broughton football team expects to show that they will be top contenders for the Division III title. David Riggs, new head coach, is intent on building Broughton back to the football eminence it enjoyed just a few years ago.*

*There are only six lettermen returning from last year's football team, but there are other returning seniors and also juniors up from last year's undefeated JV football team. With these 30 juniors and 22 seniors, the coaches hope to have two strong platoons. There is strong competition at all positions, which should encourage everyone to do a better job.*

*The CAPS will use multiple offenses and defenses throughout the season. The greatest weakness that the CAPS will have will be inexperience on offense and defense.*

*Again this season Broughton will play one of the toughest schedules in the state. For the first time in four years the Broughton CAPS will open up with a home game against Greensboro Grimsley. This season's first four games are here in Raleigh, which should boost the CAPS enthusiasm and determination. The CAPS then travel to Durham before returning home for the next weekend's homecoming game against Wilson Fike, the state champions for the past three years. The next game with Sanderson will surely be the biggest rivalry of the season. Three more games close out the season, the last being played against Durham.*

There were several key ingredients that I thought would have to be part of any football team. I assume I learned these things from having been a player in high school as well as in college. I am not sure if there is any certain priority of these ingredients, but most of these are needed.

First of all I felt that **confidence** in playing any sport or really doing anything is so important to people. If people do not have confidence in what they are doing, they will not do their very best. Confidence comes from knowledge and knowing the subject matter. If I had to discuss and carry on a conversation about business investments or the computer world we live in today, I would probably be very quiet in that discussion because I do not have a lot of knowledge about those topics. However, if you want to discuss golf, football, or the Bible I would have a lot to say since I have studied those topics and participated in them. So I knew our coaching staff would have to coach fundamentals to this team in order to get them ready for a long season.

Second of all, I felt that in order to build a real **TEAM,** everyone had to play a part and feel like they were contributing in some way. The more players who played and felt part of the team, the more chance you have to form a cohesive team. Many of these players had not played very much since only seniors had been playing the previous year. Yet, in talking to many of the players in my visits with them and from just listening to them, I knew they were hungry for victories, and most of them loved football and just wanted to play. As I was planning for the upcoming practices and games, I decided early on that we would play platoon football. We would try to find our best players who loved to hit people since football is a contact sport, and put them on defense. If we had some players who were good enough, we would let them play both ways some, but I felt like the fewer players who were playing both offense and defense, the more players could play somewhere. Also if you had a separate offense and separate defense, the players would all get to practice at their positions on one side of the ball and therefore improve at a much faster rate as the season progressed. One of the problems with this idea is that we only had 5 coaches, and two of those would be working with the Junior Varsity players, and only three of us would be able to coach the varsity team. So I had Robbie Evans coaching the offensive line and defensive ends and linebackers. John Thomas coached the offensive ends and the defensive line. I would then coach the defensive backs and the offensive backfield. Coach Thomas would head up our defense, and I would head up our offense. I guess that we would be today's "coordinators."

I have always looked at my assistant coaches as head coaches of the particular position they are working with. Again, this is part of the team concept, realizing that no one is more important than anyone else, including the head football coach or the equipment manager of the team. It is a lot like the Biblical passage in I Corinthians 12 that talks about the church which literally means community, group, assembly, or even team. "Now the body is not made up of one part but of many. If the foot should say, because I am not a hand, I do not belong to the body, it would not for that reason cease to be part of the body. And if the ear should say, because I am not an eye, I do not belong to the body, it would not for that reason cease to be part of the body. If the whole body were an eye, where would the sense of hearing be? If the whole body were an ear, where would the sense of smell be? But in fact God has arranged the parts in the body, every one of them, just as he wanted them to be. If they were all one part, where would the body be? As it is, there are many parts, but only one body." So this second key ingredient of being a true team was a must for us to get across to the players.

A third key that I wanted to be part of this team was **enthusiasm and desire.** I remember playing at Notre Dame when I was at Carolina and coming out of the tunnel at South Bend and seeing a sign that said, "Enthusiasm: If you have it, thank God for it and, If you don't, get down on your knees and ask for it." Since I was a young boy, I have always felt like desire and enthusiasm was a big part of life. It is also something that anyone can have or develop regardless of size, weight, looks, economic background, race, or age. If you cannot get excited about what you are doing, you may be in the wrong place or profession. I really believe that I accomplished many things in my athletic and educational career because of desire, hustle and enthusiasm. I knew that for this football team to be successful, we would have to practice and play with enthusiasm and desire. I began talking a lot about playing with heart. I bought about 20 different copies of Bob Richardson's book Heart of a Champion and gave them out to the players. When it comes down to individuals competing against each other and they both have equal talent, it usually ends up with the winner being the one who plays with their heart and desire.

Heart of a Champion

The final and fourth key ingredient to this season would have to be **perseverance and a "never give up" attitude**. I had learned in my playing days in Morganton and at Carolina that there were going to be some difficult times during the season and in life, but you can never give up until you have done everything you can to improve the situation.

I remember one game in high school against Valdese where our undefeated Morganton High football team was tied 0-0 with under a couple minutes left and we marched down the field to score and win the game. I remember that like it was yesterday, and I did not even play much that game due to an injury, but it taught me if people hang tight together, and never give up that you can come back. Also at Carolina, we won only two games my senior year. It was a rough season, and I never will forget Coach Lee Hayley coming by my locker after a very difficult game that we lost. He put his arm around me and told me to hang in there and not give up. I do not remember who we lost to, but I remember Coach Hayley and his words and the hug.

As the 1970 Needham Broughton football season was getting ready to begin, I felt like these four ingredients – CONFIDENCE, TEAM, ENTHUSIASM, and PERSEVERANCE – would have to be keys for our staff, team, and season. There are many other things like talent, quickness, encouragement, and luck that played a part of the "miracle season," but these four keys can be helpful in anything one does. I knew that these concepts would also help these boys to develop and be good citizens as they graduated and moved on in the world.

New Season

## TOP RETURNEES

John Holding, QB; Dave Dupree, QB-DB; Jim Bass, HB; Billy Starling, E; Phil Ficklen, E; Mark Shaner, DT; Jimmy Durham, S.

## PROMISING NEWCOMERS

David Turner, QB; Roland Massey, HB; Eric Handy, HB; Charles King, FB; Larry Height, FB; Rick Eudy, E; Jim Little, G; Kent Kistler, G; Willis Price, G; Rick Hunter, G; Dave Reynolds, T; Murray Howell, T; Jay Morgan T; John Clarke, C; Sam Beard, C; Doug Murray, LB; Charles Banks, DE; Wells Edmundson, DE; Gary Neal, T; Jim Courter, T; Steve Brubaker, DT; Geroge Lattimore, LB.

Top Returners

# CHAPTER 6
## The Regular Season

"Look for players with character and abilities, but remember
character comes first."
- Joe Gibbs

One of the best things about this team and coaching staff was that we did not get wrapped up in having to defend anything from the past several years. Our coaches did not know details about what had happened involving the coaches, the team, the school board, and other events the previous two seasons. Certainly, the players did not have anything to defend or prove except that they wanted people to know they could play the game of football if given the chance.

Everyone had worked hard in our practice sessions in August. We had pushed them hard and got them in good condition. Discipline was something that they all needed, and we were able to instill in them the right kind of discipline so we would cut down on our mistakes. We knew we were not going to beat other teams because of our speed and size, because at our own admission our team was small BUT slow, except for a couple guys. I really believe that our coaching staff knew just enough to get the players ready to play without confusing them.

Our staff would spend a lot of time trying to decide where to play each player so they could help us as a team. Putting people in the right position for them and the team was and is so important. Never did individuals take center stage, but it was always what is best for the team.

One example is the quarterback position. John Holding, a senior, had played some the previous year at quarterback and was a very intelligent player. He could also punt with the best of any punters I have had over my many years of coaching. The other quarterback was David Turner, who was coming off a successful Junior Varsity season. They both worked hard and had great attitudes. Having both of them competing for the top position of quarterback made them both so much better and therefore made our team better. There was not any complaining and griping, as I remember, from either one of them as we moved through the practices in August. Finally, we decided that David was a little more versatile and would help us more with his mobility. John did not get upset (as far as I know) but kept working hard and told me he just wanted to play. He was our punter and played a very significant role in a number of ball games during the season by putting people deep in their own territory with his punts. There is a lot of difference when a team has to go 70-80 yards to score versus 50-60 yards to score. Due to John's punts, our defense was helped a lot throughout the season. John also played some safety for us and was a good one. Having both of these boys competing for one position, but willing to sacrifice and play elsewhere for the betterment of the team was a good example of the character of this team.

### Game 1: Broughton vs. Greensboro Grimsley, September 4, 1970

The first football game for this 1970 Needham Broughton team was against powerhouse Greensboro Grimsley High School, coached by the legendary Bob Jamieson. Coach Jamieson was 63 years old, about 40 years older than me, and most people knew he was nearing his retirement. He had contributed so much to high school athletics in North Carolina. He helped start the East – West All Star football game in Greensboro in 1949. I was 24, and Coach Jamieson was such a legend, the "Bear Bryant" of North Carolina high school athletics before there was a Bear Bryant. Coach Jamieson had coached almost twice the number of years in high school than I had been alive. I knew this game would be a challenge!

The Whirlies came to Raleigh to play us, and people were excited about the opening game because it was a new season, there was a new coach and a lot of new players. Broughton had always had a lot of support from the community and students due to having successful seasons in the early and mid-1960's. The cheerleaders were some of the best football supporters we had. I remember they sent a telegram to the football team on the afternoon of September 4, 1970 for our opening game against Grimsley. You would not find that happening very often today in high school sports. So many of the sports care only about their individual sport, but in 1970 there was a lot of mutual support for all the teams.

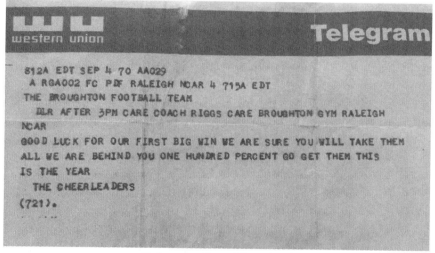

Telegram from Cheerleaders

NBHS Cheerleading Squad

As already mentioned, Broughton did not have a home football stadium on campus. They had tried in previous years to build one, but there were too many complaints about blaring lights too near the Cameron Village Apartments. People living adjacent to the Broughton High School athletic fields were simply not in favor of having lights from football and baseball games on during the evenings. In fact, when Riddick Stadium, N.C. State's football stadium was torn down and replaced by Carter Stadium in 1967, the university offered the Raleigh School System the old lights at a more than reasonable price. However, people in Cameron Village were against it and it never happened. (Finally in the 1990's, a football stadium was built for Broughton right there on its campus and has worked out fine for all concerned.)

But back then, Broughton played their home games at Devereux Meadow, the Raleigh City Minor League baseball team's home field. It was your typical football field lined off on a baseball infield. It included the dirt infield and was rough in places. The stands were pretty close to the home team's benches on the field. The visitors' stands had been brought in to set up behind the visitors' benches. You could seat a couple thousand people without too much trouble. The field was located right beside Downtown Boulevard so nearby traffic was constant during the games. We would dress at our dressing room in Holliday Gym and ride the city buses about a mile or so to Devereux Meadow.

Before we left for our home games, I was able to get the cafeteria staff to help feed us, which became a weekly routine that season. We would usually have a baked potato, small hamburger steak, salad, bread, and iced tea with a dessert. We played our games at 8 o'clock, so we would eat about 4 o'clock and then go to the gym and rest before getting dressed and heading for the stadium. Most of this was based on what I remembered we did at UNC before our ball games. Remember, the only experience I had had was my coaching and playing at Carolina, so I used what I knew and was familiar with.

As we got off the bus on that Friday, September 4, there was a lot of anticipation. We were all nervous and anxious for the game to get underway. We had a small meeting place with bathrooms behind the dugouts where we would meet after warming up for the game.

## 1970 BROUGHTON FOOTBALL ROSTER

| No. | Name | Pos. | Ht. | Wt. | Class |
|---|---|---|---|---|---|
| 10 | DAVID DUPREE | QB | 5'11'' | 165 | 12 |
| 12 | JOHN HOLDING | QB | 6'2'' | 175 | 12 |
| 14 | PRESTON RUTH | QB | 6'0'' | 165 | 12 |
| 16 | DAVID TURNER | QB | 5'11'' | 145 | 11 |
| 20 | ROLAND MASSEY | HB | 5'7'' | 155 | 12 |
| 21 | SKIP HAWKINS | HB | 5'8'' | 160 | 11 |
| 24 | DICKIE THOMPSON | HB | 5'8'' | 155 | 11 |
| 26 | JIMMY DURHAM | HB | 6'0'' | 165 | 12 |
| 30 | MACY FALKNER | LB | 5'9'' | 180 | 11 |
| 31 | RANDY PROCTOR | HB | 5'8'' | 165 | 11 |
| 32 | LARRY HEIGHT | FB | 6'2'' | 222 | 11 |
| 33 | MARK CAUDLE | HB | 5'8'' | 135 | 11 |
| 34 | JIM BASS | HB | 5'10'' | 158 | 11 |
| 36 | CHARLES BANKS | E | 5'10'' | 170 | 11 |
| 38 | VANN HINTON | HB | 6'0'' | 160 | 11 |
| 40 | ALLAN PARNELL | HB | 6'0'' | 165 | 11 |
| 41 | JIM LUMSDEN | FB | 5'11'' | 170 | 12 |
| 44 | CHARLES KING | FB | 5'11'' | 178 | 12 |
| 46 | ERIC HANDY | HB | 5'9'' | 160 | 12 |
| 50 | JIM STONEHAM | C | 5'10'' | 165 | 12 |
| 52 | WILLIS PRICE | G | 5'9'' | 156 | 11 |
| 54 | JOHN CLARKE | C | 5'10'' | 185 | 12 |
| 56 | SAM BEARD | C | 5'9'' | 155 | 12 |
| 60 | JIM FITZGERALD | G | 5'9'' | 170 | 11 |
| 61 | KENT KISTLER | G | 5'8'' | 165 | 11 |
| 62 | PAUL USSERY | G | 5'11'' | 180 | 11 |
| 63 | STEVE BREWBAKER | T | 6'0'' | 190 | 12 |
| 64 | JIM LITTLE | G | 5'8'' | 170 | 12 |
| 65 | GEORGE LATTIMORE | G | 5'10'' | 170 | 12 |
| 66 | DOUG MURRAY | LB | 5'10'' | 180 | 12 |
| 67 | RICK HUNTER | G | 5'10'' | 160 | 11 |
| 68 | HORACE AYSCUE | T | 5'10'' | 185 | 11 |
| 70 | DAVE REYNOLDS | T | 6'1'' | 205 | 12 |
| 71 | ASHLEY SPAIN | T | 5'11'' | 180 | 12 |
| 72 | GARY NEAL | T | 6'1'' | 185 | 11 |
| 73 | CHRIS MORGAN | T | 6'2'' | 280 | 12 |
| 74 | JAY MORGAN | T | 6'2'' | 190 | 11 |
| 75 | MARK SHANER | G | 5'8'' | 205 | 12 |
| 76 | JIM CORTER | T | 6'3'' | 180 | 11 |
| 77 | MURRAY HOWELL | T | 5'10'' | 195 | 12 |
| 78 | DAVE WOOTEN | T | 6'0'' | 195 | 11 |
| 79 | GRIGG MULLEN | T | 5'9'' | 175 | 11 |
| 80 | BILLY STARLING | E | 6'2'' | 180 | 12 |
| 81 | WELLS EDMUNDSON | E | 6'1'' | 200 | 11 |
| 82 | PHIL FICKLIN | E | 6'1'' | 185 | 12 |
| 83 | GARY STAINBACK | E | 6'0'' | 175 | 12 |
| 84 | BERNARD WILLIAMS | E | 6'1'' | 155 | 11 |
| 85 | JOHNNY FORD | E | 5'11'' | 175 | 11 |
| 86 | RICK EUDY | E | 6'0'' | 195 | 12 |
| 87 | DOUG PERRY | E | 6'2'' | 165 | 11 |

Early Roster

As I recall, I was certainly nervous and apprehensive about coaching my first game as a head coach, but I felt like we had prepared well. I remember feeling a little pressure for us to perform well since I was such a young head coach and I knew some people like Joel Long had taken some chances in hiring me to lead this program. I was more concerned about our team and me, as their head coach, representing Broughton well than I was about winning the game. We were underdogs and I had visions of us not being ready and getting the heck beat out of us and my being embarrassed. Yet I knew we had worked hard and prepared well for this opening game. So much of the coaching then and now has to do with preparing for everything that could happen in a ball game. I realized that what is so important in coaching sometimes is making decisions immediately on the spot. It was not like a coach can take it home with him and talk to people, then decide what he thinks is the best to do. I knew that the team and coaching staff had worked extremely diligently in preseason, and we would play hard.

We felt good about our defense and knew they would run to the football. A big question was would we move the ball? Like I said, I guess it did pass through my mind about getting beat 50-0 by Grimsley in my first game ever coaching, but it did not linger.

As we lined up for the opening kickoff, my heart was throbbing. Our sidelines was filled with energy and fan anticipation. As my pre-game ritual, I shook my coaches' hands and wished them luck. I made sure the players understood where the offense and defense benches would be so we could confer as they came off the field during the game. The band was playing and the crowd was thrilled for a new football season to begin. The referee blew his whistle and the football was in the air. Who would have ever guessed where this football team would take the Raleigh community in the next three months?

Greensboro moved the ball on us, but our defense came up with big plays throughout the first half. Jim Bass, one of the best backs I have had the privilege of coaching over 30 years, began his junior year with a great game, and it was exciting to know that he would be around for us for two years. He had tremendous balance as a back, and besides his determination, it was his best physical characteristic. He scored in the first quarter on a 74-yard run on the old Green Bay sweep. This would be one of the best plays for us all season. We had Jim Little, Kent Kistler, and George Lattimore, who were our pulling guards, and they did a superlative job. Jim weighed only 168 pounds, and Kent weighed 164 pounds. Even though none of them were over 5' 10", they stayed low and would flat out get after you. So often, pulling guards in this offense will run by people, but very seldom did any of these players pass anyone up. Phil Ficklin and Rick Eudy shared the tight end position, and one thing this offense needed was a big and tough tight end who did not mind getting his nose dirty and bloody and yet could still catch the football. Both of these guys could do all of this. Jim took the handoff from quarterback David Turner and dipped in and out following his blockers and took it right down the right sidelines in front of our bench 74 yards for six points. Gary Stainback was our kicker, and he put it through the goal post to give us a 7-0 lead with about 2:50 left in the first quarter.

Coach Riggs and QB David Turner

Linebacker George Lattimore

Grimsley did not waste much time before they got things going. After we were held the first series of the second quarter, John Holding punted the ball. It was received by running back Greg Ward. He caught it on the 30 yard line and took it the distance for six points. After the touchdown, Grimsley went for two points, which caught us by surprise. Thinking they would kick the ball to tie the score, our monster back Allan Parnell remembers with horror that he lined up to rush the kick. He, along with most of the rest of us, including me, did not notice that Grimsley was going for a two-point conversion. When Allan realized the formation, he was late getting over to defend the flats, and the quarterback, Jack Elkins, made a good throw to Greg Ward, the running back, for the two point conversion. After the game, the Greensboro coaches said they had decided before the game to go for two points after their first score. It was no special strategy, but it certainly worked to perfection for the Whirlies to give them an 8-7 lead.

We never threatened seriously the rest of the game. I remember we had bad field position most of the second half and Greensboro lived inside our 20 in the third quarter, but our defense played well and never did let them score again. It turned into a defensive struggle. We had not worked on the kicking game as much as we should have, and it really hurt us this first game. As a young coach, I certainly learned a lot about game preparation from my first high school game. From then on, coaching, preparing and practicing the kicking game was a priority for us.

I remember going to midfield and shaking their coaches' hands, and it was not a pleasant feeling. I was upset with the loss and with myself for the bad coaching job I felt I had done. I remember being in tears after the game, but I realized that I was the leader of this team and had to get control of my emotions. I do not remember what I said, but I knew we had to move on and get ready for the next game.

I had the whole team show up on Saturday mornings at the Broughton track and practice field about 8 o'clock to jog a mile. I did this because it was good for me to see how the players were doing and also catch any injuries that may have occurred on the previous night. I knew that it had helped me to get up and jog and loosen up after a game when I had played at Carolina, and you could take care of any minor injuries on that

Saturday morning that may help get the players ready for practice on Monday. The majority of the guys showed up on time. I allowed the ones who had jobs to miss, but if they were hurt in any way they were to let me know.

Grimsley 8 Broughton 7

Our coaching staff had decided to meet at the Broughton gym offices on Sunday afternoons about 4 o' clock. I would take the film of the game which was filmed by one of the teachers at Broughton, Mr. Smalls, to the Trailways Bus Station in downtown Raleigh. In those days, there were only a few places that would develop the 16mm football game films, and one of them was in Durham. So I would put it on the bus to Durham around midnight on Friday, and it would usually be back to for me to pick up by Sunday afternoon. Our staff would break the film down of our game and go over the mistakes as well as good things we had done on Friday night to help us prepare for our next game. We also would exchange films with our upcoming opponent so we could plan how to attack them. The typical rule was that you exchanged the films by a certain time early in the week of the game, so both teams could have access to what their opponent would be running offensively and defensively. Our coaches would also reevaluate our own players and see what personnel changes we would need to make. Since it was only the first game of the season, we were thinking that we would try to play as many people as we could to give them a chance to be under game situations. However, practice is the key. A player earned a position and playing time based on how he practiced during the week.

We had played Grimsley on Friday night and our next opponent, Winston-Salem Reynolds High School, was playing the next day on Saturday evening at the old Wake Forest University stadium. I went to scout the game and I remember being blown away by how good they looked physically and how big they were. I also was impressed by being in the large press box and the beauty of the field. Part of it may have been because it was a small college stadium and the excitement the Reynolds crowd brought to their first game of the1970 high school football season, but I was almost in awe of their football team. I remember thoughts going through my head of getting beat 70-0 by them. I certainly did not let on to any of this to my players, but I think I did share some of it with my coaching staff.

Here we were 0-1 after our first game and had visions of being 0-2 real quickly and totally embarrassed as a first year coach. I thought to myself, what have I gotten myself into? However, once we got back on the field on Monday afternoon, things began to fall into place in our preparation.

I am not sure when I did my preparation for the classes, but I do have good memories from teaching my classes. I was teaching American History and World Cultures, and that certainly kept me busy as a first year teacher. In my student teaching at Guy B. Phillips Jr. High School, I had enjoyed the interaction with students and this carried over at Broughton.

The students in my classes were eager to learn and were very respectful. I do not remember having any discipline problems. I was fresh out of my Masters program where I had learned so many things about our society and was eager to share with my students. I did not want them to be sheltered from what was going on in society around them like I had been due to my playing football. I felt like a person could give himself to a sport, a hobby, or anything of interest and spend time on whatever it was, and still be aware of life around them. So often people devote themselves to just one or two things they are involved in and miss a lot of life right before their eyes.

## Game 2: Broughton vs. Winston-Salem Reynolds, September 11, 1970

I knew one ball game did not make or break a whole season, so after the one point defeat we tried to move on and think about the next ball game. I knew we needed to tackle and block better, so we spent some time in our practices working on fundamentals.

We took the football on our first drive 65 yards. Bass scored on an eight-yard run off tackle behind Phil Ficklin and David Reynolds with a good kick out block by Charles King. We missed the extra point.

Reynolds got on the scoreboard in the second quarter on a three-yard run by fullback Bobby Deal and tied the score 6-6. Our defense in the 5-2 monster played well, and our whole philosophy was "bend but do not break." We shut them down the rest of the second quarter and even got a break by recovering a fumble. With just four minutes left in the half, we took the ball 67 yards down to the one-yard line where David Turner sneaked it over for the touchdown. We went for two-points, but failed and the score was 12-6 Broughton. Reynolds, however, did not give up and came right back at us. They drove the ball about 65 yards in the last couple minutes of the half. Jim Durham came up with a big interception in the end zone with less than a minute to go in the half. That gave us a lot of momentum going in at halftime and more than anything else began to give us the confidence we needed.

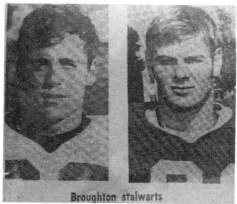

Broughton stalwarts
Roland Massey and Wells Edmundson

Football so often is a game of breaks and turnovers, and a team has to get their share in order to come out on top. That interception by Durham may have been the play of the game. Jim also knocked down a couple more passes that were crucial to keeping Reynolds from scoring. George Lattimore, Doug Murray, and Alan Parnell played very well for us at the linebacker positions. Lattimore was all over the place making tackles. Also Mark Shaner was the key to our defensive line and loved playing the nose guard position in our defense. Mark was short and squatty, but could match anyone with his strength. He had a full beard during part of the season and probably scared some centers because he looked like he was 26 years old.

Being up 12-6 at halftime was good, but we knew we had to put more points on the board, because all Reynolds needed was a touchdown and extra point to take the lead and give us our second defeat. My thinking was too much about not losing the game instead going for the win. The third quarter was a defensive battle with neither team moving the ball very much. With about 5 minutes left in the game, Turner directed an outstanding 60-yard drive for our third score. We had no penalties and no mistakes as we took it right down the field with sweeps and off tackle plays with Bass running hard every play. Again, the offensive line was fundamentally sound and began to move off the ball against a much larger defensive line. Mixed in with a couple passes to wingbacks Roland Massey and Eric Handy along with a couple runs by Height and King, we moved down the field at a good steady pace. Turner sneaked over from the one again to score his second touchdown. Our extra point was good by Stainback to give us a solid lead 19-6, and that is the way it ended. Reynolds threatened once more, but our defensive ends Wells Edmundson and Charles Banks pretty much contained them from any long running plays. Preston Ruth, our safety played an excellent game along with our defensive backs Jim Durham and Dave Dupree. It was a good win for us for many reasons.

It certainly felt awesome to get the victory over a good Reynolds team, and it gave me confidence as a coach. It removed any nightmares of getting beat 70-0 and helped me to gain some confidence in myself and our football team. I was really nervous about how we would do against Reynolds after scouting them the week before. All of this was new for me, and I realized we were in the "big time" for high school football. Our defense really began to tackle better, and our pursuit to the ball improved a lot from the first ball game. I knew we were not very big or fast defensively, so we had to make up for our weaknesses with pursuit to the ball and better tackling. We really had to play as a team if we were going to be winners on the field.

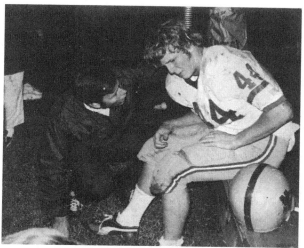

Fullback Charles King

"Otto, this is the way it is."

Jim Bass was selected as one of the offensive players of the week in the Raleigh area. He continued to run well, and his determination always picked up extra yardage after the initial hit. Jim led all rushers with 119 yards, and he also caught three passes from Turner. Charles King and Larry Height led the way with solid blocking from our fullback position. David was learning the offense and becoming a field general. I allowed him to call some plays just because I felt that the game of football really belongs to the players, and they so often know more than a coach standing on the sidelines because they are in the action on the field and can look into the eyes of their teammates. I felt like this when I was playing both in high school and college. It may have come from my growing up "sandlot" days in Drexel and Morganton when we made up our own plays in the backyard.

Jim Durham made six tackles and had one key interception and three more knockdowns and was selected as the defensive player of the week. Jim was always real cool in the secondary and played his position very well. He, like our whole secondary, did not have much speed but played great zone defense in the backfield.

Reynolds Game

So here we were with a 1-1 record after two games. Few people thought we would win many games, but with that victory over Reynolds we were almost halfway to the total number of victories that had come about in 1969. I knew after this game that we could compete in any game. I could tell the boys were intelligent and they played smart. Out of all the games that year, this one was the most important for this 24-year head coach because I thought that we may get blown out by them. This gave me confidence in what we were doing. The kids felt super afterwards and began to play and practice with more confidence. I do not know what they thought about me and our young staff, but I knew this had to give them some confidence in us as well as themselves.

After the ball games our coaching staff would visit with the players as they were cleaning up and leaving, would begin washing the uniforms, and I would take the game film to the bus station. The night of the Reynolds game, assistant principal Bill Blackburn and his wife Peggy had asked all our coaches and wives, other administrators, Ed Mclean and his wife Lois, and several other people who were part of the athletic department to get together after the game. I felt like I was walking on a cloud. I will have to admit I was feeling proud of the way we performed that night. It was so good to get together with other people who were part of Broughton High School and shared in our success that night. It was certainly an upbeat gathering, and those people made us feel so welcome to be part of the Broughton family. It gave our coaches' wives an opportunity to be with other wives, and it began a life-long friendship with many of those people.. It was also good to get away from the coaching duties for a short time. I believe these get togethers after the games this first season helped me develop a habit of trying to get our coaches and wives and others who were part of our football program together wherever I coached. I was certainly lucky to have Marie, who loves football and was our number one fan, who is very warm to others, fun to be around, and loves people. She is a great coach's wife and has probably had as much influence on the boys I have coached as I have. These times also gave other coaches and their wives a chance to be together in a social environment other than on the field coaching. Friendships within the coaching staff's families have a lot to do with the success of any program, and this was a place after the games that helped mold and unite our coaching staff family. Robbie Evans was not married, but was dating his future wife, Lavinia. John Thomas and his wife Brenda were pregnant with their first child. Mac Caldwell and his wife Suzie had three small children at the time. Mike Kral was not married at the time, but usually would attend our staff get-togethers.

## Game 3: Broughton vs. Enloe, September 18, 1970 (Double Header)

By this time in our season, I was feeling confident in our team and coaching staff. So I began thinking a lot more positively about what this team could accomplish and become. This new positive thinking was 100% due to the players performances and attitudes. This is an example where the players influenced the coach rather than the coach influencing the players. I was fired up about the rest of the season.

We had to soon forget that great 19-6 win over Reynolds because we had to get ready to play Enloe High School in a very special game that would help high school football in the Raleigh area. Raleigh City Athletic Director Carroll King had come up with the idea that the four Raleigh city schools would play a doubleheader football game at N. C. State's new Carter Finley Stadium.

The doubleheader was being held to raise funds for the city of Raleigh's athletic program, both junior and senior high schools. Carroll King said the night of high school football's primary three objectives were:

1. To help balance the current deficit.

2. To make possible a broadening of athletic programs.

3. To make new friends and fans among the adult community in order to raise interest in high school football.

The games were endorsed by Mayor Seby Jones, the Raleigh Chamber of Commerce, Merchants Bureau, and the Council of Civic Clubs of Raleigh. N.C. State Athletic Director, Willis Casey made the new Carter Stadium available at a minimum operational cost. It was to be a special night for high school football. Sanderson High School and Ligon High School were to play at 7:00 p.m., with Enloe and us playing the night capper about 9:00.

Coaches Roberts, Harrington, AD Carroll King, George Thompson, David Riggs

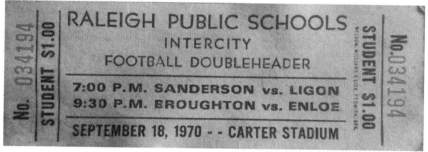

Student Ticket

As in most high school communities today in 2016, there was no tax money used in any way for school athletics. The operating costs for most schools came directly from gate receipts and booster clubs made up usually of parents of the players of the athletic teams. The Friday night football doubleheader was titled "Family Night for the Raleigh Public Schools." The hope of all involved was to have a big crowd that could see the four high schools play football and raise some money for all athletics in the Raleigh City Schools for the kids to be able to play sports. The cost of tickets was $3.00 for adults and $1.00 for students. It is a shame today that inflation has raised tickets for football games in high school to as much as $6.00 per person. A family of two adults with two children cost $24.00 to see a game today. I wish there was a way where students and young children could get in for a couple bucks, but we live in a different age today than back in 1970.

Needless to say the players were more than pumped to have the chance to play in a college football stadium in front of a lot of people. There was a lot of additional publicity the week of the game at Carter Stadium mainly because the games were put in the public's eyes due to trying to raise some money for all athletics in Raleigh. Back in 1970, none of the high schools had soccer programs, very few athletics for girls, and only Broughton had a cross country team made possible because of volunteers. Several times during the week of the game, we needed to provide players to be at Carter Stadium to have their pictures taken and action pictures to be taken with the players of the three other Raleigh Schools. The head coaches were asked to have a short news conference and picture day also involving the doubleheader. All of this interfered with practices for our team. I just wanted to coach and prepare our team, but I was learning that other things come along with being head coach. We sent Mark Shaner, one of our co-captains, Jim Bass, our leading ground gainer, Steve Brewbaker, one of our defensive linemen, Jane Holroyd, our head cheerleader, and others to Carter Stadium to participate in the publicity for the Friday night special doubleheader.

WARMING UP — Getting ready for the big high
igh school doubleheader Friday at Carter Stadium
re these four players: left to right, Broughton guard
Mark Shaner, Enloe guard Tommy Lee, Sanders
tackle Bill Terry, and Ligon end Frank Williams. E
loe faces Broughton, Sanderson plays Ligon.

Double Header

Enloe High School was coached by George Thompson, who had built a good reputation when he was at Kinston. One of George's assistants was Dick Knox, who later would be a great contributor to the North Carolina High School Athletic Association as assistant executive of the association throughout the 1980's, 90's and through 2008. Avery Tolley, Ansel Glendenning, and Wilson Hickerson were also some of George's assistants, and they each were good high school coaches. As I think of these men, I cannot help but think of so many high school coaches who gave so much of themselves to the players they coached. So many things are not appreciated until long past the time they are gone. I did not know all of these men well individually, but I do know through conversations I had with them that they loved coaching and they wanted to have a positive influence on the kids they coached. And they did.

George, along with his staff, was so kind and gracious to me, a young 24-year-old first year high school coach who probably thought he knew more than he did. George, along with Jim Brown at Sanderson, accepted me without any problems as their colleague and fellow head coaching friend, and that meant a lot to me in 1970 as well as it does today. George was a funny man and very giving. His daughter, Kay Koenig, worked with the NCHSAA for years and helped me, as well as many other high school coaches, in getting jobs, hiring assistants, and understanding a lot of what the NCHSAA could do for us. George coached for many years and then retired from Enloe in 1979 when he helped open up the new Athens Drive High School. The new head football coach to run the football program selected with George was David Riggs. I served with George for several years at Athens Drive when he was athletic director. I still remember story after story about and by George. He always would say when he had a weak athletic team and would lose a ball game that "it was like going bear hunting with a switch."

Facing Enloe was going to be a tough and important football game for us. In fact, Caulton Tudor, a sports writer for the *Raleigh Times,* called it "Broughton's biggest game in three years." I, again, did not know all that had gone on in the past few years but I did understand that this game was a big test for us mainly because of the environment and because it was against a strong rival school in Raleigh.

Jim Bass(BHS), Charlie Muldrow(LHS), Larry Larson(SHS), Julius Branch(EHS)

Julius Branch was one of the best backs in the history of Enloe High School football and he was the main man. He was a tough shifty back who could run and catch the football. Enloe had beaten Cary earlier in the season, but had lost to Fayetteville Terry Sanford the week before we were to play them in the doubleheader. I do not have much memory about playing them at Carter Stadium, but I do remember it was certainly a different atmosphere than playing at Devereux Meadow. I believe there were close to 10,000 people who had attended the doubleheader, and many of them stayed for both games that September 18<sup>th</sup> night.

We scored our first touchdown with five minutes to go in the first half. Jim Bass ran the ball well again, and David Turner completed several passes when needed. Bass ran the final two yards to give us a 6-0 lead at half-time. The second half opening drive was one of the better drives we had had up to this time. We took the ball on our on 33-yard line and drove it the length of the field for our second score. It took us 19 straight running plays with Turner sneaking it over the final yard. Most of the yards were gained by Bass and fullbacks Larry Height and Charles King. The touchdown put us in control of the game with a 12-0 lead and took over seven minutes. Jim Bass was continuing to prove he was one of the better running backs around with another 100 yard-plus game. Of course, the thing I remember so much was our linemen getting off the line of scrimmage getting after people. John Clarke, Kent Kistler, Jim

Little, Rick Hunter, with the help of Jim Fitzgerald, Murray Howell, Gary Neal, Dave Reynolds, and Jay Morgan all played well and helped open up holes for us all night long.

Why can't we go back in?

Our defense led by Shaner, Brewbaker, Corter, Banks, and Edmundson continued to improve. Our linebackers of Lattimore and Murray ran to the football like crazy and kept the "D" all fired up. Our secondary, Ruth, Durham and Dupree, played smart, tough, and was very football-wise that night, just like they had been the whole season. Our defense forced a fumble later in the fourth quarter, and Bass took it over the last two yards after a short drive. One of the key plays in that drive was a 19-yard pass from Turner to Roland Massey. It was 20-0 after our try for two was successful. Enloe scored in the fourth quarter as Julian Branch had a three-yard touchdown run to give them their only score for the night.

After the game, I knew we were getting better, and the boys were loving to play the game! Our passing game was coming along with Turner improving and Roland Massey, Billy Starling and Phil Ficklin catching the ball better as each game was played. We were now 2-1 for the season and 1-0 in our conference. The conference season was the key to get to the playoffs because only the conference champions would qualify to participate in the state playoffs at that time. I knew and felt as a coach that the key to our team was improving as the season progressed. In all my years of coaching, the idea of improvement in every game was so important to being successful. I knew one victory or one loss did not make a season successful or a failure, but the goal was to improve and get better. I felt like this team understood this and was on its way to accomplishing it. Next up was a tough non-conference opponent and a traditionally well-coached football team – the Rocky Mount Gryphons.

Carter Stadium Win

## Game 4: Broughton vs. Rocky Mount, September 25, 1970

Rocky Mount was a state powerhouse in all sports. Danny Talbott had made Rocky Mount famous in the early 1960's by his ability in football, basketball, and baseball. I played football with Danny in college at UNC for several years. He was a great one.

Rocky Mount was 3-0 for the season and was tied with Wilson Fike and Goldsboro for first place in their Division II 4-A Conference. So we knew it should be a grueling game. However, they were coming to Raleigh to play us in Devereux Meadow.

It was a big crowd that filled the Meadow that night, and they did not have to wait long before the fireworks began by both teams. Rocky Mount kicked off to us, and Jim Bass caught it on the ten-yard line. He followed his blockers up the middle and then cut to his right running near our bench. Jim, with his great agility and balance, was hit a couple times early on, but kept running toward our goal line. He made it the last 40 yards without being touched and put us ahead immediately 6-0. The try for the point after was blocked.

Jim Corter   10-1-70

Shaner and Ford looking on

On the ensuing kickoff, Rocky Mount returned it and got good field position on the 35-yard line. On the very first play, the Gryphons wasted little time in moving the ball when Pete Thompson broke off tackle for

44 yards down to the 18-yard line. Three plays later, Roscoe Batts threw a ten-yard pass to Thompson to tie the score. The extra point was wide right and we had a 6-6 tied ball game. A lot had happened in the first three minutes of the game, and it looked like it was going to be a high scoring game. After a couple of exchanged punts, Bass gave us great field position after his 33-yard punt return down to the Rocky Mount 14-yard line. Larry Height, our big fullback who alternated with Charles King, blasted up the middle for a ten-yard touchdown run thanks to super blocking by John Clarke, Jim Little, and Dave Reynolds. Our pass for the two-point try fell incomplete, and we were up 12-6.

The two defenses began to really play from this point in the game until the beginning of the fourth quarter. Both teams played hard and hit hard and neither yielded any scoring play. David Dupree recovered a Rocky Mount fumble to stop the Gryphon march in the third quarter. The ball was deep in our own territory and we were unable to move the ball. John Holding, our punter, had to punt from our own end zone on the first play of the fourth quarter. The big defensive and outstanding lineman from Rocky Mount, George Jones, broke through our line and blocked the punt, and Karnell Kimbel grabbed the ball on the two and fell into the end zone for the touchdown. Howard McCullough kicked the go-ahead point, and Rocky Mount led 13-12 with 11 minutes to go in the game.

Both teams moved the ball up and down the field without either one getting much of an advantage. Then we had a big play from our defensive squad. Charles Banks, our talented defensive end, broke through on 4th down and deflected the punt to give us the ball on the 49-yard line. We moved the ball with our running game, and then Turner hit Starling on a rollout pass and we had a first down on the 20-yard line. We could not get it in the end zone, so we tried a field goal from the 6-yard line. Macy Falkner was our field goal kicker at this time, and Preston Ruth was our holder with John Clarke our snapper. Macy split the uprights to give us the lead at 15-13.

With only about three minutes left in the game, we had some terrible communication which had to be my fault. Someway, I am not sure how, our kicker thought we were trying for an onside kick, BUT no one else on our team knew. To this day, I do not know how that happened, but it certainly gave the Gryphons excellent field position. They got the ball on their 46-yard line with just minutes left in the game. Rocky Mount's Walter Sherrod ran the ball several times down deep in our territory. Batts then threw to Pete Thompson again for the decisive score with just over a minute left in the game. Jim Corter and Steve Brewbaker blocked the extra-point and we were down 19-15. We could do nothing with the ball the last minute, and we left our home field with a heartbreaking defeat. Even though Rocky Mount was a first-class team and we played them tough, nothing could take away the hurt in our guts over that defeat.

Quarterback David Turner

Losing in football leaves an ache in most players' and coaches' stomachs. As a coach, I do not understand why most of us feel the losses are so much lower than the wins are high, but I believe in general that is true. Sometimes as a coach goes through the season, he remembers the losses much more than the wins. Life is that way sometimes too. One can have ten good things happen to them and one bad thing, but often will remember the one bad thing.

As I thought back about that game, I realized that we had played hard with a lot of desire, but had made way too many mistakes. We had a punt blocked, fumbled the football at the one yard line, and had horrible communication on the onside kick. Our offense moved the ball and our defense played well as usual, but the all-important third part of a football game, the kicking game, was a disaster and ultimately cost us the game.

So here we were 2-2 for the season and had actually performed well enough to be undefeated. However, I honestly believe we were learning that to be winners consistently the entire team, including me, had to do the little things right. So often a win in a football game can be traced back not so much to a big play or tackle, but to the fact that the team does the little things correctly, and I believe that this is so true in life also. A few good things can happen to you in life every once in a while, but what is important is how you are doing in the little things. One good thing about our losses was that they both came against non-conference foes, and that meant that we were 1-0 in our Division III 4-A conference. Our next opponent was a key one because it was against the conference team of Durham Hillside.

Difficult one to get over

Tough Loss

## Game 5: Broughton vs. Durham Hillside, October 2, 1970

Our next game was to be against Durham Hillside with their famous coach, Coach Russell Blunt. Coach Blunt was in the midst of a rebuilding season with the Hornets. He was an excellent coach and had earned an excellent reputation in high school football. Coach Blunt was another coach who accepted this young 24-year old coach just out of college. In later years he and I corresponded from time to time, and he encouraged me so much just by showing interest in what I was doing. Most people in Durham and people involved in the NCHSAA know of Coach Blunt's successes, and they were many. As good a coach as he was, I remember him as a better person. I would love to know some of the hardships he faced in the coaching ranks as he started out and coached through the 1950's, '60's, '70's, '80's, and '90's with all the prejudices and discrimination that went on. I realize there were many more Afro-American coaches like Willie Bradshaw who learned under

Coach Blunt who also had to face many prejudices and mistreatment as they started out coaching. Coach Blunt was inducted into the National High School Hall of Fame, and his Hillside track team won the State Championship when he was still coaching in his 80's. What a man and coach!

Coach Russell Blunt

A year later in 1971 I wrote Coach Blunt and his staff after Hillside got blown away by Enloe High School and just told him I admired the way he and his staff and team fought until the very end. They showed great spirit and fight, and it certainly showed up as a never give up attitude. A lot of teams will give up and throw in the towel when they are getting beat bad, but not Coach Blunt's Hillside team. They made a tremendous impact on me and helped make me a better coach as the years went by. I would later leave coaching for about eight years as I went into full-time ministry working in Raleigh and in Fairfax, Virginia. In 1989, I left the full-time paid ministry and came back to coaching at Sanderson High School. After the newspaper published an article on me getting back into coaching, I received a letter from Coach Blunt along with the copy of the letter I had written him in 1971. In the letter, Coach wrote, "I have kept this letter you had written me over 15 years ago. I kept it among my "special letters" because a coach does not get too many nice letters especially from his rival coaches. It is great to have you back in the harness again. Sincerely, Russ Blunt."

I still have that letter from Coach, and it has meant a lot to me over the many years of coaching. Coach Blunt coached into his nineties and developed many young boys and girls into outstanding men and women. I hope I have had just a fraction of an impact Coach Blunt had over his many years of coaching.

Hillside was not a very good football team in 1970 and came into our game without a victory. Our defense was getting better as the season was progressing. The linebackers played such a key to our 5-2 monster defense, and George Lattimore, Doug Murray, Allan Parnell, Jim Lumsden and the rest of the crew swarmed to the ball. With Wells Edmundson and Charles Banks at our defensive end positions containing anything running wide and turning it into our defensive line of Jim Corter, Mark Shaner, and Steve Brewbaker, our offensive opponents were finding themselves facing a formidable test. All three of our defensive backs were so very good, and all three played smart football. Dave Dupree and co-captain Jim Durham played our zone pass defense really well, and neither one would hesitate to assuredly hit you. Preston Ruth and John Holding played our safety position, and they both were intelligent football players and understood the game. In our defense, the safety was the last player for us between the football and our goal line. Preston always knew that if he got beat deep on a pass that it was his fault and he would be in "hot water" with the secondary coach who was me.

As we progressed through the season, I felt that we needed to be a little more versatile on the defensive side of the ball. When I was coaching the freshmen team at UNC the previous year, I realized that a change-up defense presented other teams some difficulty rather than staying in one defensive front. Linemen always have trouble adjusting and blocking different fronts, mainly because it confuses people. As I have said, one of the keys in anything one does in life is to understand your job. If you are confused or do not know what your role is in your job, then you really cannot go full speed ahead with confidence and you will not be able to do your very best.

Kistler, we got this!

Coach Thomas – Stinkin'

Our staff talked and shared ideas about a new defense as a change-up. I was familiar with the 4-4 defense that was becoming popular with a lot of the college teams. We ran the 4-4 at Carolina, and I loved the blitzing aspects of the defense, and it was a very easy defense to shift to out of our basic 5-2 monster defense. We also had the players who were smart enough to understand and play it. We did not want to get real fancy with it, but certainly wanted to use it enough to confuse our opponents. We practiced it during the week before the Hillside game and thought it would be a good game to use, since Hillside was not having a very good season and we were favored. I thought it would certainly help us down the road if we could perfect it and the players could understand it.

We unveiled it against Hillside and it went well. We kept them out of our end zone and dominated the game. We limited the Hornets to a total of only 49 yards in rushing and passing. While our defense was dominating, our offense continued to get better controlling the ball on the ground as well as being able to throw when we needed to. I always tried to use the pass as a supplement to our running game and used it when the opponent least expected it. I learned somewhere early in football that you should throw on running downs and run on passing downs. That can be risky at times, but you have to take risks in order to win sometimes. The same thing applies to life also. One cannot always continue to do the same thing the same way all the time. There will be a point in life when you have to step out and gamble or take a risk in order to grow and get better in anything you do.

We took the opening kickoff and drove it down for a touchdown. David Turner had several excellent completions to Eric Handy that totaled about 44 yards. From the ten-yard line Jim Bass powered his way into the end zone for 6 points. Macy Falkner, who had really improved his kicking by his hard work, added the extra point and we were up 7-0.

Our defense swarmed to the football next time Hillside had the ball and we forced a fumble recovered by Charles King. We got good field position thanks to our defense which often put us on the opponent's side of the fifty yard line. John Holding hit Billy Starling, our leading receiver, for a 35-yard touchdown immediately, and we were up 13-0. We missed the extra point. Our defense led by Banks, Edmundson, Shaner, and Murray along with our solid defensive backfield shut out the Hornets the rest of the half, and we led 13-0 at halftime.

In the third quarter, our offense controlled the ball with the running of Bass, Height, King, and Massey. Turner directed the running game to perfection and we scored our third touchdown with Larry Height running it over from the 3-yard line. Turner ran the two-point conversion after a tremendous fake in the backfield and we were up 21-0.

Both David Turner and John Holding had good games at quarterback against Hillside. They combined for more than 207 yards in the air and more than 110 on the ground. Both of these players understood what our offense was about, and more important than this, they understood their teammates and their abilities. Players play together better when they truly understand their capabilities of who they are playing with. Sometimes that is missed in today's game of football.

I always believed in playing everyone who practiced if at all possible, even though our main objective was to win the ballgame. The 21-0 lead gave us an excellent opportunity to play everyone on the team. It is so beneficial for the players and the team as a whole when every member of the team has an opportunity to play in a game if at all possible, whether it is football, soccer, basketball, or whatever. It makes parents and relatives proud of their child and hopefully reassures the players that they are making a contribution to the team. Sometimes coaches, myself included, do not do a good job of getting players in during ball games. So much is going on during the games, and you are constantly so focused on your team improving to the point that you sometimes forget what really is important - which is every player on the team.

We were able to play everyone this game, and it gave us joy and excitement to see the people play who usually did not get in very much. I have observed over the years that often the starters get more excited about good plays the substitutes make rather than plays they themselves have made.

It was a relief to get our second conference win and be tied with several other teams for first place. I did not worry much about weeks down the road, but I tried to concentrate and keep our coaches and players concentrating on the very next game. I have always been pretty good about staying focused on the game of the week and stay away from thinking too far ahead and saying "If we can beat so and so in two weeks or if we can win the next two games" then this will happen. If I as a coach or as a player think about anything other than the present game, it can cost you if you are not careful. We were 3-2 overall and headed in the right direction. I knew if we could just keep improving week by week that we could still be in the running for the conference championship. In all honesty, playing in the playoffs, much less playing in the state championship game, was the farthest thing from my mind.

In fact, it had not even entered my mind at all.

Homecoming was our next game against Wilson Fike. I would learn a lot about homecoming games as we worked our way through the week.

Great Conference Win

**Game 6: Broughton vs. Wilson Fike, October 9, 1970 (Homecoming)**

Homecoming Parade

Wilson Fike High School football was well known across the state of North Carolina. They had won three State Championships in a row and had dominated high school football in the state. They had graduated All-American Carlester Crumpler who ended up going to East Carolina University. He had been an unbelievable running back for Wilson Fike. Coach Henry Trevathan had just resigned from the Fike job, and one of his knowledgeable assistants took over as the new head coach, Gary Whitman. They had continued their winning ways under Coach Whitman and were coming in to Devereux at 4-1 looking for another victory over a Raleigh team.

Fike had been relying on a very strong running game as usual and a very stout defense in their winning ways. The rivalry between the Wilson Fike Titans (formerly the Cyclones) and the Broughton Caps had been one of the most hotly contested rivalries over the last few years leading up to this 1970 game. Both teams were coming into Devereux off winning games.

Broughton had created great traditions for their homecoming games.

There was always a big pep rally in the gym and a parade in the Cameron Village area on the day of the game. You do not find this happening very much anymore because of so many other things going on. However, back in 1970, most students and faculty of the school had some interest in the homecoming game and parade and all the hoopla surrounding the Friday night football game.

Homecoming Parade

Homecoming

We were coming into this game with a lot of confidence. Our offensive line of John Clarke, Jay Morgan, Dave Reynolds, Jim Little, and Rick Hunter had played very well against Durham Hillside. Shaner, Lattimore, and linebacker Jim Lumsden had helped the defense hold Hillside to very few yards the week before. We had had some injuries, but Roland Massey, Jim Durham, and Kent Kistler were all hoping to be back at full strength. Injuries can easily affect the outcome of a game. The average sports spectator may never realize how important it is for a team to be physically healthy, especially a high school football team. You always hope that the back-up players will play their best, as they often have to play for injured players. The mark of a good team is not just the starting 22 players but the whole squad. All play a part in winning or losing each game. I learned this more and more as I gained more experience in coaching and working with teams. I really believe that is why the high school football game is such a great team sport, because everyone has to play a part in practice especially, but also the games themselves. That is why I continued to emphasize that we are all links in a chain, and if that one link of our chain breaks, then the whole chain will collapse. Each player needed to practice as if a win or loss on Friday night depended on him.

Like all the other games we had played, we tried to focus and concentrate on the one game we had before us. Our strategy and concentration was totally on beating Wilson Fike. I do not remember much distraction from the game because of it being homecoming, but I am sure most of the 17-18 year old players were thinking about it being homecoming, the dance after the game, alumni coming back, and more.

We knew it was going to be a difficult game and especially a defensive struggle since both teams' defenses had played well against some good opponents. Neither team moved the ball very well in the first quarter. We got a break in the second quarter when Mark Shaner hopped on a fumble on Fike's 17-yard line. Jim Bass had a great run with superb blocking by the offensive line and took the ball to the two-yard line. David Turner sneaked the remaining two yards behind our center, John Clarke, and guard Jim Little to give us a 6-0 lead. Macy Falkner kicked the extra point and we led 7-0 the rest of the half.

We continued to have some injuries to key people, but our backups faithfully rose to the occasion when they were called on. One of our defensive backs, Jim Durham, was nursing a severely bruised foot. Dickie Thompson filled in superbly for Jim and made some key tackles and defended the pass well.

Eric Handy

Early in the 4th quarter, Fike drove the ball 63 yards for a tying touchdown. Dennis Wilkerson, Fike's quarterback, threw a 12-yard pass to Willie Williams for the touchdown. They kicked the extra point to tie the game at 7-7 with about 7 minutes to go in the game. Other than a 5-yard drive early in the second-half which ended on the 15-yard line, we did not move the ball well. Jim Bass, Charles King, and Eric Handy all ran hard, but we were not consistent enough to get the ball in the end-zone for a score.

Captain Mark Shaner

With less than three minutes to go, Fike's quarterback, Dennis Wilkerson, completed a huge 37-yard pass to wingback Tommy Davis. That gave them a first down on the nine-yard line with only 19 seconds to play in the game. It took them three plays to get it in the end-zone, but John Howell crashed over from the one yard line with 2 seconds left in the game to give the Wilson Fike team the victory. The extra-point was good, and we were once again on the wrong end of the scoreboard 14-7. It truly was a heart-breaking game, but very hard fought by both teams. That was our third close game that we actually played well enough to win. However, it was good training for us to hang tough and play hard and never give up. Life is so much like that, filled with hurdles, tragedies, mistakes, and heartbreaks, but one must learn to keep moving and progressing forward regardless of what happens to you. It was very discouraging to us as a staff and team to get so close, but not close the deal. I told the players after the game that it would be hard to fight back from a loss like this but that they could do it; they had done it before. We played real sound football except for a couple plays, and it hurt us. But we will be back. We're that kind of a team.

We were 3-3 for the season and 2-0 in our conference. We were staying optimistic and we all, coaches and players, were learning a lot life lessons. Yet, it would have been better to learn some of those lessons while we were winning some close games. That time would come in the near future, and that is why I look back at some of these losses helping us in the long run. Again, it is a lot like life – you sometimes cannot see how some difficult times and things you go through really teach you and help prepare you for the future. Bad things are going to happen to all of us, but the key is how we are handling them and how we respond in the midst of troubles and defeat.

Broughton's David Turner about to be racked
Fike's Billy Rodgers moves in for the stop

Turner on the Run

Wilson Fike Wins

Even though we had another close loss, there were good things that I saw. Other than some breakdowns at crucial times which we could remedy, our defense was sturdy. Charles King, Mark Shaner, Doug Murray, and Steve Brewbaker all played well on defense. Once again, Jim Bass ran well and gave a super effort. Our offensive line blocking left a lot to be desired, but again I felt that it was nothing that could not be fixed and corrected with work and focus. Coach Robbie Evans was an excellent teacher and coach, and I knew he could and would get his players to improve. Robbie was a good offensive lineman himself for Broughton in the 1960's and of course started for the Wolfpack of N.C. State in college, so he knew what it would take. As we will see later in the season, Coach Evans accomplished a great deal with his young men.

Next up for us were the Sanderson Spartans, which was the key rival game in Raleigh. Remember Sanderson and Broughton were both under the same roof at Broughton High School in 1968 for a semester because the buildings at Sanderson were not completed until later that year. Thus, the Sanderson football team practiced on the front lawn of Broughton while the Caps practiced on the practice field. Also, when Sanderson opened up, a good number of Broughton football players as well as a large number of students left Broughton because they were reassigned to Sanderson. The attendance lines were redrawn by the school board in 1968, and many friends were split up, which helped make this a natural rivalry game. We knew it would be a hard-hitting and tough football game.

Sanderson had some big physical players along with some speedy backs. They had lost several close ball games, but had played well through the first part of the season. Sanderson had been bitten by the injury bug, and that had hurt them a great deal. They still had Paul Wilder, Charley Norkus, and Don Norton who were the foundation of the team. Sometimes in rival games, players all of a sudden get better and healthier.

### Game 7: Broughton vs. Sanderson, October 16, 1970

David Reynolds, Jim Little, John Holding

The game against Sanderson was definitely a rivalry game and very important because it was a conference game. I had felt pretty good about our team because we had been in every game and could have easily won them all if we had not made big mistakes. However, all the mistakes were correctable, and that was my responsibility to correct them.

Jim Bass had been our strength on offense with his great balance and determination in running the football. Larry Height and Charles King had given us the punch that we needed, and we had decided to build our offense around the running game.

Our defense had been led recently by nose guards Mark Shaner and Jim Corter, linebackers George Lattimore and Doug Murray, and our defensive ends Charles Banks and Wells Edmundson.

Both teams brought their "A" game defensively the first half, and the hitting was pretty intense. Sanderson had planned to shut down Bass, and they certainly did that for most of the game. There was no score in the first quarter, and both offenses had trouble moving the football. Sanderson did penetrate deep in our territory in the second quarter and had a good chance to score, but Preston Ruth intercepted a Spartan pass on the 19-yard line to stop the drive.

Roland Massey

We got the ball with about four minutes to go in the first-half after a good Sanderson punt put us back on our own 20-yard line. David Turner went to work against the Sanderson defensive unit, who had played a great game so far. Turner completed one pass of 14 yards to Billy Starling and then came right back with a completion to Roland Massey for another 16 yards. Jim Bass broke a long run of 35 yards behind the blocking of Jim Little, Kent Kistler, and Charles King. Eric Handy and tight-end Phil Ficklin combined for a great double team block on the run also. After the Spartan defense held on the first three downs, we decided to kick a field goal. With only 23 seconds left, Macy Falkner kicked it through the uprights for a first-half lead of 3-0.

The third quarter continued the defensive struggle, and neither team could move the ball with any consistency. Sanderson took possession after a John Holding punt that went out of bounds on the Sanderson nine-yard line. John had punted very well for us all year and had served as a key weapon in several games. It was a great advantage for us to have someone who could be a threat to run, pass, or kick the ball. His best attribute in the punting game was he kicked the football so high that we got very few run backs. Little things like the kicking game are a must in order to win championships. I felt confident with John punting the ball, and we always got good coverage from our special teams.

With just over ten minutes left to go in the game, Sanderson's offense drove the ball down the field. Charlie Norkus, the Spartan's quarterback, directed Sanderson all the way down to our nine-yard line, where they fumbled and we jumped on it. Two plays later we gave the ball back to them with a fumble on the ten-yard line that was recovered by Sanderson's LeBaron Carruthers. Our defense stiffened up, but Faison Hicks, the running back from Sanderson scored the touchdown from the one-yard line to give Sanderson the lead 7-3 after Paul Wilder's extra point kick.

We received the kickoff and returned it to the 33-yard line. We had only about five and a half minutes left in the game, and we had struggled on offense all game against a good defensive team. Coach Jim Brown, who was a wise and good coach, had come up with a good plan to stop our running game and especially Bass. However, Bass did not need much daylight to get going, and I was hoping it was just a matter of time before he broke loose. We ran our 46 lead play off tackle with our center John Clarke and Jim Little double-teaming and our tackle, Dave Reynolds blocking on their defensive tackle. Larry Height blocked on the linebacker in the area and Doug Murray, our other guard, threw a key block. David Turner gave the ball to our number "34" and off he went. After breaking several tackles, including one big hit by defender Larry Larson, Bass broke toward the sidelines with the Spartans chasing him. As he was hit on the sidelines, he then tip-toed down the field, and the last 12-15 yards he somehow kept his balance. To this day, I can still see Jim being low to the ground and staying in bounds and staying on his feet with superb balance. He got the ball in the end zone on one of his best runs of the season and maybe his career. Our offensive line coach, Robbie Evans, who had blocked for backs like Leon Mason and Bobby Hall at N.C. State, termed Bass's run as "the greatest one I have ever seen." Coach Brown agreed and said "You can stop Bass for most of the game, but all he needs is one or two plays and he can break it open." That is exactly what Jim did on that run. I wish I had a film of that play because it truly was one of the best runs I remember a high school back having on a team I coached.

Touchdown!!!

Macy Falkner kicked the extra-point to give us a 10-7 lead with about four minutes left. After our defense shut down Sanderson's offense, we got the ball back with just over three minutes left. I was just hoping to run for a couple first downs and run the clock out and get out of Devereux Meadow that night with any kind of a win. Bass ran off tackle for four yards. On the second play we ran the old Green Bay sweep play from our 46-yard line and off Bass went again. He took it to the end zone for his second touchdown within a couple minutes. We were up 16-7 and got away with an awesome victory. Sanderson deserved a lot of credit for the way they played and almost pulled off a major upset. At the end of the day, we did what we had to do to win the game. We still had made some mistakes, but we were beginning to cut many of those down to just a few.

Jim Bass and David Turner

We were thrilled with the win over our rival, but it also put us 4-3 overall, and an important 3-0 in the Division III conference. As I said earlier, I was not thinking about an undefeated conference season, a state championship, or what team we were playing two weeks down the road. I was just thinking about one game at a time. I knew we had one of the best running backs in the state and a group of boys who were playing very hard on the field. Those things by themselves gave us confidence and helped keep us focused on the task at hand. Our immediate task at hand would be a super talented high school football team from Fayetteville, North Carolina. Many thought they were the best football team in the state.

Breakaway Bass

## Game 8: Broughton vs. Fayetteville Terry Sanford, October 23, 1970

After defeating Sanderson 16-7, our team had to make the trip to Fayetteville and play 6-1 Terry Sanford High School. Fayetteville is a military town and as far as we knew was full of transient kids, tough and military, of course. So far this year we had not played out of town, and the whole experience was different from what we were accustomed. We gathered after school in the gym with our travel bags. It was about a two-hour trip, and it was all different from any game we had before. So here we went to meet a very powerful team. They were one of the best teams down east and were making a good run in their conference just as we were in ours. They had a highly touted quarterback in Frankie Townsend and a tough-minded defensive unit. Fayetteville has always had a reputation of hard hitters and tough kids. They still do today. Some of the best football has always been played in Fayetteville and still is. Many of their players were from military families at Fort Bragg and were perhaps more accustomed to adjusting to challenging times.

We made the bus trip down to Terry Sanford thinking we could win the game which would set us toward the last two games of our regular season in pretty good shape for the end of the season. We had had a pretty good week of preparation as best I can remember.

We kicked off to them and played pretty good defense the first series. The next time they got the ball, they took it right down the field and scored an early touchdown on a seven-yard roll out pass by halfback Chip Bishop. They kicked the point after and were ahead of us 7-0 early on.

We responded with a touchdown of our own in the second quarter. We drove the ball the length of the field with a couple David Turner completions to Eric Handy and Billy Starling. Our wingback, Roland Massey, took the ball in for our first score from the 5-yard line. Macy Falkner once again kicked the point after, and it was a tie ball game. It would remain that way the rest of the first half.

What happened the second half that night, I really do not know, but it was not good. As we began the second half, we began to feel that we were a little in over our heads. We began to get some injuries. Jim Corter and Jim Little both with concussions and Jim Lumsden with a knee injury. Townsend ran and threw the ball well the third quarter and helped lead the Bulldogs to three second-half touchdowns. He threw a 17-yard pass to Rodney Evans for a touchdown to give Terry Sanford the lead for good. The extra-point made it 14-7. They controlled the football most of the second half so we did not have many opportunities to score.

Eric Handy

We could not move the ball after receiving the kickoff and got backed up deep in our own territory after several mistakes by the offense. Even though we were only down by 7, we had been dominated by them the whole ball game. John Holding went back in our punt formation and was kicking from about the fifteen-yard line. It looked like the gates of heaven opened for the Bulldogs to come in to our backfield and block the punt. John did not have a prayer, and the punt was blocked and recovered on our one-yard line. On the very next play, Townsend sneaked the ball over for their third touchdown and kicked the extra-point to make it 21-7.

After not being able to move the ball on our next possession, we kicked it away again. Once more, the Bulldogs marched the ball down the field deep in our territory with just a few plays. Their fullback, Keith Merritt, ran it over for their final score, making it 28-7, thus completing the rout.

Not only was the loss embarrassing and by such a large margin, we got the "stuffin" knocked out of us. It seems like Bob Womble, Harrison

Ward, and Robbie Jones, our trainers and managers were busy taping anything that did not feel right. I remember we were bruised and battered badly. I recall feeling humiliated as a coach, and I even shed some tears by myself on the way to Raleigh. The bus ride back was a long and pitiful one. We were beaten down quite a bit and I believe both coaches and players knew we had been handed our lunch. Most of us were very demoralized as a team. I honestly believe we may have thought we were better than we were. In a blow out loss like we had, our team could have easily languished in a pity party.

Harrison Ward, Bob Womble, Kerbaugh, Robbie Jones

After being tied with Terry Sanford at halftime, 7-7, many of us had felt like we could play with anyone in the state. I knew we had taken a beating physically, but we had to give credit to them. They were very good. Several of their players went on and played college football for Southern California and several other major college teams. I remember reflecting on our way back to Raleigh that night that we had to develop attitudes of never giving up and responding positively to adversity. I still felt like we were a good team and still could be successful, but it would not be easy.

Even though the team had resembled a mash unit the night before, when they arrived for our Saturday morning mile jog and check-up, something had changed. The players were no longer down. In fact some of them were fired up to prove we were better than the performance we had displayed the night before. This team decided to make something positive come out of the disappointment and loss we suffered from the night before. The big question was: could we get back to where we were a couple weeks ago after such a defeat? I was not sure.

As a player at UNC, I had been through some difficult and tough losses as well as some great victories. This is where those days at Carolina having those experiences paid off. We won only two games my senior year at Carolina, but I remember my coaches telling us to keep working and hang in there and never give up. Those were difficult times, but it made me a better person in a lot of ways. I am convinced that my perseverance in the coaching profession came from a lot of experiences from my playing days. I would need all the help and experiences of bouncing back that I could use after the terrible defeat from Terry Sanford.

We did lose several people during the ball game and knew that we would have to start depending on some people who had not played very much that year. In the long run, I believe it helped us several weeks later when we were in the state playoffs. On our way back to Raleigh that night, it was hard to see "down the road."

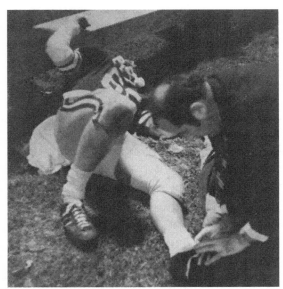

Dr. Dameron works on Doug Murray

Jim Lumsden, our starting Monster in our 5-2 defense, had played super tough for us since early in the season, but he blew his knee out against Terry Sanford. He was one of several players who got hurt in this game. Jim actually had what we call today a torn MCL, but he had played the whole second half with it. Our team doctor, Dr. Thomas Dameron operated on him the very next Monday and we lost Jim for the rest of the year. This was a blow to us and to him. He ended up on crutches on our sidelines during our games, and several of the boys remember him challenging and encouraging us every step of the way. That was his spirit, but also was typical of the boys on this 1970 team. In fact, Jim got so "into it" during the State Championship game at Carter Stadium, he accidentally broke open the cast on his leg which Dr. Dameron had to tape back together that day. Dr. Dameron was very loyal to our football team and was always willing to look after our players. He along with Dr. Hugh Thompson and Dr. Walter Hunt opened up Wake County's first General Surgery Practice with a focus in Orthopedics in 1959. We appreciated all that he did for our Broughton team.

After grading the film of the Terry Sanford game, our staff did not have much to talk about. I decided against showing this discouraging game film to the players and just move on toward our preparation for the next game.

John Holding remembers that I said, "Well, we are still undefeated in the conference and we have two games left with Ligon and Durham. If we win those two games we win our conference, and off to the State Playoffs we will go." He and others thought to themselves, *Wow, our coaches still believe we are winners. Let's do it.*

## Game 9: Broughton vs. Ligon, October 31, 1970

Next up for us was Ligon which was the only "black school" high school in Raleigh. We had four black players on our varsity team and about seven on our junior varsity team who attended Broughton by choice. Ligon always had something to prove and always had a couple of really good players. This year it was Charlie Muldrow. Charlie was a speedy and tough running back. He could squirt through the tiniest hole in the line and was very able to take it for a score anywhere on the field.

We knew we needed to be ready. Probably more important for us than a lot of physical preparation was our overall mental outlook and attitude. A team could easily be discouraged after a defeat like we had suffered at Terry Sanford. Our preparation for Ligon began on Monday for our players as usual, minus watching the previous week's game film. Still undefeated in the conference, the prize of a conference title and automatic entry into the state playoffs was still there for our taking. Win out and we controlled our own fate.

Coached by Frank Roberts, Ligon had lost some tough games. They had played very well at times, but were inconsistent and were on a five game losing streak. Knowing this, we practiced even harder during our week of preparation. I was afraid that we would let up and take for granted that we would beat them. High school players are usually smart enough to know if they are better than their opponent. However, after the way we had played and the whipping we took at Terry Sanford, I was not sure if we could regain our composure and show up to play like the team we had been earlier. I remember working hard on fundamentals that week, and I knew we had to tackle better or we would not beat anyone.

The game was scheduled for Friday night at Chavis Park, but it rained so hard that the game was postponed until the following night, which was Halloween. The night was wet and chilly and the field was quite muddy and certainly affected both offenses. Towards the end of the first quarter, led by their quarterback Ronnie Burrell, Ligon was driving down the field when Jimmy Durham intercepted one of Burrell's passes. He had a great run back with good blocking from the defensive team, and he returned the interception all the way down to our 44-yard line. We gave the ball to Bass, and as usual, he produced. He carried the ball three times and took it down to the 6-yard line. With some good blocking by John Clarke and our whole offensive line, Jim took the ball over for the first score to end a solid 56-yard drive. Gary Stainback kicked the extra-point to give us 7-0 lead.

Our defense really came to life as Ligon took the kickoff back to midfield. We continued to mix up the defense by running our 4-4 and 5-2 monster defense. We had some backup players subbing because of injuries suffered at Terry Sanford. Those injuries actually ended up helping us in an important way. I believe by playing more players rather than the same ones who had dominated play all year, our entire team became closer and we grew a lot in our relationships. Also, confidence, excitement and encouragement was increasing among players, fans, and parents..

George Lattimore, Doug Murray, and the whole defensive line really stiffened up against Ligon in the second quarter. After a bad snap, a swarming defensive stunt called by Coach Thomas, Ligon found themselves deep in their own territory. On fourth down, we put pressure on the punter Elrold Whitaker and we ended up tackling him on the twelve-yard line.

Times Photo by Steve Adams

Caps' George Lattimore (65) has foot hold
Charles Banks (36) comes in to help on Ligon's Elroid Whitaker

Banks and Lattimore

John Holding stepped in at quarterback for us. John had played in a lot of games, but David Turner had been our starter. John was a good passer, and on his third play, he hit Roland Massey on a 13-yard touchdown pass to make it 13-0 for us. We went into halftime with the lead and felt pretty confident where we were. John Holding was a very good pitcher for the Broughton baseball program throughout his

Broughton days. He also went on and pitched for N.C. State University for three years and had a successful career.

John Holding

In the third quarter, the field worsened from the rain the day before. Defense was the name of the third quarter as play was held between the two 30-yard stripes. Penalties hurt both teams and very little was accomplished.

Late in the final quarter, our defense shined again from great play and great hustle. Macy Falkner intercepted a pass from his linebacker position and put our offense in super scoring position. Ligon held tough for three downs inside the 5-yard line, but Bass broke the goal line on a short run to give us a 19-0 lead with only a couple minutes to go in the game.

Thanks to some of Ligon's mistakes and some great play by our defense, we ended up with a victory. Even though our offense sputtered, our defense held Ligon to minus yards for the game. So our defense was pretty stifling this night and our offense was good enough to help to give us the win. This was the start of an amazing defensive run that would ultimately define this team. Here it was the end of October and with the season winding down and winter just around the corner, football was just about to consume us all to a degree we never thought possible. This win put us in pretty good shape in our conference and propelled us toward a huge game the next week against Durham High School. By the way, earlier in the week during practice, a flock of geese flew over the practice field, but only a few guys noticed.

Beginning of Shut-Outs

## Game 10: Broughton vs. Durham Senior, November 6, 1970

Another good week of practice after the Ligon game in preparation for Durham High School. It was going to be a game for all the marbles in our conference, so we knew we had to work diligently to prepare for the game.

As we finished practice on the Thursday before the Durham game, something happened at the end of practice that caught more and more of our players' and coaches' attention. When we were coming together as a team at the end of our walk-through practice, another flock of geese flew over in a V formation. One of the players claimed, "That's a sign of **VICTORY** for us for tomorrow night against Durham." We all laughed and agreed it was a good omen for us.

Listen to me!

We were grateful to be playing our last regular season game at home at Devereux Meadow Stadium. This game would determine the 1970 Eastern 4-A Division III Championship. We were tremendously excited about the fact that we were playing for a conference championship, and the winner would advance to the first round of NCHSAA4-A playoffs and would meet either Burlington Williams or Greensboro Dudley the next week.

Both Broughton and Durham were undefeated in our conference, with Durham having a big non-conference win over Wilson Fike, who had defeated us earlier in the season. Durham had a ball-control offense and a stingy defense and was very similar to our team. Neither one of us were picked to win the conference, but both teams had played well enough and consistent enough to be in the conference championship game. Durham had a solid one-two running attack with Tommy Hayes and Mike Mangum. Jim Bass had been our main man in running for an average close to 100 yards each game this season.

Statistics going into the game indicated that we had the advantage in the passing game, thanks to 1st string quarterback David Turner. Billy Starling and Roland Massey had been our leading receivers and both had been very dependable. Defensively, we had great play by many players, but especially by middle guard Mark Shaner, halfback Jimmy Durham, sound end play by Wells Edmundson and Charles Banks and stalwart play by Steve Brewbaker who was one of the few players who played both ways at tackle.

Bring it on!

Cheerleaders Leading

As we kicked off to Durham, the atmosphere at Devereux was fever high! Both teams had the support of a tremendous crowd who came to see some championship football. After a scoreless first quarter during which neither team threatened the other, things started to pick up in the second quarter.

After we stopped Durham and forced a punt, we had the ball on our own 31-yard line. As we began our drive, we went to our "bread and butter" play with Bass running around the end on a sweep. With good blocking we were picking up good yardage as we moved the ball from our own territory into Durham's side of the fifty. I always felt as a coach if something was working, we should keep running it until the opponent stopped us. That was what we did with Jim Bass and the lead blocking of Larry Height and Charles King at fullback.

Out of the seven plays in which we moved the ball down to the five-yard line, Turner gave the ball to Bass six plays. On the last play of the drive, Jim made an outstanding run, twisting, leaning, driving across the goal line. Jim had made so many of these runs during the season, it had almost become expected. At times, I had worried about our team just watching and waiting until Jim broke a long run or did something beyond belief so that we would score. Regardless of how good a back is, he cannot do it by himself without a lot of help up front. So we were up 7-0 after Gary Stainback kicked the extra-point with about eight minutes left in the half.

Durham came right back and took the ball on their next possession right down the field. With runs and passes, they moved the ball down to the 6-yard line, where our defense really stood tall. Chris Morgan, Brewbaker, Otto, and Lattimore really played big at the goal line and forced Durham into a field goal try. When the ball was snapped they actually faked the kick, and Tommy Parker passed the ball to Ralph Etheridge and it fell incomplete in the end zone (Tommy Parker became the Athletic Director of the Durham City Schools in the 1990's after he had coached at Northern Durham High School for several years.) We went into halftime with a 7-0 lead knowing we were in for a tough and hard-nosed 2nd half of football.

The third quarter was a lot like the first quarter, with very little offense, but with rugged defense. We did take the ball once and had a decent drive down to the Bulldog 12-yard line, but they held us on downs.

In the fourth quarter with about eight minutes left in the game, our defense stopped them and forced a punt. We got the ball on our own 49 yard-line and took it right down the field for 51 yards to score. Bass scooted around the end the last 11 yards for a touchdown. We missed the extra-point, but had the lead at 13-0 with about three minutes left in the game. Our defense finished the game with the shutout, not knowing that that shutout was one of many more to follow.

Steve Brewbaker played one of his best games ever with eight unassisted tackles on defense and blocked very well on offense. Larry Height and Charles King had some crucial 3$^{rd}$ down runs as well as opening up some holes for Bass to do his thing on the ground. Bass not only had great balance and determination in his running, but he was so good at using his blocks. Our coaching staff had moved some Junior Varsity players up to the Varsity team since they were playing so well on the JV team. It was a risk in some ways, but we felt like Larry Otto and Sandy Goodwin and others could help us, and they did. You never know how some moves like that would affect the chemistry of the team, but I was only interested, to be honest, in getting the best players on the field. Otto played some good ball for us during those last few weeks, and it really paid off having him on the Varsity.

So here we were in early November with a Division III Eastern 4-A Championship. We ended up 6-4 overall and 5-0 in our conference heading to the N.C. State Championship playoffs. Winter was just around the corner and we were still playing football! August seemed so long ago in some ways, but it seemed like it had been a flick of the finger in other ways. All the summer workouts, fourth quarter drills, late nights breaking down film, the weekends planning strategy, the pressure of being a first year head coach, etc. - everything seemed worth it there at the end of our regular season.

Yet I knew we needed to continue to improve. Winning the conference thrilled the parents, players, Broughton student body, and the city of Raleigh. I do not remember very much about teaching American and World History classes, but I do remember walking down the hallways of Broughton and into my classroom and the students being fired up about our football team and what the boys had accomplished that season so far. Better things were ahead. We would be on our way to Greensboro the next Friday night to take on Greensboro Dudley High School which was the main "black high school" in Greensboro.

Conference Champs

We had had several injuries both major and minor, but Dr. Dameron, who was the chief orthopedic doctor at Raleigh Orthopedics, had been our team doctor all season. Dr. Dameron was sharp and took excellent care of our players. He was always at our home games and attended many of the away games that Broughton played. He was one of those many people who contributed to our Championship run but got very little credit.

After our victory against Durham, our conference selected an All-Conference team. I certainly felt like we had a lot of players who contributed and played so well during our season. We did have three who were selected as prep All-Stars: Jim Bass, Mark Shaner, and Steve Brewbaker. We were very proud of these three players because they made a very significant contribution to our team. However, I honestly believe that our entire team, including the three all conference players, realized that it was a TEAM that had accomplished so much in such a short time. Without these three, we probably would not have won our division, but the same could be said about many more of our players who were essential to our team's success.

All Conference

So, the playoff brackets were complete and post season play was ready to begin the next week.

**The 4-A Playoff Agenda for the first round:**

Gastonia Ashbrook (10-0) at Charlotte Olympic (8-2)

Raleigh Broughton (6-4) at Greensboro Dudley (9-1)

Fayetteville Sanford (9-1) at Goldsboro (9-1)

Winston-Salem Atkins (7-3) at Charlotte Garringer (9-1)

**Chapter 7**
The Playoffs

"Champions are champions not because they do anything
extraordinary but because they do the ordinary things better than anyone
else."
- Chuck Noll

Bernard, Shaner, Spain

## Quarterfinals: Broughton vs. Greensboro Dudley, November 12, 1970

The week of November 9, 1970 was an interesting week for us as we
began preparing for the first state 4-A playoff game at Greensboro

Dudley High School. This would be Broughton's first playoff game appearance since 1966, when the Caps defeated Durham High School for the Eastern Regional title. It would be my first ever playoff game as a head coach. I attempted to treat it like any other week of preparation. We certainly were pleased to have been 5-0 in our conference, and I personally felt like we were playing our best football of the season. One key is to be playing one's best at the end of the season rather than at the beginning of the season.

Our blocking had been outstanding against Durham. Tackles Jay Morgan and Steve Brewbaker, guards Jim Little and Kent Kistler, and center John Clark all did a tremendous job. Jim Bass once again ran well, and the two fullbacks of Larry Height and Charles King were super lead blockers and even getting better. David Turner continued to direct the offense in a brilliant way as he had matured into a very good high school quarterback.

Coming to get you!

Defensively, linebacker Larry Otto and our secondary of Preston Ruth, David Dupree, and Jim Durham played every game with sound fundamentals. I still felt it was a true team defense and a bunch of guys who wanted to hit and would run to the ball like crazy. Our 220 pound nose guard and co-captain Mark Shaner had played consistently all season. Charles Banks and Wells Edmundson were very sound fundamentally as defensive ends, and tackle Steve Brewbaker continued to play well both ways. Lattimore and Murray were hard hitters on defense. Our kicking game had continued to improve in the return department, and John Holding continued to boom the football in his punts, which consistently gave us good field position against most of our opponents.

Greensboro Dudley held a 9-1 record and had played very well on both sides of the ball. They liked to control the football with their running back Richard Williams, who was a 191 pound bruiser. Coach J.A. McKee had done a solid coaching job with the Panthers and like us were enjoying a lot of momentum coming into the November 12th Friday night game. Even though their offense was powerful, the impressive factor about Dudley was that they were stronger defensively than offensively. We knew it was going to be a tough assignment, but we were looking forward to it.

Overall we were healthy. We had lost Jim Lumsden in the Terry Sanford game to a knee injury and we had missed his leadership, but Larry Otto had played well since we brought him up from the JV team. Coach Thomas always had the defense ready and well prepared. We watched and studied film so much as a staff that we knew their favorite plays from the specific formations. Our players recognized the formations and began to call out the play even as the offensive team got into certain formations. In fact, one of our linebackers, Doug Murray, remembers he and George Lattimore calling out, "Watch out for the sweep" or "...the lead play" or "...the isolation," and it really surprised the Dudley players as the game progressed.

We had another solid week of practice even though the weather was getting colder. Oh, by the way, the flock of geese flew over again in the V formation right over the practice field on Thursday, and all of us certainly took notice again.

Game time was at eight o' clock at Grimsley Stadium. Grimsley Stadium was the main city stadium for Greensboro, and the Greensboro schools shared the stadium. Most people already were talking about a Fayetteville Terry Sanford vs Greensboro Dudley game the next week. Terry Sanford seemed to be favored to win the 4-A State Championship.

Our Broughton student body was pumped up about going to Greensboro for the playoff game. In fact, they organized about ten buses to make the trip to Greensboro. This was a little unusual even back in the 1970's, but the whole school was enthusiastic about following the football team. I believe parents also chartered a bus to the Friday night game.

It had rained some during the latter part of the week, and we knew the field was going to be wet and nasty, but we did not realize how bad it would be. The smell was like a sewer, but the field still gave good footing.

As we pulled into the parking lot at Grimsley Stadium to dress for the ball game, I could not help but think that it was less than six years earlier that I had laid in the same dressing room getting a shot of Novocain in my hip from my dad to help me play in the annual East-West high school all-star game. I do not think this would be allowed in high school today, especially if there was any possibility of furthering the injury. Neither as a coach or player would I feel okay about this being done to players today. Our Broughton team was assigned to the west side of the field house. We put on our equipment in the dressing room, then walked to the field, imagining what it would be like in four hours after the game. Would we be celebrating, or would this be the last game of the 1970 football season for us? To be honest, I thought that Dudley had much more speed and size than we did, but I also believed in the boys who were on our football team. There was a toughness about our guys that could not be denied. But very few people gave us a chance.

I distinctly remember listening to the Dudley team chanting, singing, and clapping in their dressing room as we finished putting our game uniforms on. I knew from this atmosphere that we were in enemy territory and we were not playing just a conference game. I will have to admit I felt a little intimidated by all their singing and realizing this was a first round game of the state championship, but I was not about to let that show.

In fact, doubt had been voiced in a Greensboro newspaper and also by some Raleigh citizens and sports reporters that the Broughton Caps, with only a 6-4 record, a first-year head coach and a team small in size, should technically not even be in the playoffs, much less have a chance to handle a team of Dudley's stature, a team that suffered only one close loss during the year. I remember using that as a motivating factor as I talked to our team before we went out for the opening kickoff of the game. I knew the wet field would be a factor, but I also knew a good start to the game for us would be a key.

Doug Murray

We kicked off to Dudley and held them the first series to force them to punt the ball. We began our first series on offense on our own 26-yard line. We started with running our "bread and butter" sweep play with Jim Bass and the blocking of our offensive line. We moved the ball without a lot of trouble into Dudley territory. David Turner came up with a big throw to our tight end, Phil Ficklin, on a difficult third down play. That was the play that kept our drive alive and gave us our sixth first down on their nine-yard line. Two plays later, Bass scored on a quick burst up the middle from the three-yard line. The extra-point was blocked, and after seven minutes into the game, we were ahead 6-0.

After we kicked off to them, our tenacious defense held them once again for very little yardage and forced them to punt. This time we started our drive from our own 49 yard-line. Larry Height and Eric

Handy picked up a few yards the first couple of downs. Then Turner, after a good fake to Bass, hit sophomore Sandy Goodwin, another of the several sophomores who had been moved up from the JV team, for a 40-yard pass for a quick touchdown. I believe that pass and touchdown caught Dudley by surprise, and it really gave us the confidence we needed. We went for two points, and Turner hit Bass in the flats for a successful try, and we were ahead 14-0 with 7:35 left in the first half.

Our defense had great play from Brewbaker, Gary Neal, George Lattimore, Mark Shaner, David Dupree, Preston Ruth, and Jimmy Durham. In addition to Bass and Turner, our offense received consistent play from both wingbacks, Roland Massey and Eric Handy.

Our defensive team again stopped Dudley in their tracks after our next kickoff. As several players said, "Their offensive line was shocked when we began to call out their plays even before they ran them at the line of scrimmage." Our coaching staff had studied enough Dudley film that we felt like we knew their favorite plays from certain offensive formations. Our defensive coordinator, John Thomas, had shown his defensive squad these formations and plays over and over and over at practice during the week of the game. All of this seemed to be paying off.

Towards the end of the first half, we had once again forced them to punt after we had pushed them back seven yards in the first three plays of that series. They punted the ball out of bounds at the Dudley 43 yard line, and then thanks to a penalty, we began our drive on the 38 yard-line with under six minutes to play in the opening half. Turner was throwing the ball as well as he had thrown all year long. Amazingly, he was on target all night and completed eight of eleven passes for a total of 130 yards and threw only one interception. On our third touchdown drive, Bass made an excellent reception, running down a pass from Turner and carried the ball down to the 15 yard-line. With just about four minutes left in the first half, Charles King plowed ahead for two yards, and then Bass scored his second touchdown of the evening after a 13-yard scamper off tackle. Macy Falkner kicked the extra point for a 21-0 halftime lead that must have shocked a great majority a lot of people in the stadium. Having that big a lead of 21-0 would be like 40-0 today considering today's clock stoppages and the fast speed and the passing offenses. We were thrilled to be ahead by three touchdowns at halftime, but still knew we had to keep playing hard and smart.

Dickie Thompson

What do you think?

In 1970, if there was a tie game in the playoffs, the tie breaker would go to the team who had the most total offensive yards at the end of the game. We had so dominated the game the first half that we had 199 yards to Dudley's 9 yards. We were certainly in control of the game, but I still did not feel we had the game won. Our guys were confident, but not cocky, and they knew we had to come out and keep playing with intensity. That we did in the second-half.

Dudley barely even crossed midfield in the first half, and our defense continued to play with a tremendous fire and desire. I honestly believe our players were better prepared than a much more talented Dudley team. At times our offense moved the ball the second half, but never could mount a consistent drive. Our defensive secondary faced a lot of passing by Dudley in the second-half, but out of twenty passes, they only had four completions. The only threat by Dudley was near the end of the game. They took the ball down to our nine-yard line but had three straight incomplete passes. On fourth down, Shaner and Brewbaker threw Lewis McKoy, Dudley's quarterback, for a 20-yard loss and ended any threat of scoring by the Panthers.

As the game came to a close, you could feel the sense of pride and confidence we were continuing to gain. It was not a cocky attitude that showed any kind of, "I am better than you" mindset, but a genuine belief that we could play with anyone IF we played together as a team.

Coach J.A. McKee said, "I knew Broughton had improved during the season, but I did not think that the game would end like this." He was shocked and disappointed, but Dudley had had a good year. After all, we knew only one team would end up with a win at the end of the season, and everyone else would end the season with a loss.

I did not comment to the sports writers that most people had in fact given us very little chance to win. I did say that our team had come a long way since the start of the season, and we were peaking at the right time. We had played the whole season well, and actually had been only out of one game during the season, and that was the second half of the Terry Sanford game when we lost 28-7. I said that I felt we had a few excellent players with talent, but overall what made us winners was our desire because we had a bunch of determined boys who wanted awfully bad to win.

On our trip back to Raleigh after our 21-0 win, we stopped to eat a post-game meal at a restaurant. Everyone was talking about the next game against Terry Sanford and getting a chance to play them again and redeem ourselves. Then all of a sudden, someone came in with the news that Goldsboro had beaten Terry Sanford 19-12. Some players were disappointed that we would not get another shot at Terry Sanford, but others did not care who we played. I guess I was feeling super we had won, and I did not know much about Goldsboro, but I was not totally disappointed that we would not have to play Terry Sanford again.

Going to Semi-finals

The bus ride back to Raleigh was a happy one, and listening to the players sing or try to sing made me feel so satisfied for them and all they had accomplished up to this point. The players had worked so hard since the beginning of the season, but so had so many other teams. I knew that you had to be pretty good to get to the semifinals of the State Championship, but I also knew you had to have some luck.

We had now shut out the last three opponents, and our defensive unit began to get the credit they had always deserved. I felt like our defense had become our offense at times because they had given us such great field position throughout our season. Our dominant defense was something that we and others began to talk a little about. I remembered Coach Bear Bryant had once said, "You win games with offense, but you win championships with defense." We were after a championship.

It was getting late into November now, and the weather was turning colder. That meant that practices would be in colder weather, and that is not pleasurable even when you are getting ready to play in the State semifinals. We knew the game would be at good old Devereux Meadow next Friday at eight o'clock. We had seriously begun to win the attention of the city of Raleigh with three shutouts and only two more games to play for the State Championship of North Carolina.

Even though it was cold during that week, we still practiced daily for 2-2 ½ hours in order to prepare ourselves or for Goldsboro. We watched and studied film just as hard as we had done in week two of the season. We knew that our preparation had helped get us where we were, and we were just too close to the championship to let up at all. We had cut down on some of our individual time and instruction, but added to our team periods in our preparation. Practices were still intense, but we did not feel like we had to stay out as long as we had earlier in the season. Of course, we had our 4th quarter drills at the end of every practice, and they became more important to us mentally than physically. I still wanted these young men to believe that as we entered the fourth and final quarter, we were in better shape than our opponent because we had worked harder and conditioned better.

As we finished that Thursday practice, I felt grateful that we would be playing at home at Devereux Meadow instead of having to journey to Goldsboro. Oh yes, guess who showed up during practice on that Thursday afternoon. You got it, the V flock was there right on time.

### Semifinals: Broughton vs. Goldsboro, November 19, 1970

Goldsboro High School was coached by Gerald Whisenhunt, and the Cougars were outstanding. The team was led by their tailback Bobby Myrick and blocking back Dan Kepley. Bobby Myrick went on to play at ECU and then played for the Ottawa Rough Riders in the Canadian football league. Dan Kepley played linebacker at ECU after graduating from Goldsboro and played 10 years in the Canadian football league for the Edmonton Eskimos. Both were great high school players. Coach Whisenhunt was a very smart football coach and seemed to be a powerful motivator. His teams played with a lot of hustle and desire. You give him talent like Myrick, Kepley, receiver Gene Hagans, linebackers Paul Southerland and Charles Coley along with Warren Campbell and Ricky Lewis, and you definitely have the ingredients for a strong and athletic championship team.

They were coming into our game with a 9-2 record and had just beaten Terry Sanford 19-12 in the quarterfinals the week before. They were known for the big plays by Myrick, and their kicking game was an excellent part of their attack. Coach Whisenhunt and Goldsboro were still running the single-wing offense, rarely used today. A lot of the spread teams in the 2000's are a lot like the single wing of old. You have a quarterback running the football as well as passing the football, and there is a great deal of misdirection in the backfield.

Impossible Dream

For this crucial semifinal game, I felt like we were pretty confident and healthy. I was honestly not thinking about the possible State Championship game next week. I was just focusing on Goldsboro, and I believed our players were doing the same.

That Friday night we had our good pre-game meal in our school cafeteria, thanks to the ladies in the school cafeteria along with a couple of parents, and then headed to the wrestling room to rest before heading to the dressing room to dress for the game. I am not sure if we realized it at the time, but this would be the last time a high school football event would be held at Devereux Meadow, since Sanderson High School's new Gregson Stadium was opening up next year for them and also for us to use as our home stadium.

As we left for Devereux on the city bus, as we had done for all our home games, I sensed our players were focused, serious and ready to play. I remember telling them we would have to <u>play all four quarters</u> and <u>give our very best</u> in order to be able to play that one last game.

Goldsboro brought 4-5 busloads of students into Devereux Meadow, and we certainly had an awesome Raleigh crowd supporting us. The crowd was estimated at over 6,000 people, which filled Devereux Meadow. It was one of those ideal November nights for football. Goldsboro kicked off to us to open the game. We started our opening drive with our sweeps, off tackle plays, and passed when we needed to. We took the ball in 15 plays down to the Goldsboro three-yard line, where Goldsboro's defense really got tough and stopped us on third down. We sent Macy Falkner in to try a 20-yard field goal. It was wide left, and after a good solid drive, we came away with nothing, and momentum shifted to Goldsboro.

Goldsboro took the ball from their three and drove it down inside our 30 yard-line on 12 plays. Bobby Myrick did most of the damage along with the fullback, Dan Kepley. Our defense stood firm and forced them to throw the ball. On third down, Myrick tried to hit their favorite receiver Gene Hagans in the end-zone, but our halfback David Dupree came up with a great diving interception in the end zone.

We got the ball on our own 20, but did not move the ball enough for a first down. John Holding punted on 4th down and sent a booming kick to put Goldsboro deep in their territory. Neither team could muster up much offense the rest of the first half. I was hoping the missed field goal would not come back to haunt us later in the game. Both of our teams had explosive backs in Myrick and our Jim Bass, but I knew that the defense was the core strength of each team. We had to stop any long runs and plays by Myrick, and we needed to break a long one ourselves in order to be victorious. The two defenses slugged it out the rest of the first half.

Coach Evans explains to Roland

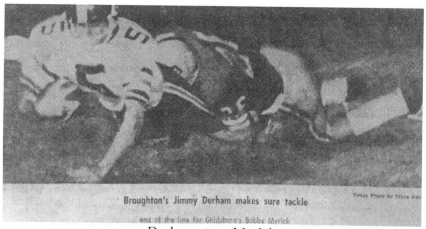

Durham stops Myrick

Goldsboro kicked off to us to begin the second half. Bass took the ball on the first play of the second half and rambled for a 12-yard gain down to our own 48-yard line. On the very next play, Turner gave the ball to Jim again on a trap play. Our center John Clarke along with guard Jim Little double-teamed the nose guard, and Kent Kistler trapped and opened up a hole for Bass. Our tight end Phil Ficklin along with tackle

Dave Reynolds threw excellent blocks on their linebackers, and we had several people downfield hustling to get in their secondary's way. Both Billy Starling and Eric Handy were hustling to get blocks ahead of Bass as he broke through the line of scrimmage. He broke toward the sidelines and was headed for the goal line. At the 20, the final Cougar defender made a valiant effort to knock Bass over. Jim's unbelievable balance somehow kept him on his feet, and the little 158 pounder prevailed. I remember the crowd erupted behind us, and the Caps were on the board. Jim's run was similar to several other phenomenal runs he had that year against Grimsley, Sanderson, and Durham. I do believe that out of the 30 years I coached high school football, I have yet to see a player with Bass's balance.

Jim Lumsden Encouraging

Macy Falkner made the extra-point, but a 15-yard penalty forced us to try again from the 22-yard line. We missed that try, but we were up 6-0. The touchdown came barely 50 seconds into the second half. The rest of the game was an outstanding defensive game played by two stalwart teams.

Goldsboro could get no closer than our 36-yard line, and that came with just over three minutes to go in the 4th quarter. Myrick completed a pass to his favorite receiver, Gene Hagans, to give them a first down on our 36-yard line. Just when the Cougars seemed to have the momentum to move in for a final score, our defensive end, Charles Banks, who had been so reliable along with our other end, Wells Edmundson, put a heavy rush on Myrick. Banks and linebacker George Lattimore both tackled Myrick on the 43-yard line and forced a fumble. Banks with his quickness and hustle got off the tackle and out-scrambled everyone for the ball. That gave us pretty good field position, but more than anything, it took the ball out of Myrick's hands.

Broughton Band

Our defensive ends, Charles Banks and Wells Edmundson did not receive as much credit as our secondary or our linebacker trio of Lattimore, Otto, and Murray, or our tough-minded defensive line of Corter, Shaner, Brewbaker, and others, but they were a very integral part of the defensive unit. They were consistent, tough, and smart the entire game and season. The other defensive players knew that the opposing runners would be coming toward them because Charles and Wells were going to keep them from getting outside and turn them back in toward the interior line and linebackers. As we played and competed week in and week out, players like ours with such superior attitudes made our jobs as coaches extremely satisfying. It truly seemed as if the entire team did not care who got the credit as long as we accomplished our goals.

After Banks recovered the fumble, we drove the ball down to Goldsboro's 16-yard line and took up most of the last three minutes of the game, which was very important. Goldsboro had one last try with 16 seconds left, but our defense rose to the occasion once again. Four straight shut outs in high school football is awesome anytime, but especially in the playoffs.

Charles Banks

Broughton 6 Goldsboro 0

Needless to say, we were ecstatic and overjoyed to beat a talented Goldsboro football team. It was a little ironic in that we had stopped them from scoring on a long play and we ourselves had scored on a big play. We had players like David Turner, who had really developed into a field general for our team. He, like a lot of our players, was not real flashy nor super fast, but he was reliable, consistent, and constantly improving and developing every day. That was such a key.

It was a difficult loss for Coach Whisenhunt and his Cougars. They had had a very successful season, only losing two games before they came into Devereux Meadow. He said, "In all honesty, I think we have played better football teams, materially speaking. But, they have desire. They hustle and they have the momentum too. They are a good football team. We have beaten teams three times the talent they have – E. E. Smith, Terry Sanford, Rocky Mount, Wilson Fike – but talent does not make much difference when you play football the way Broughton does," he said. "They have great spirit and determination, and they hustle and will hit you."

Caulton Tudor wrote in the *Raleigh Times* the next day that, "Maybe – just maybe – Broughton was in her finest football moment at Devereux Meadow last night. The final 6-0 count on the scoreboard simply said the Caps were 1970 Eastern 4-A Champs; it said nothing of the road behind. Save remarkable tailback Jimmy Bass, tackle Steve Brewbaker and middle guard Mark Shaner, Dave Riggs' first Broughton team would likely match up slim in ability lineups, but in quantities of heart and guts, the Caps have few equals."

As a head coach, I could not have been any prouder of our team. I continued to reiterate the fact that we were talented, but we had something else every championship team must have, and that was the idea that ALL of us were needed in order to be successful on the scoreboard. The thing this team ran on could not be measured in a scouting report or picked up on game films. This was just a team – an old-fashioned TEAM that worked together for everyone else involved. There was no way I could shut up talking about them. By the way, that was our fourth straight shut-out.

Even as excited as we were to have a win over Goldsboro and to have an opportunity to play for the 4-A North Carolina State Championship, we still knew we had <u>one more game</u>. Not many people will ever remember the runner-ups in any final championship game.

## Headed Toward the State Championship Game

"It's the repetition of affirmations that leads to belief. And once that belief becomes a deep conviction, things begin to happen."
- Muhammed Ali

Defense

The location of the State Championship game alternated between the East and West and it was the East's turn to host. Therefore, we were hosting the final game in Raleigh for the 1970 State Championship game and we were thrilled! The North Carolina High School Association had arranged with the Raleigh Schools and N.C. State University for the game to be played at State's Carter Stadium on Saturday afternoon. Tickets were going to go on sale early in the week. The price for students ahead of the game was $1.50, adults $2.00, and all tickets at the gate were $2.00.

We knew we would be playing either Charlotte Olympic High School or Charlotte Garinger High School. They played in Charlotte Memorial Stadium for the Western Championship the Saturday night after our victory over Goldsboro.

On that Sunday morning, I found out we would be playing Olympic High School, coached by Joe White. All I knew about them was that they had an All-State halfback Randy Rhino who had already signed with Georgia Tech. Olympic was a team a lot like us. They had a good defense and a great running back who was the key to their offense.

I honestly cannot remember when we exchanged films with them, but I certainly remember being extremely impressed with Rhino and the offense that Olympic had. Obviously, we felt positive it was going to be another close and tough game, and we would have to play our BEST to win – and be a little lucky too.

Getting Ready

A lot was written in the newspapers that week about some of Broughton's past great teams and seasons. Even though Broughton had won several Eastern State Championships, they had not won the State Championship since 1961 when Coach Clyde Walker led the Caps to the State Championship. The quarterback of that team was Larry Honeycutt, and the offense was built around the running backs of Austol Youmans, Buddy Cayton and fullback Bob Denlinger. The defense in 1961 was led by stars Billy High, Harold Landis, Fred Fletcher, Griffin Dodd, and Earl Johnson.

The 1963 Broughton team finished 8-2 but did not participate in the playoffs. The next playoff team for the Caps was in 1966 when they defeated Durham 21-0 to win the Eastern Regional 4-A Championship. The 1966 group finished 11-1, and it too was led by a great defense that gave up just 52 points. The defensive forces were highlighted by end Sonny Leach, tackles Bryan Cheek and Lee Coleman, linebackers Charlie Baker and Bill Brafford, and backs Jimmy King and Al Godwin.

We had an intense practice week in preparation for the State Championship game. School was out on Tuesday due to Thanksgiving break, but we kept our usual practice schedule as best we could. On Thanksgiving Day we practiced that morning about 10:00 a.m. so families could still gather for lunch or dinner and have special family time. A number of our players had relatives visit for the weekend mainly due to the Championship game that was to be played on Saturday.

We had our walk-through on Friday and completed our final preparations and reviews for the game Saturday. That very chilly week we had searched the sky for the geese to fly over, but sad to say, they were a no-show. However, I do not think many of us thought that meant that we might lose, but several of the players did mention the geese not showing up. I encouraged everyone to get a good night's sleep and to be at the school to dress by 10:00 a.m., and then we would depart to create our destiny at Carter Stadium.

# The Sports Observer

### by Dick Herbert

There was genuine concern just two years ago that Needham Broughton High's football program was hurt so much by the loss of students to the new Sanderson High that the Caps would not be able to compete on the high level of the past.

Today the Caps are preparing for the Saturday game at Carter Stadium that will determine the North Carolina champion in the highest of the four scholastic divisions.

*Obviously young Dave Riggs, who took over as head coach this season, and his players deserve the plaudits and support of the many Raleigh sports fans who for many years have been enthusiastic followers of scholastic sports.*

Riggs apparently has been able to convey his way of playing to his players. As a Carolina back he went about his assignments in a manner which delights any coach. He was small, but he would crash into any opponent at more than top speed. Some worried that some day he would break in two throwing himself with such abandon against the young giants who opposed him.

The Caps won their division title by shutting out Durham. They reached the state championship game by blanking Greensboro Dudley and Goldsboro.

The talent may not be as impressive as that of other Broughton teams that got this far, but the zest with which the Caps play is just as effective.

Now it is fortunate the biggest game of all will be played in a great stadium in the afternoon. Raleigh should be there in full force.

Dick Herbert's Article

## State Championship: Broughton vs. Olympic, November 27, 1970

"It always seems impossible until it's done."
- Nelson Mandela

Everyone Came

Students - Lance Ferrell

Riding the bus to Carter Stadium, I remember that there was just about complete silence on our short ride from Broughton through the Oberlin Road neighborhood, down Wade Avenue and on to Duraleigh

Road to Carter Stadium. The boys all year had done an excellent job preparing themselves mentally for some difficult games, and I expected the same for this one, even though there was no doubt that this one had an extraordinary feel to it because we were playing for the High School N.C. State 4-A Championship and it was taking place in a college stadium.

About 50 minutes before the game started, we sent out our specialty people, our punters, kickers, kick receivers, quarterbacks and receivers. It was truly a beautiful, sunny day, and Carter Stadium was a perfect setting for the final game of this miraculous season for the Broughton Caps. I remember that the sky was bright blue with hardly any clouds in the sky. The wonderful variety of colors from both sides of the stadium brought even more excitement and electricity to pre-game warm ups. About 25 minutes before kick-off, the rest of our team came on the field with Coach Thomas for warm ups. A small airplane flew over pulling a huge sign that said, "GO CAPS - WIN." Our fans loved it and the noise level in the stadium escalated greatly!

Getting Ready To Go To Work

We won the toss and elected to take the ball. Olympic kicked off to us, and we brought it back to our 22 yard-line. From there we took it 78 yards for the first score of the game. It was a drive of 13 plays that could not have been drawn up any better. We mixed our sweeps and off tackle running plays in with a couple passes. It was a typical drive for us with nothing real fancy, but very consistent and very few mistakes. The final play of the drive was a ten-yard pass to Charles King, our fullback, from our steady quarterback, David Turner. Macy Falkner kicked the extra point through and we led 7-0 with 6:18 left in the first quarter.

On the kickoff, Gary Stainback kicked the ball into the end zone. The referee threw the kickoff tee toward our sidelines (Harrison, you forgot to go get it.) and it hit me in my Adam's apple and I hit the ground immediately. The game went on even though the coach was flat on his back. After a few minutes, Dr. Dameron said I was okay and I began coaching again.

The Caps Fans

Olympic came right back with the running of Randy Rhino and Bobby Cook. However, the defense stepped up, and Charles Banks threw their quarterback, Eric Sadler, for a seven-yard loss and forced a punt from the Trojans. Both defenses played pretty well the rest of the half. Olympic's Rhino had a good 25-yard punt return in the second quarter, which sparked a good drive for the Trojans. Olympic then took the ball for 60 yards in 16 plays all the way down to our 4 four yard line. On fourth down with less than a minute left in the first half, Sadler pitched the ball to Rhino, and he bobbled it for a second, and our defense was all over him. He got down to the one-yard line, but not in the end zone. That was a huge stop for us at the end of the half and it seemed that our whole defense had hustled to the ball. Our boys took a knee and the first half ended with us ahead 7-0.

Bass Gets Another One

We went into the dressing room feeling pretty good, but realizing that we were in a fight for our lives in the second half. I remember several things happening in the locker room during the halftime. Our coaches, as always, put our heads together to plan for the second half. We decided that we would change a few things, but did not want to go away from what had gotten us here, so we decided to keep the ball on the ground

and pass when we needed to, but pull a couple plays out that we had not
shown the first half.

Eric Handy vs Olympic

As the halftime was coming to an end, we all gathered together, and
Larry Height said in his robust voice, "If we don't keep playing hard, we
are going to lose this game!" I was pretty spirited as a young 24-year old
head coach, but overall, I was usually under control. However, I do
remember going off on Larry in the locker room, but some players told
me years later that it had served to get them even more fired up. I
grabbed Height and hollered, "Don't you use that word 'lose' again today
because we are NOT going to lose!! We have worked too hard and for
too long to lose this ball game, you hear me? Now let's go win this
championship!"

The second half was a battle. Little scoring, lots of defense. It was a
lot like the first half in that we controlled the football for most of the
half. In the fourth quarter after exchanging punts, we took the ball on our

own 40-yard line. After a couple of running plays by Height and Bass, we called a halfback pass. Turner handed the ball off to Roland Massey, our wingback who was left handed, and he started around the left end and pulled up and threw about 26 yards to Billy Starling who took it down to the 13 yard line for a huge first down. Billy had actually lined up on the wrong side of the field, but was football savvy enough to know where he needed to end up on the play. He ran a corner route instead of running a post, and Roland hit him perfectly in stride and we were in scoring position.

Murray & Lattimore Closing In

Our Bread and Butter

A couple plays later Bass scored on a seven yard run, and Falkner once again came through with the extra point, and we were up 14-0 with only about seven minutes left in the game. Once again, our defense took over by shutting down Olympic's running game. They bent a little, but never did break, and we ended the game with our fifth straight shut-out and the State Championship!!!

As the clock ticked down to the final seconds of the game, we - and our sidelines - erupted with pure joy and excitement. The scoreboard at Carter-Finley Stadium read Broughton 14 and Olympic 0. The referee blew his whistle and lifted the football up in the air, ending the 1970 4-A Football State Championship game. The Broughton students jumped out of the stadium stands and onto the field hugging, jumping, hollering, and celebrating with players, cheerleaders, coaches and parents and fans. It had been a long and tough battle between two great fundamentally sound football teams who had given their all for 48 minutes.

Is Jim Corter airborne?

Charles King and Billy Starling

As I shook hands with Coach Joe White and the coaching staff from Olympic High School, I was overflowing with pride. When I turned back to our sidelines, I saw our players dressed in their purple jerseys and gold pants and gold helmets. The uniforms were covered with sweat, grass stains, and some with a little blood. I remember having tears in my eyes and I was filled with joy and sense of accomplishment for these young men. How in the world did this happen? How did a bunch of undersized, inexperienced boys become a State Championship football team?

As students and parents poured out on the field, the players were just running around hugging each other with sheer, unadulterated thrill and euphoria! I remember my wife, Marie running on the field wearing a BHS corsage with her blond hair flying. She was way beyond excited, jumping up and down screaming, "WE WON!! WE WON!!" Mr. Conrad Hooper, the Raleigh School System Superintendent, presented the N.C.4A State Championship team trophy to us, and we were more than exhilarated to receive it.

I actually don't remember much about what happened after the game. My dad and his wife had come from Morganton and were staying with us for the weekend. We went out to eat with them to a restaurant on Western Boulevard and rehashed the game. I was feeling such pride and happiness over this TEAM - these amazing kids. I did not realize at the time what a major event and achievement it was to win the State Championship. I had always been so focused on competing and playing the game, either as a player or a coach, that I did not get too wrapped up about boasting or wanting to be in the victor's circle. I do remember being very tired and exhausted because it had been a high pressure ballgame, and it had been a long season with long hours every week, even for a young 24 year-old coach. After eating, I think we just went home and went to bed pretty early.

In the days and weeks to follow, we would realize more and more what this team had attained. I believe the boys and the fans and coaches came to appreciate our accomplishments even more as the days went by.

Mr. Caudle, the manager of the then prominent Sir Walter Raleigh Hotel downtown in Raleigh, offered to let us have the banquet room for a State Championship Banquet. The parents organized it and really put on a good show for us. It was a coat and tie affair and pretty fancy for a high school football banquet. I don't remember the entire menu, but I do remember the "Baked Alaska" dessert; it was brought out burning with flames, plus it tasted great. This was a time before they gave rings out to State Champions, so we got trophies for all the players, managers, and coaches. I still have mine, and it is the only trophy I have out that is not boxed up in the attic.

I attended a 90th birthday party for David Turner's mother recently at Jim Lumsden's home in Raleigh. As I walked into his study, he jumped up and said, "Look at this, Coach Riggs!" and he proceeded to show me and everyone around us his trophy from the State Championship. He said, "The arm is broken and the plaque is missing, but it is the most important trophy I have. You know, people can take away your money, your house, and a lot of things that belong to you, but no one, no one can take a State Championship away from you." I thought how true that is. Those trophies probably did not cost more than $15 even back in 1970 and they cannot talk, but they say a whole lot.

As I reflect over those months from June through December of 1970, I was truly a fortunate and blessed man to be at <u>the right place, at the right time, with the right people.</u>

It's all over, Baby!

Number 1 Fan, Marie Riggs

WE DID IT!

Dave Dupree

Phil Spence, Tim Marriott, Don Harris

Finally a smile!

Number One!

Rick Eudy gets a hug.

John Clarke, Jim Durham, Rick Eudy, Dave Dupree, Doug Murray.

Celebrate!

Coach Robbie Evans

14-0

Champs!

Jane Holroyd, Charles King, Marie Riggs

All Heart

# CHAPTER 8
## What happened to these champs?

"That's the thing about football. Once people can play together, they
see they can live together."
- Eddie Robinson

Like all other coaches, people always would ask me, "Are you going
to have a successful team this year?" I certainly learned over time that
what <u>really</u> makes a team successful is not necessarily what their won-
loss record was, but how the players turn out 20, 30, and 40 years later.
As I look at the 1970 Broughton State Championship team, the record
was successful, but more than that, most of the players have truly
contributed to others' lives and to our great country. You will agree as
you read about what these young men have accomplished with their lives
and where they are now.

This chapter will include the following for each player:

1. Preseason comments *in italics* from the Pigskin Preview written by
Broughton's Student Information Director, Tom Wagoner.

2. My comments and thoughts from my memories and also from
recent times spent, when possible, with some of them.

3. Players' memories/reflections, comments, brief biographies, etc.
obtained from conversations with them or from written responses to
questions I asked of them.

### 1. HORACE AYSCUE

*Junior---5' 9"---185---good spirit---Really wants to play---Needs experience and more speed.*

Horace did not play very much during the season, but he contributed to our championship run by his "behind the scenes" work of running the opponents' defense and offense. Horace was not a starter, but he helped us win many games by his consistent hard work in practice of holding dummies and being on our scout team. I do not ever remember Horace complaining about playing time or anything else pertaining to football. He was one of the many "unsung heroes" who is on every successful high school football team and is just as important as a player who played in the games on Friday nights.

I have not been able to locate Horace during the writing of this book.

### 2. CHARLES BANKS

*Junior---5' 10"—172—Loves to play football---Very quick---Should help us this year.*

Charles was a very dependable defensive end in our 5-2 and 4-4 scheme. Charles always did his job of turning the offense inside and keeping the ball from getting to the sideline. If he did make a mistake, he would make up for it with his cat-like quickness. Charles was a good tackler and had fun playing his position. He was a very quiet friendly player and was liked by his teammates. One story Bernard Williams tells on Charles was one game when Charles came out of the game, Coach Thomas told Charles "Now let's be tougher and go in there and get ferocious." Charles turned to Coach and said, "Okay, Coach, what number is Ferocious?" I do not know if that is a true story, but that sounds like Charles. He was always polite, hard-working, and very dependable.

Charles was one of our outstanding black athletes. He had experienced some discrimination as he grew up in Raleigh. He went to his first white school when he was in the 6th grade and remembers being called names and spit upon as he walked to school. Coach Ed McLean, who was the basketball and track coach at Broughton in the late 1960's, helped get Charles and Phil Spence to come to Broughton. Phil played basketball at Broughton and went on to play on the national championship team at N.C. State in 1974.

Charles worked three times a week at IHOP while attending

Broughton, including during football season. He recalls he was supposed to work the afternoon of the state championship game in 1970 since it was a Saturday. However, when his boss found out Charles was playing, he let Charles off and the boss and his son went to see Charles play in Carter Stadium. Charles went to Fayetteville State and Laurinburg Junior College immediately after high school.

One of the churches that our football team visited on Sundays during our season was Watts Chapel where Charles and his family attended. Several of the white players remember going to the all-black church during the season. It was their very first time worshipping at a black church.

Charles Banks

Charles' father worked for the railroad for most of his life, and Charles began working for the railroad after attending Laurinburg Junior College. He said that the football workouts and discipline helped him a lot in his work for the railroad. It prepared him to work hard and focus on doing the best he could do. Charles has had some problems in his life, but has worked through them and is doing well. He worked for over 20 years with the railroad and then retired with full disability. Charles has a son who was a good football player for Millbrook High School in the 1990's. Charles's mother is still alive at 89 and Charles is living at his home where he grew up and taking care of his mom. Charles is still a good looking man.

### 3. JIM BASS
*Junior---5' 9"---160---May be one of the best backs in the area--- Always hustling---Good blocker.*

Jim Bass was one of the best backs I had the privilege to coach in my career. He had the best balance of anyone I have ever seen. Jim grew up in Raleigh and played on little league teams with a lot of the other players on the Broughton championship team. He could do it all on the field. Jim was tough, had good hands, was a good blocker, and a shifty runner. One person does not make a team, but if there was one player on this team who made such a huge difference, it probably would be Jim Bass. One of the best characteristics Jim was blessed with was his humility. He always worked hard and never thought he should receive special treatment. Jim was the star of our team, but if you were around him, you would never peg him as the "star." Jim was also a tremendous baseball player also and was quite a star in high school.

Jim had a younger brother, Craven, who was in special programs at Broughton, and he and Jim always had a close relationship. In fact, Craven lived with Jim and his wife in Boone, and Jim took care of him and loved him dearly. Craven was always a staunch supporter of his brother.

Jim was one of the players from our State Championship team who was transferred to Enloe High School in 1971 because of integration and forced busing that began that year in the Raleigh City Schools. Jim played football and baseball at Enloe his senior year. We hated to lose him, along with quite a few other players who were caught up in the transfer system the year after winning the state championship. His dad came to me to see if there was any way for him to stay at Broughton for his senior year, but I had to tell him unless their whole family moved into the Broughton district he would have to go to Enloe where he was assigned. Mr. Bass and his family could not afford to move at the time, and we were all sorely disappointed.

Jim went to the University of South Carolina after graduating from Enloe. He worked hard for the football program there under Coach Paul Dietzel. While in college, he married his USC sweet heart, Vickie Beasley. After a couple years, both Jim and David Turner transferred to Appalachian State in Boone to finish college.

Jim and Vickie remained in Boone, worked in real estate some and were apartment managers. Vickie died in 2013. Jim loved the outdoors and was quite a fisherman and hunter. Jim's brother Craven lived with him until Jim's recent death in 2016.

As I think back about Jim Bass, I think about his being a true winner and competitor.

At Jim's memorial service, David Turner provided the following eulogy:

"Sometimes life is so short. You know, even with all his heroics and all his accomplishments, I never once heard a boastful word come out of Jim's mouth. He never spoke of his personal successes and accomplishments, which were many, but he spoke only of the team's success and the successes of his teammates. You just can't beat that. After high school, Jim and I went to South Carolina to play football for the Gamecocks. Our freshman year we were roommates.

"That year Jim started dating a freshman cheerleader named Vickie Beasley. Most of you know her as Vickie Bass, Jim's wife of some 38 years. I think Jim had reached a turning point in his athletic life and was beginning to branch out and pursue other goals and dreams. We both transferred to Appalachian State in Boone. Jim and his new wife Vickie, and me just trying to do something new. After a while, I was struggling with things. One year I came back up to start the new school year but had nowhere to live. I was just kind of listless with little direction. Jim and Vickie took me in and let me live with them. Jim saw I was in need and he did what he could do to help me out. He was being a good friend and I needed the help.

"After we both graduated from ASU, I went back to Raleigh but Jim stayed in the Boone area and made a new life for him and Vickie. He has been up there ever since right up until the day he died. I know Jim has made a lot of dear friends up in Watauga County. He's been there over 40 years. We have all made good friends throughout our lives, but as I stand here today, I can promise that none of you will find any better friends than what you've got sitting around you right now, right here. We've got to take care of one another. If there is a friend in need, go to them. Talk to them, listen to them and be there for them as best you can. Life is way too short and we just can't afford to do anything less. So reach out when the time comes. I know Jim Bass would. He did for me and for a lot of you and so should we all."

Jim and Vickie Bass

### 4. SAM BEARD

*Senior---5' 9"---151---A good little scrapper---Small, but a lot of desire.*

Sam was a back-up center and played a little linebacker for us in 1970. He is another young man who worked and practiced hard on a daily basis. Sam brought a lot of fire and spirit with him to practice as I remember. Sam was always ready to serve in any way for the good of the football team.

I have not been able to locate Sam during writing of this book.

## 5. GORDON BLAKE

Gordon graduated from Broughton in 1969. He has always been a faithful athletic fan of the Broughton Caps. I really believe his blood flows purple and gold and a little red for the Wolfpack. Immediately after graduating from Broughton, Gordon served as Custodian of the athletics facilities at Broughton High School. During my years at Broughton, Gordon made sure all the athletic facilities were above average. He helped me a tremendous amount in adjusting to being the head football coach. He made sure I knew the history of the athletic program to keep the standards high that had been set before me. Not only was he diligent about his responsibilities around the campus of Broughton, he made sure the equipment for our football team was taken care of during the season. He has remained a friend throughout the years since that famous season in 1970.

Coach Ed Mclean and I had the privilege of being at his wedding in 1993. Gordon is retired and lives in Statesville, N.C. with his wife Pat. Gordon's mom still lives in Cameron Village next door to Broughton and is 92 years old.

### Gordon's Memories/Reflections:

Gordon recalled Jim Bass's outstanding runs against Sanderson and Goldsboro. He also remembers a person from the N.C. High School Association being on the sidelines during the Goldsboro game who was recording the total yards for each team. Back then, if there was a tie at the end of the game, the winner would be determined by the team who had accumulated the most yards.

### Gordon's Bio:

After graduation from BHS and then working for the Broughton High School athletic department, he worked for Revco Drug store for 8 yrs. Then he really enjoyed working for the next 8 1/2 years for the Athletic Department at N.C. State. For the rest of his life, he worked for security in Charlotte and in Statesville before retiring in spring 2016.

Gordon and Pat Blake

### 6. STEVE BREWBAKER

*Senior---5' 11"---185---Good athlete---Can play several positions for us---Good strength.*

I remember Steve being very solid, intelligent, and fundamental in all he did on the football field. This was much due to his dad being a top assistant coach at North Carolina State during this time. Coach Brewbaker was well-known by high school coaches and always was kind to me. He raised a fine young man. Steve played both offensive and defensive tackle and was one of several players that we felt confident in allowing him to play in multiple positions if we ran into injury problems. Steve was knowledgeable enough about the game of football that he adjusted if he needed to. He was quiet, hardworking, and gave a lot of effort regardless of where he played on the field and he would hit you. Steve never got a lot of credit, but he was one of those champions a football team needed if it was going to win over others. He received a football scholarship from N.C. State.

### Steve's Memories/Reflections:

My most important memory is that you and your assistants treated the players like a dad would want his son treated. No profanity was allowed by coaches and players without punishment. That led to a nurturing environment rather than the hostile attitude seen so often. Long hair was tolerated as long as it didn't interfere with performance, which was unique at that time and a tribute to the freedom of expression allowed.

Even though I never had long hair, I appreciated the fact that we were free to be individuals. Once the season began, the blocking and tackling was very limited so that by Friday we were ready to hit people. This was so different from my prior experience where all we did was scrimmage and weren't fresh for games. We ran our plays over and over so that we were never tired during games.

I have lots of good memories, but still feel guilty that I got blocked into Jim Lumsden and he was out with a knee injury. After that season, I signed with N.C. State and started at guard and was a captain on the freshman team, then moved to center and lettered as a sophomore. I decided to go into medicine and told Coach Holtz that I was quitting football to focus on my grades, but I was just sick of him and his staff who were the opposite of you.

**Steve's Bio:**

I went to medical school at Wake Forest, then moved to Wilmington for a four year residency in OBGYN and remained in Wilmington in private practice. My wife Freda and I have been married for 35 years and have a daughter, Amy, who is in veterinary school, and a son, Carey, who is an anesthesiologist in Savannah.

Steve and Freda Brewbaker

My health is good, and I play golf at least three times a week and take our two rescue dogs out on the boat to swim and run on the sand weekly. I look forward to the book and thank you for doing it and for the influence you had in helping us be better men. I lucked into marrying a beautiful and kind woman.

## 7. MARK CAUDLE

*Junior 5'8"---130---Small, but good hustler.*

Mark played a wing back for us in a back up role. He had good hands to catch the ball and worked hard at his blocking skills. I never heard any complaining from Mark. He was another player who tried to improve every practice.

I have not been able to locate Mark during writing of this book.

## 8. JOHN CLARKE

*Senior---5'10"---182---Good hustler---Looks like a good center.*

John was another one of the Broughton warriors who was not very fast, strong, or quick, but he had the desire to make up for lack of his natural ability. He was a hustler and would get after you at any time. Playing center is a very important position and not an easy position to play. He had to deliver the football every time perfectly to our quarterback. I always said if we could not get the snap off, we could not run any plays. John was smart on and off the field, could handle a lot of defenses, could adjust easily and still snap the ball on time. He was a key to our offensive success.

### John's Memories/Reflections:

The memories begin much earlier than that season for it was the prior years that set, for me anyway, the actions that were to come. Specifically, I started playing football in the 5th grade but was never able to play in a game of pee-wee football due to "missing weight." However, I practiced constantly with the team and was assured of a starting spot if I met weight, but was always a couple of pounds heavier. So it was not until the 8th grade at Daniels that I got going on football and then, was not selected for the team, but it was a lesson in perseverance that I have not forgotten.

Growing up in Raleigh in the 50's and 60's was a different time than now or even a few years later in the 80's. Raleigh was a small town with just 3 high schools and even Enloe had only opened in 1962, so it too was an off shoot of Broughton. Sanderson was opening for the first time in 1968 but Raleigh was nothing like it is now. My point is as you grew up in Raleigh, you always knew your path in school provided your family did not move around. All my neighbors went to Broughton and it was a great school with a State Championship in football in 1961. Sandlot games were prevalent and no one wore pads or a helmet even if we were playing tackle ball. You had the opportunity to play with older faster kids and that only made you want to get better or be left behind.

The disappointment in not being selected for the 8$^{th}$ grade team did not last long as the new season for the 9$^{th}$ grade approached. I ran in my Converse All Stars every day throughout the summer to get into shape and be ready to make full contact. Coach Harrington loved the old Oklahoma drill or as some would call it the Hamburger Drill. I wanted to prove myself early and volunteered first to be the defensive side tackling whoever was running. Three straight contacts and hard hits ensued and I fully remember throwing up afterwards. But my energy and enthusiasm was evident to Coach Harrington and being a "senior" made the team. I played offensive line and mostly at guard. Coach often put me in on defense as an end. Aycock was our arch rival school, followed closely by Carroll. Aycock featured some big fellas and we wanted to beat them, especially their big strong running back Julius Branch. We did not beat them and lost pretty badly...35-0 but the seeds of the future were planted. The kids from Martin also did not beat these kids either. We thought that we were going to get better and whip these kids one day. Remember, no one at Daniels or Martin was going to go to Enloe and the Aycock kids were going to go to Enloe...revenge would come.

10$^{th}$ grade was almost guaranteed you would be on the JV team and not the Varsity unless there was an injury or need. We came together as a team, but slowly and again, we did not beat the Enloe JV team but we did score on them for the first time. Our Varsity team also did not beat Enloe in '68 or '69, but the games were intense. Early in practice, Coach Honeycutt tested me out at center and they liked what they saw, so center was to be my position going forward.

Junior year, 1969 meant a chance to be a starter, but competition was tough at center with Ronnie Vereen holding down the job. Coach Stutts was a tough coach and fought hard for our team with the school board on budget cuts. Few of us knew anything about what was happening behind the scenes. Each day at practice, you could only do all that you could to get noticed and maybe make second string. That is exactly what happened and I was ecstatic to get the shot, then Vereen went down with an injury and Coach Stutts moved me to starter. Two practices later, Coach Stutts called us in for a team meeting and informed us that he was being fired. Clearly, devastating news and what did it mean for the team? Buddy Stewart would be named interim head coach and he immediately decided that only seniors would play. My starting spot was gone and he moved me to third string behind Vereen and Dan Garner.

On the bright side of that news, we got to scrimmage as the weekly opposing team offense against the Broughton starting defense. Here was my chance to show the coaches what sort of decisions they were making by not playing me. I gave it my all only to hear them yelling at the defenders but not praising our work. I also got to play with several guys on the JV team when we did scrimmage and got to know David Turner well when he came up to play quarterback. This sort of treatment set a tone in me that I was going to get my job back at some point if I just kept trying and working hard. Coach Stewart left many of us with a bad taste in our mouths but it did not curb our enthusiasm to come back for that senior season once we heard a new coach would be coming to town and Stewart was out.

Early summer in 1970 allowed for lots of gatherings of kids in various places, usually a drug store such as Johnson's on Fairview Road or Northside to talk. Word quickly spread in June that my side of town was going to be rezoned and all of us east of Hayes Barton area would be going to Enloe. We were seniors and that did not seem fair at all. Parents all over protested to school officials that redistricting was not fair to the seniors but no decision was forthcoming. Then it was official, no changes would occur that year; we could go to Broughton and graduate and I could get my chance to be a starter playing football.

I liked almost all aspects of what Coach Riggs and his staff brought to the team. As soon as our schedule was released, I set a goal on paper that we would make the playoffs. So instead of just a 10 game season, I wrote that we were going to play 13 and win the 4-A State Championship. All we had to do to qualify for the playoffs was to win our conference and that was a goal we were going to achieve.

Those two-a-days were hard and long and Coach Riggs and Evans (and the other coaches) built what would be a great tool to keep our mostly undersized bodies in proper blocking position to push back or knock down an opposing player. The large wooden forms were set up so that you would hit yourself in the head (helmet on, of course) if you came up too early from your stance, so learning to stay low made a big difference for us. Coach also did something that I would later learn made a lot of impact: wide stances or gaps between each position. This setup forced the opposing team to spread out too and with our speedy Jim Bass in the backfield, you only needed to hold your man back a few seconds and Jim would be gone.

I remember sitting down on an early summer evening prior to school starting for a one on one meeting with Coach Riggs. We discussed goals and most of us stated that we wanted to win Raleigh for sure and our conference. Beating Enloe was a critical element for our success but so were the other games that were non-conference. Goal setting is something that has stayed with me from that meeting and one that I still frequently use by writing down, "What do we want to accomplish?" Others have stated it as, "What does 'done' look like?" State Championship was what "done" looked like for me.

Greensboro Grimsley was the first game and we all got it into our heads during those 4th quarter drills that you cannot go undefeated unless you win your first game. We learned a lot during that game but lost 8-6. We needed to score more points but our defense was playing pretty well too. Getting a good kicker was also going to be important and during the season, Macy Faulkner would emerge as our place kicker. Game film would show us too that we had the skills but were missing a few assignments and were not as fast off the ball as we should be. We were smaller than most of our opponents so getting off the line quickly was crucial.

The drill that I recall to improve that skill was the blocking crawl. Staying down and driving a dummy forward for a 10 yard push got us faster. We had those four position races too where we all "sped crawled." I recall being one of the faster people on the team in those races. Practice makes perfect only if it is perfect practice. Doing something over and over again until you have the skill down is something I carried forward too in life and work. Some coaches now refer to that as "want to" but it is a desire to be the best and be an achiever.

Winning that first game against Winston-Salem was great and we got to play at home for the second time that season at good old Devereux Meadow which was a baseball field converted to football for our high school. Broughton used to play at Riddick Stadium on Friday nights on the campus of NCSU, but they demolished the field and turned it into a parking lot and sending us to play in "The Meadow."

The most memorable game of the regular season (for me) would be the Enloe game. The city got a great idea to have a Raleigh High School double header and play the games at Carter Stadium. This game was going to be big as we were the nightcap and would not start until around 9 pm. No one went home after school and we all stayed around in the wrestling room on the mats to rest. It was a long rest and then we finally got the call to go downstairs and get dressed. Some of the guys were not taking the game as seriously as needed, perhaps laughing and joking around too much. I dressed very nearby to Jim Bass and I vividly recall him standing on the bench and yelling at all of us "to get serious." That moment was a lesson in leadership too. Jim and I had been friends since first grade and he along with so many of us had known each other for most of our lives and felt comfortable talking about almost anything. Time to get serious and we did.

My memory of that evening was my ability to move a much larger opponent anywhere I wanted to take him. I credit that skill with the drills of practice, stay low, come off the ball quickly, and drive your man backwards. If they stand up with you being so low, they were going to fall down. Either way, open the holes for the backs. During the third quarter, we held the ball for almost the entire quarter…nearly 10 minutes straight. We knew we were going to win after that even with their big Julius Branch. That game was a change point in the season. We knew we could play with anyone and win, we just had to do it together. Heck, we had been playing together most of our lives and now was the time to do exactly that. Execute together, stay focused and you are most likely going to succeed. This lesson too worked on my sales teams when we had to rely on each other to win for the entire team.

Several losses followed, but none in the conference, which meant we were going to go to the playoffs. The Rocky Mount, Wilson, and Fayetteville games (each a loss) made us all realize we were good but had to be perfect if we wanted to beat a physically superior team. I am pretty sure chop blocking is now illegal for lineman, but it surely was not illegal in 1970 and we learned to use that technique when going up against physically superior teams. The point of our execution that became most evident was during the last two games of the season against Ligon and Durham and then the three playoff games where we were undefeated and unscored upon. No one can beat you if they cannot score! Those next three games were not going to be losses as we were all goal setters and achievers.

I especially recall the Goldsboro game as one of my best games. My man was the future star linebacker for ECU and the Canadian Football League Toronto Argonauts, Danny Kepley. Danny was so fast that I had to angle to where the play was going in order to get in front of him. The first play from scrimmage he hit me so hard in the jaw that I saw stars and now I believe it is called a concussion versus, "You got your bell rung." I fondly remember that we had designed plays for the first 3 or so plays and in this game, they worked to perfection going straight down the field but stalling out at the 3 or so and we did not kick a field goal, but we held them scoreless in the first half and it was all tied up 0-0.

Coach Riggs was a UNC grad and got game film from Bill Dooley of the UNC games. UNC had Don McCauley at halfback and had a great designed play that we emulated and practiced all week long. We had not run the play in the first half but after a riveting halftime talk by Coach Riggs, we immediately went out and ran "16." This play went to the right side of the line but basically we all "drove" our man wherever he wanted to go. The play might look like it was going to be a pass play which would freeze the linebackers as the offensive line was collapsing backwards. David Turner simply handed off deep in the backfield to Jim Bass and he took off for over 10 yards on the first play against Goldsboro. It was important for us to get as many yards as possible because in the event of a tie, the winner was determined by most yardage. Our confidence was high after that one play and the play came in from the sidelines to run "17" which was the exact same play just to the left side of the line. Bass took off and screamed down the left side of the field with Kepley in chase but Jim was not to be caught. 6-0 and that is the way it stayed. We beat a team that had beaten all of the teams to whom we had lost. We were avenged and going to the Championship.

Coach Evans was a NCSU grad too and I am guessing had something to do with getting our Championship game played at Carter Stadium. Two games in one season on a field that was awesome is something most high schoolers will never experience. We all had developed our good luck clothing of a specific under garment that we had worn in all of the victories and did not want to change now. We wore our home purple jerseys with gold pants for all of those last 5 games. For me, it was a cut off sweatshirt, but we were not playing at night but during the day and it was warmer in the bright sunshine than under Friday night lights. After warmups, we had to come out of those sorts of clothes and minimize so as not to overheat. Glad we all had a tee shirt to wear. I was honored by my teammates to be the first onto the field and to run through the paper barrier welcoming us to the game. It was exciting running down the slight hill onto the field from the field house and I vividly recall thinking, *Do not fall down as I would be trampled by the rest of the team!*

We won and we kept Charlotte and their great back and future Georgia Tech great, Randy Rhino, off the scoreboard. Olympic had a designed play to Rhino that our coaches had picked up in game film. The game film work by our coaching staff was incredible for they were able to spot multiple tendencies and it helped us. Olympic got down to inside the five-yard line with maybe only one or two downs left to play. The score was 7-0 in our favor but we had to hold them. Then we all saw it from the sidelines and on the field. It was the formation we had observed in the film study and it was going to be a quick pitch to Rhino out of the backfield. Our defense nearly jumped off sides, but we did not get called and we stopped Rhino in his own backfield. We got the ball back and then drove out of that hole, scored and were crowned the 1970 State Champions.

What I Learned From The Season:

I learned to goal set, never ever give up, keep fighting, prepare, prepare, prepare and work as a team. People do not care how much you know until they know how much you care. We did care about each other. Practicing for anything in business prior to engaging with the customer was how we worked at Johnson & Johnson. Numerous role play exercises that made me think back to those hot summer days of running the same play over and over until it was second nature. Observing what your opponents do when you engage them helps set the tone for how to respond. We worked frequently on those sorts of drills in business too. What happens if we do X, how will competition respond? What actions can we be prepared to execute? Look back at what you specifically did on a sales call was the same as film watching exercises. Learn from the positives and the negatives as you can always do better.

I enjoyed listening to Bob Richards' motivational talks that Coach Riggs played for us. Specifically, the lecture on HEART. You can be the biggest and the strongest but you might not win if you are not playing the game with all of your heart. I kept motivational tapes in my car as I drove around town to prepare me mentally for the sales call I was about to undertake. Those life lessons were also passed along to my children as positive imaging to see yourself completing the task and doing it well.

**John's Bio:**

I attended NCSU for two years and during my freshman year thought I would like to try freshman football. Coach Evans had spoken with Jim Donnan (both played at NCSU together) who was one of the assistant freshman coaches. Coach Donnan got a better job with UNC and my ties to the staff were gone. The college game is not the same as the high school game and it was apparent to me that as a walk on, I could not pay for school without working and could not play football if I worked and went to school. After two years, I was not sure what I wanted to do with my life but I had an ambition to find out about motorcycles and that industry. After 2 years, it was clear that profession was going to go nowhere. I married Anne Rouse, a fellow NBHS class of 1971 grad and she had finished at ECU. She encouraged me relentlessly to go back and finish my degree which I did, graduating in 1978. Anne is a trained speech therapist with a strong interest and skill in stuttering therapy.

I enjoyed science and medicine and wanted to get into sales. The pharmaceutical industry was a perfect match for my background and goals to incorporate science and selling. I worked in various capacities for JNJ for 30 years. In 2008 at age 55 I got an opportunity to retire and I decided to take it. We lived in Baltimore for 12 years and in NJ for 10 years before I returned to NC to finish out my career.

As I mentioned, I am married to Anne and we have two children, Jessica and John Randall. Jessica is married and has one girl and a new son. She is an Emory University undergrad and earned her JD from Georgia State University. She is presently working for the United States Foreign Services as a Consular Officer stationed in Bogotá Colombia. John is married and has a boy and a girl. He is a double major graduate from Clemson University and works in the finance department for JNJ and lives in NJ.

Anne and I found our "retirement home" during a visit to the beach in late 1999 and bought it thinking we would eventually get here full time. Since I traveled extensively, I was able to move here and work from our home in Pine Knoll Shores. We both volunteer on a couple of boards and enjoy being out of the rat race. We took off to Atlanta late in 2009 and bought a condo near my daughter's home as she was going to have her first child in March of 2010. Her husband, Oscar, was traveling with his job and she was finishing law school at Georgia State, so a few extra hands were needed to help out. Being able to devote full attention to a child was not something I personally got to do the first time around, so this event was going to be special. I can only tell you that we have an incredible relationship with our granddaughter Camila. We were with her almost every day from birth to about 3. We worked out with our daughter that after she got her feet on the ground and opened her office, we were going to sell the condo and move back to NC. We did so in September of 2012. We did not get the same opportunities with the other ones, but it is a different set of circumstances. My daughter in law decided to be a stay at home mom until the kids are older and then she might return to her work as a civil engineer (M.I.T. grad too!). My son-in-law, Oscar, has done the same and is at home full time with their two kids. We are very proud of him and he has become a US citizen as well. It was a long process, but what a fantastic ceremony to witness when he was sworn in as a citizen with people from over 100 countries becoming part of our great country.

John and Anne Clarke

## 9. JIM CORTER

*Junior---6'2"---175---Not much experience, but really works hard to improve---Has desire.*

Jim was a tall, skinny kid in high school. I remember looking at him early in the season and wondered why he was playing football. However, it did not take me long as we prepared for the upcoming season to learn that Jim was a technician on the football field. He fits right into the group of players we had who were not fast, strong, or quick, but loved the game and had a big heart of desire. Jim did not want to disappoint us as coaches and therefore gave extra effort in all he did. He was very intelligent in the classroom (someone told me he made a perfect score on the SAT), but he also carried that intelligence to the field. He knew a lot about leverage and learned he had to use that leverage to move his opponent and he did. He made big plays throughout the season at his

defensive tackle position. I remember Jim fighting hard to improve and
was very proud of his accomplishments without showing off in any way.
He went about his business in a very quiet and determined way. Jim is
now a professor at Columbia University.

**Jim's Memories/Reflections:**

I think of that experience, and of you and the other coaches, quite
often. It was an intense set of experiences and as educational as anything
that happened in high school. You were an inspirational and flexible
leader, and it was a pleasure to play under you and the coaches and learn
from you.

Why did I play football? I had always loved sports, and there was a
feeling in my family that football was the only "real" team sport. My
father had been a football standout at his small-town high school in
Pennsylvania, and he definitely encouraged my older brother and me to
play. For one thing, he hoped we might get college scholarships – raising
four kids on a college professor's salary, the cost of education was
something to worry about even in those days. This worked out for my
brother Carl – he graduated from Broughton in 1965, and attended
Davidson on a football scholarship. An interesting family side note –
before we won the State Championship in 1970 (with me playing nose
tackle and defensive tackle, as a junior) the last time Broughton won it
was 1963, and my brother was a junior starting at defensive guard. A
funny coincidence, in my opinion.

One thing I loved about football was being in shape. You and the
other coaches worked us out pretty hard (I'll say some more about that
later), and I think I was in the best shape of my life in those days. That
made me feel remarkably healthy, and gave me both physical and social
confidence. I felt like I could walk into the street and stop a car. Maybe
that was a bit dangerous to imagine, although when you think about it,
that's roughly the job description of a defensive tackle. Although I was
tall and skinny, I had strong legs. Some guy I met in those days showed
me a trick, that he (or I) could pick up the front end of a VW bug, just
squatting it using the front bumper. So that was a minor hobby among
some of us for a while.

On the other hand, let's face it, football has some physical risks.
Playing nose tackle and defensive tackle, when we were all a bit

undersized, was not a stroll in the park. I got a concussion in that tough game at Terry Sanford H.S. in Fayetteville, was basically knocked out. I stood up after the play, was standing there woozy, and I fell down two or three times getting to the sidelines. I tried to claim I was ok, could go back in, but I remember Coach Thomas asking me, "What's your name?" I tried to give him a sarcastic look back, to show that was a silly question, but I don't think I actually answered. He turned away with a slightly exasperated look, and I went to the hospital to be checked out. My father was allowed to ride with me. The doctor diagnosed a mild concussion, and advised that I not play again that night. My father made sure to get that message to the coaches when we returned to the stadium.

And you, no doubt, recall that my senior season ended early when I tore up my right knee in practice. We were doing an offensive line pass blocking drill, and Coach Thomas asked for defensive line volunteers to jump in to provide a pass rush. I was pushing my man back, but the defensive guy next to me, Skip Hawkins, just made a quick move and shot the gap, and his offensive lineman, having missed him, decided to cut-block me to look like he was doing something useful. He landed on my knee and the knee essentially bent backwards and sideways. I believe I probably broke the team rule against cursing at that point. Dr. Dameron at the Raleigh Orthopedic Clinic attended to me and I had surgery a day or two later. They removed the meniscus, and repaired most of the ligament damage. But in those days they did not know how to repair a broken ACL, so they just left that unrepaired, which is how it has been.

Most of the guys on the team, and several of the coaches, including you, came to visit me in the hospital. That support was appreciated, of course. I have to give some special credit to Skip Hawkins, who came and gave me a book, Seven Days till Sunday, about the NFL. It contained a long passage about Gayle Sayers, the running back, who completely blew out his knee – they replaced ligaments with muscle strands to try to repair it, but through incredibly hard work, he came back enough to play in the NFL again. That was inspiring and encouraging. I asked Dr. Dameron what the long-term consequences would be, and he shrugged and said, "You'll probably have arthritis in it when you're older." That also was reassuring, and turned out to be pretty accurate. I have favored and protected that knee all my life, and worked out carefully to strengthen it, and I still walk with a slight limp sometimes, but I have led an active life. I fenced in college, played full-court basketball longer than any of my friends, still do downhill skiing and backpacking. So I can't complain.

I think one important lesson football teaches is how to be on a team. People often use military metaphors to describe football. Part of me thinks that is silly, and trivializes the sacrifices that our servicemen and women make, and the intensity of combat experiences. But there are definitely some similarities. A football team is a hierarchical organization, the coaches are the leaders and set the rules (hopefully, fair ones – again, more about that later) and strategy, the players are the troops. And it teaches you that sometimes in life, you just have to take orders and execute them fast, on the spot, no backtalk. So that's a form of mental discipline, to understand that a team has to function top-down sometimes, there has to be a coherent plan. Maybe you're not in charge of formulating the plan, but you are in charge of executing it. They say that to be a good leader, you have to know how to be a good follower, and team sports teaches you that. Another reason why the military metaphor is not so far off, is that there is some physical danger, and some fear (at least there was for me), and a lot of intensity, in football, and that breeds camaraderie and team closeness. I mentioned fear – practice at conquering fear was part of the growth for me – sometimes, on the team bus on the way to a game, I was afraid, quite frankly. But once the game started, there was only the flow and the "battle," and the fear was forgotten. The last thing you want to be in a quick strategic physical game like football is tentative.

Being an athlete in high school brings some respect and status from other students. Maybe that's in part because being athletic is a respected thing in and of itself, and no doubt because success is admired (when the team is successful). But I think part of the respect is an acknowledgement of the hard work involved, and the self-discipline that that work requires, but maybe even the danger.

Here are some further reflections about football and our Championship year. Some of the comments below will seem obvious, and some you may disagree with or remember differently, but here goes.

Earlier I talked about the physical aspects of playing football, being in shape and injuries, so maybe I should talk a bit more about the positive aspects. First, playing football is good discipline; I always made my best grades during football season, because I would come home from practice, do my homework, and go to bed. I had no time or energy to goof off or get in trouble, except on weekends.

I do love football; it's still the only sport I spend significant time watching (except for a little college basketball.) Besides its intensity, football is remarkably complex in its strategy. It's like chess in real time, with parallel moves. It was an intense experience to play football, and I remain very proud of being part of our State Championship team.

The main credit for our Championship belongs to you, the coaches. Of course, it's a little hard to point fingers - football is such a team game. What you, the coaches, did both reacted to and affected what we did, and the strategies no doubt took account of our strengths and weaknesses as players. One lesson we learned from you was not to point fingers after a loss, to take it as a team failure, that everyone could have found something to do better. And "failure" doesn't seem like the right word, maybe "falling short of the goal" comes closer. If you do your best, no reason to hang your head after a loss. But "best" does not mean perfect, so there is a reason to focus on what you individually could have done better.

OK, here's the most amazing memory – it's related to that last comment. There was a point in the season when our record was 4 wins and 4 losses. And you gave a speech, saying, "Don't get down. I know 4 and 4 doesn't seem like a good record and our season seems like it's slipping away from us. But you know what, we could still be State Champions! We haven't lost any conference games." I think our first reaction was to laugh; it seemed like a wild exaggeration. But after we thought about it, we had to admit you were right. That was quite a prediction. As you know, we did not lose a game after that, and we won the last five by shutouts.

I remember the final game of the season, the Championship against Charlotte Olympic. My father said he was sitting in the stands behind a couple of college scouts. He claimed one of them said, as our team was introduced, "What a ragtag bunch! There may not be a major college prospect in the lot of them." And when I ran on to the field, one said, shaking his head, I assume, "Look at that big, skinny defensive tackle."

I was left tackle. The offensive tackle I was facing was a big skilled guy, their team co-captain, and he, in fact their offense in general, pushed us slowly up and down the field the whole game, no doubt running a lot in my direction. You put in Gary Neal in my place for some series, to see if he could stop the run better. Luckily our goal line defense stopped them every time.

But one way or another, I was on the field for the final play. They were 10 or fifteen yards from our end zone, we were up only 6-0. The play they called was a sweep left, but I guess our right defensive end and backs turned it back inside, their running back was scrambling, and Steve Brewbaker and I tackled him together. That was memorable.

I could talk about the professionalism and football knowledge you brought us. The strategies were innovative, at least to us, and the knowledge you all imparted made us an effective force on the field. This was no mean feat, given our physical limitations in terms of size and speed. I mean, on the defensive line, we were often outweighed by 50 or 60 pounds by the guys we were facing (I was a defensive tackle, 6'4", playing at around 190). But you always preached, "I want all eleven of you in on every tackle." And we came pretty close -- I thought of our defense as a kind of "killer bee" defense, where we would swarm the ball carrier. Another thing, I always had 110% faith in our defensive backfield. They were amazing, so much so that when another team would drop back to pass, I would think, as I was rushing the passer, "Haha, you fools!" Our goal line defense was also amazingly effective, when big Chris Morgan would truck in, we would use a 5-or 6-man line, line up face to face with the offense, and often "stunt," where everyone would shoot a gap.

Of course, we had to be in good shape to play that killer bee way, and we were, because you coaches worked us so hard. I remember in those preseason twice-a-day workouts in the August heat (sometimes 90 degrees and 90% humidity), I would weigh myself before and after practice. I would sometimes come off the field weighing 10 pounds less than I went out, mostly water loss I suppose. But all this had an effect -- you convinced us that we would always have an advantage in the fourth quarter because we would be in better shape than the other team. I remember we would yell "fourth quarter" at each other when the clock got to that point. This was a psychological advantage, but there was something to it.

Even before you took the job (and I'm using "you" to mean partly you individually, but also all the coaches -- coaching a football team requires a team), you had an impact on us. I remember word got around that the new coach had been coaching at the college level, UNC I believe. And I asked whoever told me that, "Why does he want to leave a college job to coach at the high school level?" And the reply was, "I think he feels he can do more to affect players at a younger age." Maybe the word wasn't "affect," but it seemed clear that your intent was to have a moral effect on the players as much as teaching them football. And as someone who comes from a family of educators, I certainly respected that motive.

But there was a certain tension to that too, partly because American society was pretty polarized in 1970, nearly as much as now. There was the Vietnam War, and most of my friends opposed it because we thought it was an unnecessary war, with terrible costs to civilians and to those who fought in it. But we kind of expected most adults to support it, and tensions ran high, with many of us thinking the war was immoral, and other people thinking any opposition to the war was unpatriotic. A Quaker friend of mine, Jonathan Tyler, got beaten up in a school stairwell for handing out antiwar leaflets. Lots of parallels to today, actually.

In any case, we also heard that you (and some of the other coaches) were devout Christians, and I think I worried a bit about how that might play out. I consider myself a religious person, but I am very private about that, and one of the things I value most about America is the freedom of religion, including the freedom not only to believe what you want, but to keep it to yourself if you want.

But I needn't have worried, you handled this part of (how you perceived) the job beautifully. It was clear that you were devout Christians, and you encouraged devoutness, but you were completely nondenominational about it. So when you said, "OK, we're going to take a minute of silence, you can pray, or you can meditate, or you can do whatever you want, but take a minute to reflect on X," that felt perfectly ok, and I did not feel any pressure to pretend I believed anything other than what I believed. Maybe the most overtly religious part of the whole program was the opportunity to visit individual team member's churches, but it was completely voluntary. I really enjoyed that, particularly visiting some of the Black churches (because who doesn't like gospel music?), and I think it was a good team-building experience. After all, another part of the polarization in society at the time was the Black-White divide, which was sometimes harder to bridge than we liked.

Other things that made playing for you a positive experience were also related to your religion and your moral educational mission, I think. One was that the team was really a just and fair mini-society. I believe that a well-run school, a well-run football team, or really any organization where teamwork is valuable, should be run like a good family, that is, with justice for all, and with the expectation that everyone treat everyone else with respect, both peer-to-peer, and up and down the ladder. That also means clear rules, no favorites and no outcasts; everyone has a chance to express their opinions. I think we all felt listened to – that was not something you can take for granted in many organizations. Little things like encouraging us to put a stereo in the locker room, and bring in our own music to listen to, made us feel that our culture and likes and dislikes were allowed, in spite of the youth-adult divide and the cultural polarization of the time. (I brought in a 45-rpm record of Joe Cocker's "Feeling All Right," maybe "The Letter" too.)

I have to mention the no-cut rule. This is a policy I really respect, and it seems like the right one for a school team, because this is something an educator (as opposed to a coach whose only mission is to win games) would do. You said, "If you are willing to come out, come to practice, and work hard, you can be a part of this team." I think the policy helps with team spirit, and makes the team a part of the larger school community. And it seems to me it helps combat a kind of privileged-athlete mindset, something that today we sometimes see the negative effects of, and that gives football and other sports a bad rep.

Another small thing that made you, the staff, seem very moral, was your strict "no cursing" rule. As adolescent boys, we were all trying to learn to curse, to try to seem more grown-up and macho. But at the same time we appreciated that you, the coaching staff, never cursed, no matter how intense things got. I can still call up a vivid flashbulb memory of Coach Thomas talking to us defensive lineman and demonstrating some technique, yelling "Throw a stinking forearm!" We heard the word "stinking" a lot.

Another way I think you were responsive to us is that I think you did a good job of guiding us out of trouble, in a quiet, low-key way. Between my junior and senior year, I did an exchange program, spending a month with a German family in Nuremburg. When I returned, Gary Neal told me, kind of gleefully, "You sent a postcard to the coaches, saying 'The beer here is excellent'." My reaction was, "You must be kidding me! I did that?" realizing I was probably in trouble. Seventeen-year-olds are prone to doing stupid things (that's part of my point here). I think I must have gone through some thought process deciding that beer was against team training rules only because it was illegal for minors to drink, so if I was in a place where that was legal, it wouldn't be against the rules. And besides, it was not during the season, it was during the summer. But back in NC, I realized that this put you in a dilemma - I had done something against team rules, raising the question for you of how to be fair but not undercut team discipline, and realizing that you probably felt you couldn't just let it slide. Your solution was to call me in and interview me about the particulars. In that meeting, you kind of led the witness, asking me if it was just the case that the family I was staying with had served me beer, since it was not an odd thing in Germany to offer a 16- or 17-year old beer. I agreed, because this was in fact true. And you didn't pry much further (there was a bit more to the story), thus you managed to handle it in a low-key way that was flexible but preserved team discipline in this kind of unusual case.

I have two small postscripts to add:

First, I have to mention another "permissive" policy you had, besides the music in the locker room, that helped bridge the "culture war" gap. And that was allowing us to have long hair -- a big issue in that day. You said, "As long as it doesn't become a safety issue by sticking out of your helmet, so that somebody could grab you by it, it's ok." You were ahead of your time -- I see dreadlocks now in the NFL, but it seemed unusual then. I think Shaner took advantage of this policy the most - good for a monster back - he looked kind of like Blackbeard.

Second thing is, I was thinking about how I personally coped with being substantially outweighed on the line by some the guys I was facing. After all, if a bigger guy hits a smaller guy, he is usually going to drive him back, that's just physics. So I remembered that I had a trick: I wore inch-long "mud cleats" all the time, in all weather. That enabled me to dig in. So I would basically hit the guy once, then make sure I got under him, even if I was practically on the ground, then just dig in. I might not have made the tackle, but we made a pretty big pile at the line that the running backs would have to go around, giving our linebackers time to get there, and maybe a one-on-one situation when they did. It's possible this "trick" may have backfired on me the next season, when I blew out my knee, because it was a bit dangerous to wear them, given that it made it easy for my foot to get trapped, but I really don't think it was a factor.

OK, that's about all I have time for today, and covers much of what I wanted to say. This seems like a good opportunity to thank you for your decision to be an educator and coach, and for all the help and teaching you gave us. I would play for you anytime.

**Jim's Bio:**

For college I attended UNC-Chapel Hill on a Morehead scholarship. I did not go out for football there, in part because of the knee, in part because they told me I would have to gain at least 25 pounds to have a chance to play as a lineman. However, I did go out for the fencing team, and made it - the coach there, Ron Miller, was willing to take people with no fencing experience if he thought they were good athletes. I greatly enjoyed fencing, lettered three years in it. I have gotten two of my children to try it as a sport here in New York City.

So I graduated from UNC in 1977 after 5 years there. I was delayed a bit because I had taken a semester off to study music full-time, like many of my musician friends. But I decided in the end I was better at school than at music. I graduated magna cum laude with a degree in psychology, and was accepted to study for a PhD there in quantitative psychology. About that time I began dating Lisa Church whom I had dated in high school. You may recall her, she was student body president at Broughton your second year there. But after a year studying in the Psychometric Lab in the Psychology Department, I began to feel I had made a mistake going to the same school for both undergraduate and graduate study – I had already taken courses with all the professors. So I applied to Stanford and transferred there. Lisa and I got married about the same time, 1979. We moved to San Francisco, where I attended graduate school at Stanford and she worked in S.F. at Stanford, I had the privilege of working with Amos Tversky, the MacArthur Prize-winning mathematical psychologist. I got my Ph.D. in 1983, and accepted a job at Teachers College, the Education School of Columbia University, as Professor of Statistics and Education. I have been there ever since, as a professor and twice serving as Chair of the Human Development department. Lisa and I had two sons, Brett and William, but we got divorced around 1998. A few years later I met my current wife, Ania Jachnik. We have a daughter, Cameron.

Jim Corter

## 10. DAVE DUPREE

*Senior---5' 10"---162---Letterman---Good athlete---Can play several positions---Good attitude.*

Dave played in our defensive backfield. I remember he was a very sound tackler. There were not many people that Dave could not tackle, and that helped prevent any long touchdown runs against us. You need someone like Dave Dupree in the defensive backfield who takes risks from time to time. He had the personality of a gambler and made several key interceptions during our season. Dave was often the voice in the backfield who made the defensive calls for our secondary and made sure everyone was on the same page.

### Dave's Memories/Reflections:

3:30 bell rings. Out into the hall, dump the books into the locker, and over to the gym. Only 15 minutes to get into those white dingy practice uniforms and out onto the rock-hard field for practice. The jostling in the locker room, the smell of atomic balm, whirlpools churning, tape being pulled off rollers and wrapped around ankles, yelling for Harrison Ward, Robbie Jones and Bob Womble for misplaced gear, lockers opening and slamming, constant laughing and grumbling between us, out the side door of the locker room and up the little hill, across the road and up the steps across the track and on to that awful field. How many times, how many days it is hard to remember, but how can we ever forget them. Coaches Riggs, Caldwell, Evans, Thomas, Kral – all standing around frowning and looking at their watches.

Those were the days and there are way too many memories to really capture, but we all have a few to share. The good ones are easy to remember. One of the most vivid memories I have, not one from the 1970 season, but from several seasons leading up to that, is chasing a bow-legged fellow wearing a green jersey, from the Enloe Eagles, down the sidelines. For years, we just could not catch him. He was bigger, stronger, faster, craftier and just plain brutal in any attempted tackle. I was not slow, but I can see him now coming around the right, or left corner, sweeping wide leaving the linemen and linebackers in his wake, and moving like a compact locomotive – his legs pumping at a seemingly unbelievable rate – heading right into the defensive backfield. Not at all like that graceful stallion, Carlester Crumpler of Wilson Fike fame, Julius Branch was 5 foot, 10 inches and 165 pounds, all compact muscle jammed into his helmet, shoulder pads and pants. You would think you had the right angle (for a shot at the ankles, but certainly not a head-on attempt), but then he shifted gears and was past you and it was a footrace down the sidelines. I can see him now in my mind's eye, moving steadily away as the Enloe crowd rose to their feet thundering. It happened so many times!!

Then came the 1970 season. I don't really remember much of the first two games – Greensboro Grimsley and Winston Salem Smith Reynolds, but I believe we played Enloe at Carter Stadium in a night game (that could be wrong, but I seem to remember that) and there was Julius. I swear the guy was 25 years old, but he was exactly the same. It seemed like deja vu all over again. Julius came around that old corner wide and the chase began…but something was definitely different. He could not turn the corner the first few times. Doug Murray, Gary Stainback, Phil Ficklin and others were forcing him really wide into cut-back situations. I'm thinking, he looks the same, runs as fast, so what's the deal? Then we must have let our guard down a little, and he gets around the corner. I have to admit, I was not looking forward to this, but Preston, Jimmy Durham and I took off – and I RAN HIM DOWN FROM BEHIND! At that point I realized that we had grown up in more ways than one. I still get chills thinking about running him down that first time. We all looked at each other as a team over the next few plays as we stopped Julius over and over and realized – we can do this and play on a level none of us had yet achieved as a team.

Somewhere in the third or fourth quarter, I remember a goal-line stand we made and I was so jacked about being able to play head to head with Enloe after all these years, that Julius carried off-tackle to our right from about the 10 yard line. He was tripped up a bit and I had a clear shot straight on and I slammed into him as hard as I could almost head to head – screaming out all of the frustration of those years past, of chasing and chasing him. In the tackle, my left thumb went into his right helmet ear-hole, and broke it straight back flat on the top of my hand. I did not even notice. We took possession of the ball and I ran off the field still screaming in the realization that something important had happened.

Coach Thomas motioned me over and asked to look at my hand. That's when I noticed the dangling thumb. Harrison Ward, our trainer, taped it and I went back in – the first time we had ever beaten those Enloe guys. That was also the start of the "dead-man defense," as Coach Joe White, from Charlotte Olympic, called it after we stopped his team lead by Randy Rhino, their star running back, on the goal at the end of the first half of the Championship game.

Coach Riggs once told us that when we hit someone really hard, always hop up (no matter what you felt like), pick the other guy up and tell him "nice run" and trot off. Preston Ruth, Jimmy Durham and I adopted that tactic as I am sure the rest of you did. I remember playing Durham and their running back, Tommy Hayes, bursting through the line and Preston (skinny) Ruth hitting him head-on with a loud crack of helmets. Jimmy Durham and I hit him in the helmet almost simultaneously, but from the sides. We were all a little shaken (Tommy Hayes had the biggest and hardest head I had ever seen and was famous for just plain running over people) and Jimmy and I hopped up, ears ringing, and we grabbed Preston and "hopped" him to his feet and said "nice run" as we picked up Tommy. PR's pupils were the size of dinner plates! I remember Coach Riggs giving that instruction to this day – his jaw jutting out, his fist clinched, other hand on someone's shoulder, telling them that doing that every time, no matter how hard the hit, offense or defense, showed the other person just how tough you were and what kind of a person you were - undefeatable, no matter what. I remember that to this day and practice that philosophy to this day.

How many times during scrimmage did we see Coach Riggs grab the ball from someone, call a play, charge through the line crashing into folks just to show us, "You gotta be tough!" And how many times have we used that line in our lives, along with all the other lessons?

So, I have to reminisce a little about the defense. ZERO points, ZERO points, allowed in the last five games. 19-0, 13-0, 21-0, 6-0. Pretty darned amazing, that 59 – 0 is. In Caulton Tudor's sports column, November 30, 1970, the first paragraph says it all, "It," mumbled Coach Joe White, "was a dead man defense all right. It killed us." He went on to say, "To tell the absolute truth, I honestly thought we could move the ball effectively on them...but I guess that is what their last four opponents thought also. To put it simple: we were just whipped."

Who remembers those awful steak and potatoes dinners we had down at that little restaurant whose name I cannot remember? In today's nutritionally driven world, that would be considered insane to eat that way an hour before a game. But it was terrific and we all felt very special to have that benefit and recognition before a home game. And Devereux Meadow – what a great place to be on a Friday night. The sound of the drums, the building murmur of the crowd filling the seats, the smell of the turf, the sun setting and the bright lights overhead against the midnight blue of the sky. And we had the best seats in the house. They were truly magic moments in our lives with all those eyes focused on us. We felt as special as most of us were ever going to feel.

I also remember the luckiest play I ever made and it was against Goldsboro, for the Eastern State 4-A Title. A defensive back's worst fear is to have someone very fast to cover and to have him get behind you. This kid was fast and had very good hands. The play faked a half-back hand off and I hesitated and half-stepped toward the line as this guy came off the line off his split-left position. He took a step inside and then turned on the afterburner and blew past me. It was a real "Oh shit" moment. We were on about their 40, so there was plenty of room to run. All I could think of was to get as close as possible and hope for a short throw. Head down, I never once looked back to see what the QB was doing, but the guy was looking over his shoulder as the goal line was approaching, so I knew what was happening. As we crossed the goal line, I remember his eyes, they were getting bigger and bigger, as his hands started to come together over his right shoulder. Coach Riggs had always told me, "Always watch the eyes. They will tell you what's happening." Never looking up, I dove towards him with my arms out, and the damned ball was just short enough and landed perfectly on my forearms. It rolled into my hands as we crashed together in the middle of the end zone in a tangle. The kid was not giving up and as we rolled, he managed to reach inside and wrestle the ball from me. The ref was right with us the whole time, and when we came up, the other kid with the ball, he gave the catch signal...and pointed to our end of the field!

Devereux Meadow went wild and we took the ball on the 20. We won that game 6-0 as Bass made the only score of the game.

All of a sudden, we were 63 boys and coaches in purple and yellow at Carter Stadium, on a Saturday afternoon, on November 28, 1970. What a day.

What happened that afternoon was life changing. No one can ever take that away. We all did well and deserved the result. The better team won. We played our best and were all equals. The defense took young Randy Rhino to the mat. We must have picked him up a dozen or so times in the backfield, patted him on the butt, and said, "Nice run," while we were thinking, *But not nice enough.* We stopped them on the ground and in the air. I was lucky enough to grab a couple of interceptions – one that I would have run back. I remember seeing a clear field down the sideline that was rudely interrupted when his diving reach snagged the inside of my shoulder pads behind my neck after I had turned the corner. (I hate it when that happens.) This game was big enough for a lot of memories, but like a lot of things in life, the trip seems more memorable than the finish sometimes.

The after party at my brother's cabin was also one for the history books. God was surely looking after all of us that evening. The floors were covered with mattresses, the furniture had been removed, Jimi Hendrix - Electric Ladyland - played loudly, and I think there was some beer involved. Someone might ask Jim Little what boys' camp we "borrowed" them from and if he ever returned them. Many people I had never seen before showed up. Several mattresses were dragged out of the house and used as cushions for doing flips off of the outside deck. Phil Ficklin, always a bit hard to understand, was completely unintelligible within a half hour. Mark Shaner got in a fight with a rather friendly tree outside I think. I was talking to John Clark as he was walking towards several of us standing on the deck, and all of a sudden, he disappeared. It took us several minutes, it seemed, to realize he had stepped into a hole in the deck surrounding a tree. Totally hilarious, as was everything that evening. Willis Price was climbing on top of the interior walls inside the house, dropping unannounced into several embarrassing situations I heard later. A good time was had by all, thanks in part to my brother, James. I seem to remember he and some of his friends dropping by at some point, opening the door, looking inside, and then shaking their heads and leaving. I have no idea what time things wound down, but these memories never die.

63 boys and coaches in purple and yellow at Carter Stadium, on a Saturday afternoon, November 28, 1970. Thank you, Coach Riggs. Thank you for believing in us.

And by the way, the dangling finger was my left thumb from hitting Julius Branch at the goal line against Enloe at Carter Stadium early in the season, I believe. It's still a quarter inch shorter than my right thumb. Was bent all the way back to my wrist. Fixed it with a little tape and went back in. Dr. Dameron set it Saturday  afternoon at old Rex Hospital.

**Dave's Bio:**

David Dupree is a founder and a Senior Partner of The Halifax Group, LLC. Prior to founding Halifax in 1999, David was a Managing Director and Partner with The Carlyle Group, where he was primarily responsible for investments in health, wellness and related sectors. Prior to that, he was a Principal in Corporate Finance with Montgomery Securities and Alex Brown & Sons. David earned a B.S. from The University of North Carolina at Chapel Hill and received his M.B.A. from the Wake Forest University School of Business.

David is also Director Emeritus of Whole Foods Markets, Inc. (NASDAQ: WFMI and a Fortune 500 company) where he served as a director from 1997 until 2008. As a Whole Foods director, he served on the Audit Committee and was chairman of the Nominating and Governance Committee.

David serves as a managing member and member of the management committee of Salem Halifax Capital Partners, a Small Business Administration mezzanine lending company sponsored by Halifax. He is currently a third term trustee of Wake Forest University and a member of the Executive Committee. David also served as Chairman of the Investment Policy Committee for the Wake Forest Endowment. He is currently Chairman of Verger Capital Management which now manages the Wake Forest Endowment as an outsourced CIO. David was also awarded the Distinguished Alumni Award recently by Wake Forest University.

David also serves as a trustee for the Potomac School in McLean, VA and is Chairman of the Potomac School's Investment Committee and is also a member of the Finance Committee and the Executive Committee.

David is married to Marijke Jurgens Dupree and has two children – Miriam (18) and Tayte (16). Miriam is an accomplished equestrian show jumper and served as the Junior Representative for the Washington National Horse Show in 2016. She will be a Freshman at Wake Forest University in the Class of 2020. Tayte is a Varsity tennis player at The Potomac School since his 9th grade year and plays both singles and doubles. He will be a Junior this year (2016). David and his wife are avid cyclists, skiers, runners and swimmers. They did their first International distance triathlon last year.

Dave and Marijke Dupree

## 11. JIM DURHAM

*Senior---6'---165---Great hustler and worker---Defensive back--- Likes to hit---Great attitude.*

Jim was one of the two captains the players selected before the season began. This was quite an honor and tells you a lot about him and how his teammates felt about him. He was a leader by doing and not talking. In fact Jim was one of the quietest players we had until he got on the field. He was a leader by example and certainly was looked up to. He was an easy player to coach because of his intelligence, football savvy, and his desire to win. Jim played defensive back and was always well prepared. He would know the scouting report frontwards and backwards and could spot things about our opponent as well as any player we had. Like so many of our players, he was very coachable and I could always trust him to follow through with his responsibility.

**Jim's Memories/Reflections:**

The team was a group of guys without "superstars" who had been playing football together for many years. Many of us started playing together at the age of nine for a team in Raleigh Parks and Recreation called "The Dr. Pepper Wildcats," coached by another "revered coach," Jim Panton. This midget team was almost professional in nature with playbook, cheerleaders, and road trips. Most of us played on this team until the age of twelve and were exceptionally schooled in the fundamentals of football by Coach Panton and his staff. We then moved on to Daniels Jr. High and Martin Jr. High and actually played against each other for a few years. We reunited at Broughton under your tutelage, and the strength of our chemistry after many years of playing together was very formidable. The strength of "the team" overcame many opponents with some individual exceptional talent, and the end result was the State Championship. Again, we were a testimony as a group of ordinary guys with ordinary talent who came together to create a powerful team.

One memory that stands out in my mind involved a practice. We had come out on the field and were just going through the motions of practice in a very lethargic manner. You became very upset, told us to get off the field, go back to the locker room, get dressed, and go home. We all ran back to the locker room, and I think in our mentality, were prepared to do just that, go home. But Jim Little rallied the troops and we all came back out on the field with a new intensity and had a good practice. The point being was that I was co-captain, but there were many, many leaders on that team who led us and contributed to the unity of the team. There was always someone like a Jim Little to "pick us up" and point us in the right direction.

And of course we owe a lot to you, "our coach," and the other coaches for bringing us together and molding us into the team that brought home the Championship.

**Jim's Bio:**

After graduating from Broughton, I attended UNC-Chapel Hill and graduated with a degree in Business Administration. I went to work with the State Employees' Credit Union in 1975 and worked as a loan officer and branch manager in Raleigh, Goldsboro, Asheville, and Hickory. In 1986, I left the SECU and joined Wheat First Securities in Hickory as a financial advisor. After sixteen years and several mergers and acquisitions, I joined Raymond James Financial in hickory in 2002 as a Registered Principal. I am still with Raymond James Financial and I do financial planning and portfolio management for my client base.

Jim and Carla Durham

I married my wife Carla (from Concord, N.C) in February of 1986. She is a teacher in the Catawba County School System. We have four children - my oldest son James (age 29 who is a logistics manager for a German company in the area called Sarstedt), my oldest daughter Lauren (age 28 who lives in Wisconsin and is a replenishment buyer for Krogers), my youngest daughter Caroline (age 21 who is a rising senior at UNC-Chapel Hill), and my youngest son Zachary (age 19 who is a rising sophomore at UNC-Chapel Hill). All four of my children were very active in AAU basketball and all had a great passion and involvement in soccer. None ever wanted to play football. Both my youngest son and daughter play on the UNC club soccer teams and we continue to travel to watch them play, now representing UNC. My daughter Lauren is getting married in August up in Wisconsin.

### 12. WELLS EDMUNDSON

*Junior---5'11"---197---Looks good at defensive end---Good attitude---Up from undefeated JV team.*

Wells was a good strong defensive end who knew how to play the position. He was patient in defending plays, and that is what we needed in our scheme. We did not need a defensive end who was only interested in hitting people at full speed all the time. At his position, Wells had to turn the offensive runners back toward our linebackers. He had to contain the offense, and that is exactly what Wells was capable of doing for us. We played a team defense, and Wells fit perfectly in our scheme. He would still hit you hard when he had a chance. Wells was smart and understood his job, as well as the game of football, and coaches and players could count on him.

Wells is a doctor in Raleigh. Several of his teammates' parents as well as some of his former teammates are and have been his patients over the years. He has been a blessing to many people. At Jim Bass's memorial service, there were 17 people who were patients of his and some would not still be here without some timely interventions by Wells.

**Wells's Memories/Reflections:**

What a great year in football for us! I was a junior, and started at left defensive end. I think it was Coach Thomas who impressed upon me to never let the runner get to my outside as there would be no help down the sideline. Charles Banks, the right defensive end, and I had an agreement that on punting downs I would go for the guy guarding the punter and he would go for blocking the punt. He blocked quite a few as I recall because my mark would cheat over because he knew I was coming after him! I believe it was our second or third season regular game when I broke my collar bone and separated my shoulder at old Devereaux Meadow. Subsequently I missed playing the next four or five games but came back in time for our playoff games like several other injured starters. I think Terry Sanford walloped us 49-0 during the regular season. Those Goldsboro kids were tough and their running star Bobby Myrick was a slippery dude but our defense was so quick that no one could score on us. I don't think any other team has been unscored on in the playoffs in NC high school football history. The highlight, of course, was playing Charlotte Olympic in Carter Finley Stadium for the Championship and beating them 14-0. Their two running backs were Georgia Tech recruits and I remember thinking it would be a miracle to beat them...but we were the Cinderella "miracle team."

I think the big lesson we all learned was that with hard work and teamwork you could accomplish anything, and it gave so many of us this mindset with which to go forward in life.

That '70 team was really a miracle with inspiration on several different levels, not the least of which was your leadership and faith.

**Wells's Bio:**

UNC Chapel Hill 1972-1976, John Morehead Scholarship, BA in Chemistry, minor in French.

UNC School of Medicine 1976-1980

Charlotte Memorial Internal Medicine Internship and Residency, 1980-1983

Boylan Internal Medicine, Raleigh, 1983-2001

Medical Director Springmoor Retirement Community, 1985 to present

Raleigh Medical Group 2001 to present

Rex Hospital Chief of Staff, Chairman Medical Executive Committee, 2006-2009

Married to Jan Swanson; children Erin Edmundson Keefer, soccer/academic scholarship Ole Miss, physical therapist; Brian Edmundson, Elon tennis/academic scholarship/NC Doubles Champion, financial analyst with BB&T

Interests: photography, gardening, French language and culture, medical-legal review

Wells Edmundson

### 13. RICK EUDY

*Senior---6'---192---Always hustling---Wants to improve---will help us out this year.*

Rick played tight end for us during the season and made several crucial catches in important ball games. Rick was filled with energy and did not back down from encouraging and getting on others. He was a talker and could keep conversations going.

Rick became a Raleigh policeman after finishing his education. Some time early during his police career Rick developed a liver disease that caused his death.

### 14. MACY FALKNER

*Junior---6'---180----Kicker---Plays fullback and wingback.*

Macy was a tough football player. He played back-up roles on both sides of the ball as a linebacker on defense and a fullback on offense. As our practices continued, I urged a lot of boys to try kicking a football, trying to find a good solid kicker for our team. Several players did a good job, but Macy's efforts and ability rose to the top. After the first couple of ball games, Macy was one of our extra point and field goal kickers.

### Macy's Memories / Reflections:

Winning the game that gave us the opportunity to play the championship game at Carter-Finley Stadium. Running out onto the field for the kick-off of the Championship game and kicking extra points.

What I Learned From The Season: That hard work and perseverance is a must for success in whatever you do.

### Macy's Bio:

Attended Campbell University, graduated with BS in Science. Worked as an Environmental Health Specialist for Johnston, Franklin and Wake County. NC State Division of Facility Services – Social Worker II, Domiciliary Division Investigator for North Carolina. Owner/CEO of National Water Technologies, Inc., Raleigh, NC.

Macy Falkner

### 15. PHIL FICKLIN

*Senior---6'1"---180---Letterman---Can play tight end for us.*

Phil was one of several on the 1970 team who had a beard and looked like he was in his 20's. He was a very reliable tight end for us and caught several passes in our run for the Championship. He was even a better blocker than a receiver, and that filled a crucial need for our type of offense. I remember him double teaming with his tackles on much larger opponents in order to open up huge holes for our backs to run through.

**Phil's Memories/Reflections:**

One of the most agonizing things Phil remembers occurred at the beginning of the season. In order to meet a team requirement, he had to run the mile for time - several times. He hated it.

One of Phil's memories was the practice when I got mad and pulled my Volkswagen and a couple of other cars on the practice field and turned on the headlights so we could finish practice like we needed to. I vaguely remember that, but Phil said he remembers that fiasco like it happened yesterday.

Phil believes that the 1970 season was the most fun he ever had in his whole lifetime. He has had some "ups and downs" in life, but he said that season was wonderful. Playing cards between practices during that summer provided bonding times and the friendships he built with the guys meant a great deal to him. He said that even though our coaching staff was not a bunch of "hollerers," the times I would say, "dad gummit" would get his attention. One of his favorite games was the victory over Ligon because we played in the rain and mud and had a blast.

One of Phil's favorite memories of a summer in high school was when he, John Clarke, and Dave Dupree drove out to California to pick up a Cobra (race car) and drove it back, and Dave's brother, Jimmy had it rebuilt. That trip was a highlight of his early travels.

**Phil's Bio:**

Phil attended Holding Tech and Wake Tech after graduating from Broughton and then went to work for IBM where he worked for over 22 years. Two years ago when I met Phil for breakfast, he was living in Apex. He shared about his two children who he is very proud of and talked very lovingly of.

Recently, Phil has developed dementia and lives in a family care home in Raleigh. Both his children visit him often. I was fortunate to visit with him in August of 2016 and he is very pleasant and we laughed a lot as I showed him some recent pictures of all of us. He is well taken care of and loves visitors.

Phil Ficklin and grandson Camden

### 16. JIMMY FITZGERALD

*Junior---5' 9"---170---Looks good at offensive guard---No varsity experience---has talent and should help us.*

Jimmy played offensive guard for our team in 1970. He was a worker and a learner, and that paid off for him as we progressed through the season. Jim filled in at times for several of our offensive lineman as we made our way through the playoffs. Jim always was a hustler and served the team well with his attitude and desire.

**Jim's Memories/Reflections:**

We (the team) were very fortunate to have young coaches take over who really wanted to win. I think what I got out of it was how to win and how to look at what I was doing that wasn't quite right and correct whatever it was. I learned how to finish and how much work it took to be a winner.

**Jim's Bio:**

Jim was born, raised, and educated in Raleigh. He graduated from N.C. State in 1976, majoring in Political Science. Since 1976, Jim's career has been in Professional Sales. He has been employed by Unisource (now Veritive) for 38 years. He has won numerous awards through the years, including being designated as one of the Top Five Sales Representatives in the Southeast for 20 years.

Jim has been married to Mona Rhyne Fitzgerald since 1983 and they live in Raleigh. Jim enjoys boating, hunting, fishing, spending time at the Pamlico River, and traveling.

Jim and Ramona Fitzgerald

### 17. JOHNNY FORD

*Junior---5'11"---174---Can catch the ball---Up from JV team.*

Johnny played tight end for us as a backup. He may have had the best hands out of all of our tight ends. He played behind a couple seniors mainly due to their experience and blocking ability. Johnny always seemed to have a smile on his face and was easy to coach because of his desire to play. I remember he was a good baseball player as was several of his teammates.

**Johnny's Memories/Reflections:**

I remember those hard practices with some talented athletes. Always remembered you said I had the best hands on the team. I tried to do my best but football was not my love like baseball. Still have people ask questions about the team. It was just special and always will be. Wished the team could have stayed together my senior year, a lot went to Enloe.

**Johnny's Bio:**

After graduating from Broughton, I went to Appalachian State and to

N. C. State. After three years I went into the haircutting business. I owned a shop for 32 years and sold it 7 years ago. I am still running the shop for the person. It's been a good business for me. It does not seem like a job. I have met a lot of great people. I remarried in June and am very happy. I still see a lot of the guys at the shop or at Bible Study or out and about.

Johnny and Renee Ford

## 18. Sandy Goodwin

Sandy was a sophomore wide receiver on our Junior Varsity team for most of the season. He was one of the fastest players on our football team. After the JV season was complete, we moved several people up to the Varsity for the playoff games and Sandy was one of them who joined us for the remaining five games of the season. Sandy had been the leading receiver on our JV team with his good speed and great hands. During the playoff games, he caught several passes that were big plays for us on our run to the Championship. One of the best catches he made was for our first touchdown against a heavily favored Greensboro Dudley team. That set the stage for that game which we won big, 22-0.

He made several other catches in the playoffs and contributed a tremendous amount to our Championship season.

Sandy died in a swimming/diving accident in Florida a few years ago. He certainly died too young.

### 19. ERIC HANDY

*Senior---5'9"---156---Not much experience but will definitely play this year---Great speed—Hustler.*

Eric was one of about seven black football players on our State Championship team. His success as a student and football player at Broughton led the way for his siblings to be successful. He lived in Rochester Heights in south Raleigh and was assigned and bussed to Daniels Junior High School when he was in the 8th grade. Eric saw and experienced a lot of prejudice and discrimination that year. The first week of school he and a few other black students were greeted with some people calling out, "nigger, nigger." This heckling lasted for about a week, and then things settled down. He also felt a discriminated against by some teachers and coaches at Daniels. He would sometimes ride his bicycle from south Raleigh through downtown and to Daniels. He remembers one time some white boys hollered at him as he rode through downtown and they actually threw a rock and hit him in his head. He said that is how he learned to ride his bike fast.

Eric was on the Junior High football team as a ninth grader but saw very little playing time. When he went to Broughton as a tenth grader, he began to feel a little more comfortable in the majority white school. He really spent a lot of time with the Broughton guys playing football, baseball, and track. His father had been a math teacher and coach at Carnage Junior High School when Eric was at Broughton. Mr. Handy came to Broughton as a counselor the year after Eric graduated from Broughton and was very helpful in the 1971-72 school year when Raleigh City Schools fully integrated the schools.

Eric had tremendous speed and was probably the fastest player on our team. The wingback reverse play was a big one for us in crucial situations, and Eric so often made big plays for us. He was a key blocker for us, and his double team blocking led the way for much of our running game. People had to respect his speed.

Eric played the clarinet which helped him get in with a different group of students rather than just athletes. He and Rick Hunter, another football player, were in a band together called, "The Keys." Eric was the lead singer, and as you can imagine, it made him feel so good to be invited to be part of that group.

One of the things that stood out to Eric from that 1970 season was our trip to Wilson Fike High School. As we walked into the stadium, Fike's students were hollering expletives at him and others and they were even spit on.

Eric thought the makeup of the team was cool. There were upper class rich kids living in big homes in the Saint Mary's and Carolina Country Club neighborhoods. There were also poorer white kids who lived near Broughton or in some of the poorer areas in Raleigh, and there were black players coming from the nearby Method area and South Raleigh. Eric became friends with most of these guys. Rick Hunter and his parents invited Eric over to their home to eat and spend the night. As he looks back at it, he is amazed that a black guy could walk in the all-white neighborhoods and walk in the Hunters' home without knocking on the door. Eric also remembers that Roland Massey would not hesitate to let Eric use his car to go home in between two-a-day practices in August of 1970.

Eric's memory about our coaching staff was that it was inspiring, and the coaches showed great leadership instead of being intimidating to the players. He was confident in playing well because he thought we were in better shape than others and that we were fundamentally sound in all we did.

The quarterfinal game at Greensboro was a memorable one for Eric, not necessarily that we beat them 22-0, but because of a lost shoe. In the plans to travel and the rush to be on the bus on time, Eric forgot one of his football shoes in his locker. He did not realize that he had forgotten it until right before going out to warm up for the Dudley game. He warmed up in a street shoe, and he was afraid to tell me, knowing that I would not be pleased, to say the least. So he and Bernard Williams, a wide receiver and special team player, plotted to take turns wearing Bernard's shoe. Bernard did not play very much that game except for special teams, so Eric was able to squeak by wearing Bernard's shoe when he was in the game.

Eric observed that the football team not only brought the players closer together, but really brought unity to the student body and whole school. The school spirit and support was unparalleled. To think that ten buses of students from Broughton had journeyed to Greensboro to see us beat Dudley High School in the state quarterfinals. In regards to the Championship game against Olympic, he just knew we were going to win. We had played at Carter Stadium in the doubleheader game against Enloe earlier in the year, so he felt like we were not in "awe" of the college stadium for the Championship game like Charlotte Olympic may have been.

As I reflect on Eric's journey through Daniels Junior High School and Broughton High School, I cannot help but think that he made a tremendous impact on his younger brothers and sister. He faced numerous hurdles to overcome due to prejudices and discrimination he endured during his growing up years. He in many ways pioneered his family's way to success. His brother, Clark, went to college and is very successful in the investing business, and his other brother, Tim, went to Duke University and is successful. He said he learned perseverance and to never to give up, thanks to his football experience. The Championship year remains one of the best things that happened to him.

**Eric's Memories/Reflections:**

1. The kickoff return that Bass returned for a touchdown after we practiced on that play all week. Perfect execution.

2. I can't remember how many times David Reynolds and I had great double teams on opposing defensive tackles when Bass came through our right side.

3. I remember getting the snot knocked out of me by the Rocky Mount D end on the wingback reverse. That play hurt---bad. I felt like having a personal conversation with Ficklin for missing that block, but he was bigger than I was. After the game I had to listen to that D-end tell me how that was his hardest hit of his life. I made up my mind not to let that happen again.

4. I remember Bernard getting knocked silly at Hillside on a kick-off. He even tried to go to their bench, hilarious. When 'Nard made it back to our bench, he asked me, "Handy, man, where we at?" I cried... it was too

funny.

5. I remember getting my shoulder hurt on the first or second play of the Terry Sanford game, and I never saw our team get man handled like that before. During this game since I could no longer play, I took my frustration out by using profanity while standing next to you. I'll never forget your look of disgust and reproach as you looked at me and said, "Eric, all that profanity." I learned a lot from you, Coach, can't ever tell you how much.

6. I learned never to quit, learned that properly prepared, I was a force to be reckoned with, I mean a force, Coach.

7. I watched you. I saw how you treated me when I was late for practice...punishment after the 4th quarter drill. That made me so strong for track. My point however is that when David Turner was being disciplined for something, you tried to kill the both of us with that punishment drill while the whole team left the field. Coach, that day in my eyes, you were the fairest of men. You killed both of us equally, no favoritism, none. I had to tell my dad that my mom was getting me to practice late...I was on time from that day on.

What I learned from the season:

1. That Larry Height was the biggest cry baby in America and he lived down the street from me.

2. That if I got one more penalty called on me for unsportsmanlike play, Gary Neal was going to mess me up because he told me so in the huddle. I believed him.

3. That Charles Banks was a man among boys; he was an outstanding defensive end.

4. I learned to block, and I mean I learned to block over there in the chutes. That drill with the linemen was my defining moment. In future years as a receiver, coaches were amazed with my love for contact.

5. At USMAPS I played beside a tackle named Ray Yakovonis who was drafted by the Vikings. He always said I hit like I was mad all the time, plus he liked the little guy talking a lot of junk – that he found amusing. Seemed like I got along with the huge linemen.

6. I learned how to improve by watching game film. I loved hearing positive comments about my play in the film room.

7. I learned the art of setting goals and achieving them. I hated I

wasn't the State 400m champ; I learned later that was due to my age and coaching. I just turned 17 when we graduated, and I was a year younger than everybody. I had the heart but not the physical stamina. Dickie Thompson and I ran with Coach Blount during the summer. Coach Blount introduced me to Leroy Walker. I was offered a scholarship to NCCU, but I chose A&T instead.

**Eric's Bio:**

Upon graduating from Broughton I attended North Carolina A&T for one year and two months. I received a football and track scholarship. My size seemed of concern and I was asked to concentrate on track; I didn't mind at all. Needless to say, I was the number 2 quarter-miler and lettered my freshman year in track.

I left the Aggies my sophomore year because my father, in his hard way of raising me, only sent me $5 to spend for homecoming. I knew that I would return to school under my own terms. I left college, enlisted in the Army, became a Medic and went to the 82nd Airborne.

While on active duty in the 82$^{nd}$, I attracted the attention of a young West Point Lieutenant by the name of Bucky Walker, a West Point Grad whose father was a Lieutenant General in charge of the European forces. After winning our Battalion Flag Championship, Bucky, who was the QB and I was his wide-out, asked me what I wanted to do. I told him my test scores were high enough and I wanted to be a cadet. A year later I was invited to attend the USMA Prep school in FT Belvoir, VA.

My year at the prep school I was the starting wide-out, leading scorer, led the team in receptions and ran a 4.45 second forty yard dash. I also returned kick-offs and punts. We had a real decent team even though we were beaten a few times.

That summer I went to West Point, and about ten of us were taken up to Varsity. Our coach was Homer Smith. The receiver coach was Ray Miklounous, a Wake Forest grad now deceased, and Steve Moore was also receiver coach, later with the Seahawks and Raiders.

They didn't play me enough because I ran track and didn't participate in spring ball. I quit and concentrated solely on track. I ran a 45.7 second quarter. Got second in the quarter in the IC4A championships. Homer Smith wrote letters to my dad asking him to talk me into coming back out for the football team. I transferred to St. Aug because of their track program with full scholarship but no coaching and no facilities.

I graduated sum cum laude in Business Management but didn't attend graduation, went right to Infantry Officer Basic Training. I have gone from E-1 to O-4. Started off enlisted and retired a Commissioned Officer. I am an Airborne Ranger and have affiliations with another special operations unit that I will not mention.

I concluded my 23 years with my last job being the Executive Officer of Fort George G. Meade, MD and 1st ARMY (East).

After the military, I worked for Harley Davidson in Milwaukee, WI as a work group advisor in the Capitol Drive sports facility. I was fast tracked through the plant and sent to York, Pennsylvania where I became the first supervisor hired to run new softail facility.

I left Harley to work for Pulte Homes in the Manassas, Virginia manufacturing facility. At Pulte, I was the plant superintendent. Then I returned to Raleigh during my daughter's sophomore year at Howard, while separating from my wife of 23 years. My mom passed in December of 2013. I reside here in Raleigh. I sub whenever I get bored.

Eric Handy and daughter Ciara

## 20. SKIPPER HAWKINS

*Junior---5'8"---157---Needs experience---Played JV ball last year.*

Skip Hawkins was one of the members of this team who did not play very much at all, yet contributed a great deal every week toward our Championship year of 1970. He would do anything we would ask of him and was proud to be part of this team. He was primarily on our scout teams, held blocking dummies, and yet still practiced to get better himself. Skip was also one of those players who would help with getting equipment out and set up for practice and always had a positive attitude.

I have not been able to locate Skip during the writing of this book.

## 21. LARRY HEIGHT

*Junior---6'2"---222---Great size---Should play for us somewhere---Good speed for a big man.*

Larry played fullback on the State Championship team and ran like a bull. His size was a definite positive for him; he was a sizable force running the football. I remember that Larry was young for being in the eleventh grade. He had started 1st grade a little early and had been successful in school.

Larry was difficult to bring down because he was so big for a fullback. He contributed some key runs in our pursuit of the Championship. Larry was one of the few juniors who played a lot. He says that winning the State Championship and playing it in Carter Stadium is a memory that will stay with him forever.

### Larry's Memories/Reflections:

Larry attended Daniels Junior High School. Not many blacks were going to white schools in the 1960's, but his grandfather was the janitor at Daniels, and that is why he went there. He feels that so many players growing up together and playing as youth helped them to be close and to be winners at Broughton. He expresses a special connection he feels with the 1970 team.

He experienced very little discrimination as a child, as best he remembers.

The 1971 football season and school year was a disaster for him, with Ligon being closed, players shipped everywhere and most of Ligon coming to Broughton. Disunited, everyone for themselves, jealousy, etc.

He reflects that it was almost like a lost year in his life.

Larry went to North Carolina Central University after graduating from Broughton in 1971. He played football there while he was on scholarship. He went to Law school at UNC-Chapel Hill and then worked in Miami, Florida for Janet Reno's office for two years. He worked as a lawyer for several organizations and now is in private practice for himself in Raleigh. My wife, Marie, and I visited him in his office in the City Market area in Raleigh to get wisdom and help for a former student of hers. She feels he belongs in a John Grisham novel as a colorful lawyer advocating for underdogs. Larry has a heart for people in prison and gives a lot of his time to help others. He is married to Yvonne and has two children.

**Larry's Bio:**

North Carolina Central University, Durham, NC. 1976 B.A., Magna Cum Laude. Major: Political Science. Attended on a four-year scholarship in football. University of North Carolina School of Law, Chapel Hill, NC 1982 - certified legal intern at State Attorney's Office, Miami, Fl. Larry served as Staff Attorney, Chief Agency Legal Specialist.

Larry is still practicing law in Raleigh and helping many people improve their lives.

Larry and Yvonne Height

## 22. VANN HINTON

*Junior---6' 1"---158---No experience---Not enough speed now but is a worker—*

Vann was a receiver for us. He did not play much, but gave good effort in all the workouts and practices. He served and practiced hard on a daily basis helping run the opponent's plays and defenses. He had not had the opportunity to play much football and this was one of his first years to be on a team.

I have not been able to locate Vann during the writing of this book.

## 23. JOHN HOLDING

*Senior---6' 2"---173---Letterman---Good passer---will definitely help us.*

John was a key to our Championship team because of his kicking abilities. He was our punter as well as our back-up quarterback and defensive safety. It always gave me security to know that we had a back-up athlete like John who was a dependable, talented, intelligent athlete who knew the game of football. He was a team player, always putting the team first, and, like so many of the players that year, he knew his role and played it superbly. Never do I remember him being upset because of playing time, even though he was a senior. John often punted so well that our opponents were forced to start deep in their own territory. Not much was said about it then, but his punting helped our defense immeasurably by causing the other team's offense to have to go long distances to score. Generally our trusty defense did not allow long drives, especially as we got into the playoffs.

John also was a good basketball player and a great baseball pitcher for Broughton his senior year. He went on to play baseball for N.C. State., an indication of what kind of athlete he was.

John recounts how important it is to him that so many boys in his class had known each other for a long time. He had known Roland Massey since they were five years old and John attended school with several others all the way through high school. He thinks that many of the guys being friends for so long contributed to the success the football team had in 1970.

John remembers having to run the mile for time before the season started. He thought then and now that the six-minute mile requirement was a tough one. He made it in 1970, but said he has a hard time driving a mile today in 6 minutes. John hated jumping those benches and dummies in the summer practices. Going through the stations without having water (so he says) was crazy. I do believe we had managers with water for them if they needed it.

During our mid-season, he recalls being late 30 seconds to the Monday practice after we were beaten so badly by Terry Sanford, and I told him to see me after practice. After the hardest practice he had ever been through, he said, "Well Coach, here I am. You said you wanted to see me." Knowing it had been a very difficult practice, I told him to see me the following day, but John said, "No sir, I want to get it over with." He could tell I was a little sympathetic with him, and I told him to run down the field and back, then go in. He knew I felt for him, and even though it was a a tardy of just 30 seconds, I was going to make him bear some consequence.

John thinks one of the keys to our season happened in the auditorium at Broughton on that spring afternoon when I first met the players and announced some things I expected. I told them we were going to have an offensive team and a defensive team. He thought I was crazy because they had just won three games with the players they had and many graduated and a lot of them played both ways. You usually had your best athletes playing on both sides of the ball in high school, and he was wondering how we were going to be any good if we did not play the best athletes. Yet, at the same time it motivated him and others knowing that more people could make the team with more individuals playing in the games. That was exactly what I was thinking. I had always thought that everyone should have a chance to play if they worked hard in practice.

**John's Memories/Reflections:**

First of all, the 1970 Championship experience has been an everlasting influence in my life, and I know it has been the same for many, many others. Looking back, there are a few points that stand out, and I will try to be brief because I think you are going to get an overwhelming response on your new endeavor of writing a book on our Championship season.

I firmly believe that football is the ultimate team game, and I think we were the ultimate team. This became so clear to me when we had our hall of fame reunion several years ago. During that weekend, many of the guys would bring up stories about Robbie Jones. I know you remember Robbie...he was one of the team managers...he died several years ago. My point is that Robbie was just as much a part of that team as anyone that put on cleats. We were truly a TEAM.

It is human nature for people to like things they are good at. Let's be honest...I was not a very good football player...Thank goodness for David Turner, because you would not be writing a book if I was the quarterback in 1970. I had much more individual success in basketball and baseball and enjoyed those sports very much. However, I absolutely loved the sport of football and being part of that team. I also learned more from it than any single experience in my life. My mother told me one time that I didn't make better grades in school because I played too many sports (she was a huge sports fan by the way). I turned to her and said, "Don't you understand that I learned more on that football field than I ever did in any classroom?" Of course, that might have been her point.

When we first met you, we were talked to like regular people. Never did you or the other coaches talk down to us. That was a new experience for us. Again, my mother...I lost her about a year ago so I guess I'm thinking about her too...She told me one time that one of her friends liked me because I didn't talk to her like she was old. I just talked to her. I don't talk down to children and don't patronize the elderly. I think it's one of my best things. It is also one of yours.

I have been managing a $50 million dollar/year company and about 150 employees now for about 15 years (not so right now with the economy, but it will be back.) I use things about teamwork that I learned from our experience every day. Like a football team, there are people from different cultures and economic status that have to work together to achieve success. I have to be able to communicate with truck drivers (whom I have the highest respect for), other production people, accountants, engineers, flaky architects to the Swedish owners. (By the way, my old shoulder pads had more personality than any Swede I've ever met.)

I have had the same core team with me now for 15 years. I am very proud of that. I truly do not know how people can manage other people unless they had a successful team experience like we did. It is the absolute foundation of my management practices.

Do not get me wrong, I had other good coaches...but the fact is you were the best and I just want to thank you and the other coaches for all you taught me about teamwork and life. You have truly influenced many lives.

**John's Bio:**

Hey, Coach, like I said...not computer literate...having trouble downloading this Bio thing. After Broughton I went to NCSU (not a curse word), played baseball 3 years until arm problems caused me to lose interest actually. I played on two ACC Championship teams which were great experiences but, in truth, was not as special as our 1970 team.

John and Jane Holding(Head Cheerleader in 1970)

I went to work in our small family business in 1976, sold business in 1995, stayed on with the new company and grew it from 1 operation with 22 employees to 6 operations with 175 employees by 2007. Really exciting times, loved it, and the basis with how we did it through my direction (and their money) came from my experience with the 1970 team and your leadership. You took a group of guys that won 3 games the year before when only the best players played both ways and you said, "We aren't doing that." I'll never forget that in the first meeting in the auditorium when we first met you, and like most of us, I thought you were nuts. Anyway, I retired, or let's just say had a parting of the ways at the end of 2013 and have not gone back to work (which I planned on doing after working out contract) because my elderly father needs me. I married Jane Holroyd in 1978 (who was the super spirited head cheerleader for Broughton in 1970), have a son John and daughter Betty Ann (who is a school teacher), one grandson 2 and half years old and one granddaughter on the way, both by John and daughter in law Jennifer. The fact is I have been very blessed in my life. Yes, I've worked hard but still very lucky. At least I've got enough sense to know.

## 24. MURRAY HOWELL

*Senior---5' 10"---195---Hard worker---Good size---Can help us this year on the line.*

Murray was a stocky lineman for our team. He played on our offensive line and played well enough to help open up holes for our running game. He was ready to play at all times, and it was good to know that we had players who may have not started all the games, but were ready and willing to help out in any way they could. Even though Murray probably did not play as much as he desired, he was one of those players who kept a positive attitude and helped this team.

### Murray's Memories/Reflections:

I live in St. Augustine, Florida and have been retired since 2007. I love it here. After Broughton I received an English degree from UNC-Chapel Hill. I still follow the Heels in football and basketball. I have traveled extensively most of my life and I enjoy each day. I actually weigh 20 pounds less than when I was a left offensive tackle. I weigh 180 as opposed to 200 lb. Our team line was undersized but very sound in its blocking and tackling. I remember starting at left tackle at the beginning of the season. I have never forgotten the cramped, smelly locker room at Devereux Meadow. I wish we had had the facilities

Broughton has now. I remember the 102 degree temperature on the bank clock in Cameron Village as we went through 2-a-days in August. We only got one water break and we were lucky someone didn't have a heat stroke. We were tougher than today's kids. Slower and less athletic but tougher. Jim Bass was a pleasure to block for. Same for David Turner.

I have kept in touch with numerous players from that team. Most of us turned out quite all right. We got a great education at Broughton that served us well through life. That season taught me to never give up. Great teammates working together can accomplish great things. We had good chemistry. I would like to think I contributed a little bit towards that Championship. I loved going against Mark Shaner in practice. I have not seen him since the 70's.

**Murray's Bio:**

I graduated UNC Chapel Hill with degree in English, then went to work for Hughes Tool Co. selling drill bits to oil rigs in Louisiana, Texas, and West Virginia. I returned to     N. C. and went to work as a utility engineer for the NCDOT in Raleigh. I retired from there and moved to St. Augustine, Florida, living the retired life. I moved back to the coast of N. C. in 2014 and still love the sea and sand. I never married; I came close a couple of times but I have no regrets. I've been following the Tar Heels my whole life.

Murray Howell

## 24. BUDDY HUDSON

Buddy was one of the JV sophomore players who we moved up to the Varsity as the playoffs began. Buddy was a defensive back and very intelligent about the game of football. Unfortunately Buddy hurt his knee and was unavailable for the playoffs.

### Buddy's Memories / Reflections:

I grew up in Raleigh all of my life with both of my parents being Broughton graduates. Needless to say, I had been going to Caps football games since I was a small child. All my life, my dream was to play football at Broughton. As a 10th grader at Broughton in 1970, my dream became a reality. At that time, all 10th graders played on the Junior Varsity. Coach Caldwell was the head coach. I started at safety and we went undefeated the entire season. In our last game I hurt my knee and missed a few days of school. I was moved up to play on the Varsity, but my knee was too badly hurt to continue. To say I was disappointed was an understatement but it didn't damper my enthusiasm and love for the team as they marched on against the odds to beat Charlotte Olympic for the State Championship.

Buddy Hudson

### Buddy's Bio:

I spent 23 years in retail, rising to be President of Hudson Belk and later President of the Northern Division with stores in four states and

6,000 employees under me. For the past fourteen years, I have run a company, PMC, Inc. as Chief Operating Officer. I also spend as much time as I can on my farm in Zebulon and raise all-natural, grass-fed beef under the name Rare Earth Farms. I am divorced and have two great sons (both Broughton graduates), my mother is still in good health at 94 years old.

### 26. RICK HUNTER
*Junior---5'10"---160---has really improved---Will help us at offensive guard.*

I remember Rick having long curly, kinky hair and was small for an offensive guard. He was one of our quickest linemen and would really stay after you in his blocking assignments.

Rick reminisces about playing guard for Broughton being fun for him because he would be pulling almost every play and blocking people on the run. Rick remembers the coaches being very inspirational during the season. He told me that I was one of his best teachers in his life along with his dad who meant a lot to him.

He remembers early on in practice my calling the team's attention to how low he was in blocking. We even stopped practice and had him demonstrate his blocking technique. That motivated him because he did not think he was very good and he knew he was not very big, but that gave him the encouragement he needed to hang in there and get better.

Rick loved baseball and had played ball in Little League, hoping to make his dad proud. Rick's dad was a dentist in Raleigh, and several of the players, Jim Little for one, had Dr. Hunter as dentist. Both Rick's parents had polio and yet still were very active in all of life. They were an inspiration to their five boys as well as other people in the community. Dr. Hunter had played football in Alabama, and that is why Rick wanted to play. Rick began playing in the 4th grade at Country Club Hills.

Because of his interest in music, Rick was in a band with several other players. He, Jim Lumsden, and Charles Satterfield were part of "The Keys" and they ended up getting Eric Handy to join them as they needed a singer. What was unique is that Eric was black, and an integrated band for teenagers was rather unusual at the time. They would practice at their different homes. Racial differences and prejudices did not enter into the boys' thinking, but the parents' generation was still influenced by prejudices they had grown up with. The band competed in the Battle of the Bands, often held in Raleigh to determine who the best band in the area was. They won several times.

### Rick's Memories/Reflections:

Thanks for all of the life lessons you taught us as our football coach in that wonderful State Championship year. The game of football, when properly coached and played, prepares one for life by teaching the values of practice, conditioning, hard work, resilience, teamwork, and how to "pick yourself up and get back in the game" when you experience hardship and adversity.

As an interesting side note, my father, Dr. Richard S. Hunter, who passed away ten years ago, was the Captain of the Alabama State Championship team when he was in high school in Opelika, Alabama. He went on to play football on scholarship at Auburn University before going to dental school at Emory and becoming a dentist. I didn't know until after Dad passed away that his football team at Opelika went undefeated his senior year. Dad was named to the All-State offensive and defensive teams as an end, and he caught at least one touchdown pass and blocked at least one punt in every game! Again, thank you so much for all that you and the coaches taught and shared with me and my teammates!

Rick and Jane Hunter

**Rick's Bio:**

After Broughton, I attended UNC Chapel Hill for two years; then Berklee College of Music in Boston MA for two years, studying jazz and classical guitar performance, musical composition and arranging; I then returned to UNC Chapel Hill and was awarded a BA in History in 1977; I then studied law at Cumberland School of Law at Samford University in Birmingham AL, and was awarded a JD in 1980; I have practiced law in Raleigh since 1980.

Jane and I were married in 1981. We have two sons, Richard age 32 and Ben age 30. I have continued to play musical gigs in my adult life including jazz, rock, R&B and classical performances. I have held every elected office in the North Carolina Academy of Trial Lawyers (now North Carolina Advocates for Justice) including the office of President.

## 27. ROBBIE JONES

Robbie was our team's red-headed, fiery manager. He was very close to many of the players, which is why he served as one of our managers. Robbie was funny and enthusiastic on the sidelines during our games. He was known to get on the referees at times and I believe he even got a 15 yard penalty during one game.

**From John Holding:**

Robbie died in his mid to late 30's mostly from life-long kidney complications. He had a transplant from his father when he was about 12 years old. I knew his mother well and loved her. I think I mentioned this before when we had our Hall of Fame Reunion; nobody's name was mentioned more in our gatherings than Robbie's. He was just as big a part of it as Jimmy Bass and the other stars and he took just as much pride in his role. I know that to be true because I helped carry his casket to his grave. It really was a special group. We were truly a TEAM.

## 28. CHARLES KING

*Senior---5'10"---175---Can play both ways. Always giving 100%.*

Charles was one of the few players, along with Steve Brewbaker, on the Championship team that played both offense and defense. Charles was a very smart player. As a fullback, he was tough and dependable enough that we really counted on him to pick up those short yardage first downs. He had good hands, and we used him some as a key pass receiver in our offense. Charles was also a good blocking fullback and I remember some outstanding blocks he made in the Championship game on the goal line. He caught a touchdown pass against Olympic in the State Championship game which put us on the scoreboard.

Charles was also one of our keys to our defense as he played linebacker in our 4-4 defense. He was agile enough to stop a running back at the line of scrimmage and also was able to cover in the flats or hook zones against the passing game. Charles was one of the more versatile players we had on the team and he loved to play the game.

### Charles's Memories/Reflections:

The magical year we spent together in 1970 has never been forgotten. Our glory days on the football field continue as a vivid memory and an inspiring time of a team that could do the impossible. Of course we all shared big dreams as we practiced in our junior and senior seasons, but we lacked a coach that believed in accomplishment as much as our teammates. After the new coaches arrived with a can-do winner's mentality, the missing ingredient was unleashed and our wistful thinking became the reality. Our unlikely team jelled and claimed the NC high school State Football Championship. What a ride that journey was ... it continues to be a lasting memory to be a part of this special team.

4th quarter was hard to forget. Especially on our final practice date when yours truly arrived a little late. My solo overtime session with you after our final practice was the grand finality of the season. Anyway, all of those extra calisthenics had to have made a difference in our preparation.

One of my greatest thrills in 1970 was when we finally beat Enloe. Since Daniels, we had lost to Julius Branch and crowd multiple times, but we finally overcame the jinx at Carter-Finley. And even though we would lose more subsequent games, this win catapulted our confidence that we could play against anyone.

The summer of 1970 was hot, damned hot, and almost as bad as the two preceding summers. The Cameron Village thermometer that you could see from the practice field exceeded 95 degrees each afternoon. Fortunately, many of us hydrated with ice-cold water as we dealt hearts in between the morning and afternoon practice two-a-days. Ficklin and I were generally the hosts to the welcome practice respite.

He appreciated very much the freedom from strict rules like not having to get a haircut a certain length or strict dress codes. Again he saw this time as change, a time of expressing one's freedom instead of having to be and do like everyone else.

**Charles's Bio:**

After graduating from Broughton, Charles attended the University of North Carolina in Chapel Hill and majored in Business Administration. Along with football, he wrestled in high school and also one year at UNC. He worked as a CPA in Charlotte, N.C., met his wife Becky there and was married in 1980. They have two daughters who attend Wake Forest University. In 1983, they relocated to Raleigh when he and his older brother, Jimmy, took over the family business.

Charles and Becky King

### 29. KENT KISTLER

*Senior---5'8"---164---a little experience---One of our best guards--- should have a good year.*

Kent played guard for us and was a guy who played football because he was so fundamentally sound. Kent was another one of our little offensive linemen who would crab, scratch, and do everything he could to block you. Kent was a "tough nut" in many ways and played through a lot of injuries that some boys would or could not have done. He would get under the opponent's shoulder pads (he had to because he was so small playing against people sometimes twice his size) and stay after you until the whistle blew.

### Kent's Memories/Reflections:

I could wax on and on about my experiences that year. As I recall, the year before most of us got very little playing time while watching a talented group of seniors struggle through a miserable season. I recall planning to quit football that quite frankly had stopped being fun for me. I had become interested in weight training the year before under Coach Ray Durham who had left for another position and decided to play my senior year when you and the new coaching staff arrived. My year was frustrating with injuries including shoulder dislocations, broken wrist and ankle injuries that still remind me some days of them. However, what is still with me is the fact that at the end of the year, I was able to play on a great team and achieve a remarkable feat. The fact that we still communicate after all these years is a testimony to that. Many of the guys on that team had played together since Pee-Wee football, and I think that led to a special chemistry between us.

### Kent's Bio:

After Broughton I went to college in Minnesota for a year, decided that wasn't for me and transferred back to NC State. I had the great fortune to work under the mentorship of a doctor in his research lab who convinced me to change majors and direction. After graduating I took a year off and worked in a research lab in Germany for a year before returning to attend Duke Medical School. Since graduating there, I went to St. Louis for an internship, then Vanderbilt for Neurology training before finally landing in Greenville, SC where I have practiced neurology for over 30 years. I have been blessed with 3 sons and a daughter and now have 2 grandkids. My youngest son is a high school junior, 6'1", 250 lbs. and after a few concussions, quit football and lacrosse and is now playing baseball. I restrict my athletics now, dislocated my other shoulder throwing a ball at baseball practice, and mainly golf and swim. My wife and I love to travel but mostly to high school games and travel to baseball/lacrosse/basketball tournaments the last few years.

I have been blessed with many great friends, mentors and experiences, and the team of 1970 is certainly one of them. I am indebted to you and Coach Evans who had enough faith in me to play a 165 lb. guard. God bless you and thanks.

Kent and Lisa Kistler

### 30. GEORGE LATTIMORE

*Senior---5' 10"---170---Great hustler and leader---should have himself a fine year.*

George Lattimore was one of our best linebackers. He was small but was one of those players who would and could "knock you for a loop." He was so sound fundamentally that he was able to use all his weight to get full contact with you. I loved to see George move laterally down the line of scrimmage to make tackle after tackle. He had a little temper as I remember, but it was so often coming from his desire to do his very best on every play. He was fiery and certainly helped energize our whole defense when we needed it the most. George was one of our leading tacklers and totally fun to watch.

**George's Memories/Reflections:**

(I haven't gone back and looked at details, so my memory may be a bit off).

Beginning of the season in August – Coach Riggs gave out something, perhaps a poem. Part of what it said was, "If you think you are lost, you are." It was all about believing in yourself and your teammates. Having played against the seniors the previous year, they seemed bigger and better, but they finished 3-7. They had suffered through a coaching change and demoralizing season. Coach Riggs along with the other coaches brought in a fresh enthusiasm and a new belief.

Our eighth game of the season against Fayetteville, was a turning point. I think we were tied at 7-7 at the half. But in the 2nd half we fell apart, and the final was about 28-7. After the game, the following week I believe, Coach Riggs challenged us that Jim Lumsden played the 2nd half with a torn up knee. We needed to give that type of effort. After that game we were 4 wins, 4 losses. But all our wins were in the conference, so we still had a chance to go to the playoffs.

We would go on and not have anyone score on us the last 5 games (I think).

I especially remember beating Enloe. We had traditionally had a difficult time through the years against their key running back. I don't remember the score but I know we won. We must have kept them from scoring if we finished the last 5 games un-scored on.

I remember the 3 playoff games:

The first game against Greensboro. I just remembered that we switched to a 4-4 defense, and that I became the 6th man on the defensive line. I was told to just fill the gaps and hold my position. I don't think I made any tackles but I think I plugged the hole. I just tried to go low and get underneath the blocker. I remember that Doug (the other linebacker) outweighed me by 10-15 pounds, but I did what the coaches wanted, and we won.

The game against Goldsboro was quite thrilling. I think it was a real defensive struggle, and we won 6 to 0. I think that they played something like a single wing offense and had a real challenging running back, small but quick. I remember we had to defend against them on a 4th down in the 4th quarter. We barely stopped them, but that stop was the difference in the ball game. I'm not sure, but I remember that Steve Brewbaker had been switched so that he played both ways, both offense and defense. I believe he was a big difference in the game.

The final game, the Championship, I remember a number of plays. In the first quarter a barrel roll was called for me to blitz and I sacked the quarterback. Right before half we were leading 7-0 and they were driving. They were inside our side of the field somewhere near our 25-35 yard line. They had a 4$^{th}$ down and did a pitchout to the half back but the pitch was a little behind, and Shaner was able to get outside and pull him down and barely deny them getting the first down. I think the key play in our drive was a pass from one of our backs, maybe Charles King, that was a bit of a trick play. They seemed to be able to drive against us on defense, but never scored. They ran right at the linebackers (myself and Doug) successfully. Rather than pursuing them, because they ran right at us they were able to make good yardage. The score by the offense in the 2$^{nd}$ half was amazing. I think we drove the length of the field. For the scoring play it was one of our bread and butter plays where both guards pulled (Jim Little, Kent Kistler), the fullback (Charles King) kicked out the end, and then Jim just had to outrun the last man, which he did. The play was a thing of beauty as each person did exactly what they were supposed to do.

What I Learned From The Season:

So often for our season, it was a game of inches. In each of the last two games, we stopped their offense on 4$^{th}$ down, but it was precariously close. It was a team effort. There was no one star. The coaches played a few players both ways (Steve Brewbaker was one I remember). But everyone had to fill their role. The "drive" in the second half of the Championship, and especially the scoring play of that drive, epitomized our season.

**George's Bio:**

* I went to Duke, and met my wife Erin there. Initially I started school as a mechanical engineering major, switched to the liberal arts college and got a degree to teach high school science (took mainly physics) and a 2$^{nd}$ major in religion (world religions). I went to India the December of '74 as part of a group from Duke and started following Jesus from an encounter there. I played on the Duke soccer teams of '73,

'74, and lettered in '74. I married Erin Duffie in the summer of '75 after graduating from Duke.

* I taught high school science for a year in Puerto Rico and surfed. Erin was an assistant librarian.

* From June '76 to May '78 I went to UVA for graduate school, obtaining a Masters in Engineering with a major in Engineering Physics. My curriculum required me to take 2 PhD Physics courses and I focused on Electrical Engineering.

* We then moved to Vermont and worked for IBM in Essex Junction for 13 years. All 4 of our children were born in Vermont.

* We moved to Austin Texas in 1991 while working for IBM, and we remain in Austin as our primary residence.

George Lattimore

* I have worked in the "computer and mobile communication technology industry" since 1978. My major focus has been circuit design for memories and support of processor designs for computers and mobile devices such as cell phones (cpu/risc/dsp processors). I have worked for three companies in both circuit design and leadership/management: IBM,

Analog Devices, and ARM Holdings. I have been employed by ARM since Jan 2008. For the first 5 years with ARM I was the Austin site manager for the Physical IP Design team. Since May of 2013 I have been supporting the Patents Team in ARM under the ARM Legal Department. I have been named as an inventor on more than 50 granted patents during my career. Now I am employed in the legal support of ARM patents. I have been working part time since September of 2013, working 6 weeks in the office in Austin and then taking two weeks off. During my two weeks off, I am often in N.C. at Wrightsville Beach. I also currently manage some real estate holdings.

* My wife Erin and I have 4 children (three are married) and 5 grandsons. I am active in our church in Austin. I currently serve on several boards of charitable organizations. My hobbies include surfing, cycling, fishing, and playing bluegrass banjo.

### 31. JIM LITTLE

*Senior---5'8"---168---Good blocking guard---Wants to win bad--- Gives 2ⁿᵈ and 3ʳᵈ efforts.*

Jim was a starting guard for us. He was probably the best pulling guard we had. I remember I used to love watching him in practice and in games pulling down the line of scrimmage on our sweep play ahead of Jim Bass. Jim was a good blocker and did not mind hitting anyone in his way. He was tough and very smart on the field and practiced as hard as anyone I can remember. He used his small size to get underneath the opponent and cut them down to clear the way. I do not think Jim ever thought that he could not get the job done as an offensive lineman. He was a joy to coach.

Jim has fond memories, like so many others, about growing up in Raleigh and playing for the Dr. Pepper Little League football team. They played against a lot of the same players who would end up on the same team at Broughton. He played at Daniels Jr. High School and enjoyed it very much.

Football gave him a parameter of seeing that if he would fight hard, work hard, and never give up, then he could accomplish anything. He and Rick Hunter spoke very highly of Robbie Evans, who was their line coach. "Robbie was big but had a good demeanor about him and coached in a way that made you want to please him by doing good."

**Jim's Memories/Reflections:**

There are so many memories, and unfortunately many I have forgotten. One of the amazing things about that season has been all the people who remember that season who were not a part of the team. Countless people when asked where I went to High school and when, "So you were part of that Championship team that beat Charlotte." One of the other comments is, "You are too small to have played." When I tell them that Kent Kistler, the other guard, was less than 165, they are amazed. Truly one of the incredible things about our team was that we had to be one of the smallest teams in the state and only had maybe 3-4 guys over 200 lbs. I remember looking at the roster and seeing that we were always listed more than we actually were. Where we lacked weight, we made up in speed and heart. You and Robbie Evans had us guards pulling on most all off tackle and sweeps and one of the real pleasures of that year was pulling around Ficklin on the end and catching a linebacker focused on Bass and laying them out. Now that was fun!

Summer two-a-day's! Other than watching the Raleigh Federal Time and temperature clock hit 3 digits in August, easily seen from the practice fields, I loved the one on one drills, hated the yellow salt pills taken by the handfuls. Who knew you could take too many, Sam Beard?

Other memories: getting my clock cleaned in Fayetteville, coming out and not remembering where we were playing or who. Sitting out 2 series and heading back in. Having Willis Price's parents take me to the hospital instead of the bus ride home. Robbie Jones, despite his size and health issues, riding herd on us all and being a real part and spirit of our team.

One of the things I remember during the playoffs was watching during late Oct. - Nov. practices for the geese to fly over the practice field. This was before geese were a fixture of every golf course, and were pretty rare. Every week they would fly over and we would stop and cheer as a good omen and good luck sign. If I remember, you had a few good luck superstitions, was it tape on your belt?

Our team was a special group. That so many of us have remained in contact and friends these last 45 years has been the real success of our Team. The entire season drew us together. We did not have any one huge star that dominated the team, and had only a few that went on to play in college. We played for each other and that is what made us successful. What an important life lesson that we gained from that experience. Our team and the experience we had gave us much more than we ever expected. Thanks to you, Thomas and Evans for all that you did for us.

**Jim's Bio:**

After graduation, I went to Elon and graduated with an Economics degree. Preston Ruth and I went through Elon together and traveled the country during the summers.

I have been fortunate to have spent my career in Raleigh working in commercial Real Estate finance and development with several different companies. Currently CFO of Keystone Corporation for the last 20 years.

I married an Elon Girl 36 years ago, LuAnn Little, who is a teacher and mom to our two sons, ages 28 and 30. One is married and both work and live in Raleigh.

I have been a lifelong member of 1st Presbyterian Church. (Thanks to you and so many others for showing us what a strong faith and belief in God is. It's a shame that expressions of faith are not allowed in the schools any more.) My other passions are fly fishing for trout, tennis, biking, and being in the NC mountains.

Jim and Joann Little and sons

## 32. JIM LUMSDEN

*Senior---5'11"---170---Not much experience, but will play for us---Could be great help at Fullback.*

Jim Lumsden was a tough and rugged football player. He had long hair and played with a chip on his shoulder. I think of Jim as one who never backed down from anyone on the football field, either an opponent or teammate. He made many a key play for us on defense and was like many of his teammates, very reliable. He played most of the Terry Sanford game with a torn MCL without knowing it. That would be his last game, but his encouraging enthusiasm was with us on the side lines of the remaining games of the season.

Soon after my retirement, I enjoyed a completely pleasurable lunch with David Turner and Jim and heard great stories from both of them and they motivated me to write about the season.

Jim also told me the story about he and David Turner being dropped off at the age of ten or eleven at the old Riddick Stadium by one of their parents. Some man outside the gate to the stadium gave them tickets to the N.C. State game that Saturday. This would never happen today for sure.

Jim and David remember so many of the Broughton players growing up together, playing with and against each other in Pop Warner football on the North Hills team, the Pepsi team and other teams. Funny story about young Rick Hunter coming back into the huddle at the beginning of a Pop Warner game saying with tears in his eyes, "I have Doug Murray in front of me, what am I going to do?" Another story about their going out to flip the coin and were horrified by seeing Doug Murray (linebacker on the 1970 team) with a mustache, beard and hair on his legs in junior high - in junior high - oh my goodness.

Jim talked a lot about the talent in the junior class and added that his senior class of tough guys really made the 1970 team what they were. He said his class was "pissed off" about not playing as juniors, feeling like they were just as good as some seniors on the 1969 team, but the coaching staff played mainly seniors. They felt they had been used as whipping boys, but it really made them tougher and prepared them for playing under the new coaching staff. So when that 1970 class of players became seniors, they just wanted to play for the love of the game, not necessarily for any glory for themselves.

David Turner and Jim both remember our coaching staff getting down and doing a lot of the work and exercises with them, which impressed them. I would do neck isometrics on the ground without a helmet and Robbie Evans would drive the sled to show them what he wanted.

They remember our coaches saying, "We will get there; run it again."

**Jim's Memories/Reflections:**

Everything was new, finally. After years of the same (bad) coaching, including ridiculous player favoritism and dull, 50's style schemes for offenses and defenses, we had a new, young, exciting coaching staff that unified rather than divided us. We had faith for the first time that merit on the practice field would be rewarded with playing time. We were willing to do anything to turn things around, and we were 100% behind our new leadership, who after all were only a few years older than us.

Starting with the summer sessions, we knew it was going to be different. The spirit in the locker room was electric, even in the dog days of summer. We knew we could be pretty good, and we were offended that the newspaper predicted a 3-7 season for us. Of course, when we had "AAA" players in the previous years, we had 3-win seasons, and now those guys had graduated, so I guess we couldn't blame the paper for expecting little from us.

For some reason, we really cared about each other, far more than we had ever experienced before, and we cared about and followed every single play on both sides of the ball. The times had something to do with that – old barriers were breaking down. For evidence, witness the end of the Cavaliers and the other social clubs that had dominated social life at Broughton for at least 20 years. Also, witness the genuine love and friendship between the black and white players, who for the first time in my lifetime hung out together away from school, at least to some degree.

We were undersized, probably by a long shot, but at least on the defensive side, multiple years of being (unfairly) labeled "scrubs" and being sacrificed daily against the first team, had prepared us for playing bigger and tougher than our physical size would indicate. Best of all, we linebackers and linemen (and monster men!) could afford to play every down with truly reckless abandon, because our defensive backs had shut-down talent, and passing against them was virtually impossible.

What fun we had, after we figured out we could play with anybody, and after beating Sanderson, best of all!

I remember the play that (sadly) ended my season, at Fayetteville Sanford, the only team that really manhandled us. We were up 7-0 in the 2nd quarter when their big guard knocked Brewbaker back so hard he rolled my right leg up, trapping my foot, and I heard the MCL snap. However, I wanted to keep playing so badly that I just put an Ace bandage on it at halftime and finished the game.

I was so depressed afterwards that I didn't go to a few games, at least until a large part of the team came to me and dragged my butt – crutches, cast and all – down to the sideline for the final run to the championship game. What a day that was (and, I have to say, what a night too)!! Yes, I broke my cast--it was from the hip to the ankle-- at the game, jumping up and down after one of the scores! I was the only injury at that game I think – Dr. Dameron was there and he fixed it up as I recall just after the game was over…all I know is that I was able to make it to the party afterwards – by the way, that party was LEGENDARY. It was out at Jimmy Dupree's, near Lake Anne, really in the woods in those days. We could play the music loud, yell and scream and celebrate and no neighbors (or cops) would be around to complain. Dupree had laid a bunch of mattresses (set up on the ground off the deck, we used to collect from the leftover mattress rejects from Camp Durant and lay them down in the back of the vans). People were doing flips and swan dives off the porch - it's a wonder nobody got seriously hurt - what a time! Nobody got home before dawn, but the parents were OK with it, as I guess they thought we deserved to celebrate our most unlikely and thrilling victory!"

(Some of Jim's reflections and memories are included also in the Introduction of this book and I thank him for allowing me to use them.)

What I Learned From The Season:

I think we all learned what miracles may be accomplished by individuals, when they believe in and are driven by a common purpose. By rights, we had no business winning the State Championship. Nor is it at all probable we should have been able to shut out so many teams. But we had Jim Bass and therefore 14 points we could count on at minimum, and if we could stop the other team, well, then we win."

**Jim's Bio:**

I went to UNC, where I got a history degree but played in bands semi-professionally until 1979, when I went back to Chapel Hill for an MBA. I began a financial career in 1981 as an investment banker with Kidder, Peabody and Merrill Lynch Capital Markets in New York. In 1986, after returning to Raleigh, North Carolina, I became President of Loadmaster Corporation and Lawyers Title of North Carolina. In 1992, I founded and served as Managing Partner of Franklin Street/Fairview Capital, which sponsored and managed private equity investment pools. In addition, I was a founding general partner of The Halifax Group and Oberlin Capital (a federally licensed SBIC).

Jim Lumsden

From 2005 to 2012, I served as Executive Chairman of Cobrek Pharmaceuticals, a specialty pharmaceuticals firm in Chicago acquired in 2012 by Perrigo Company. Currently I am a director of American Timberlands Company and president of Fairview Land and Venture, LLC. In the past I served on a number of private and public corporate boards, including First Federal of Raleigh, Gregory Poole Equipment Company, Cherokee Sanford Group, and Eastern Standard Insurance Company. I participated in various professional and civic organizations, including Young Presidents Organization, the Raleigh Arts Commission (Chairman), the N.C. Museum of Art Foundation (Chairman), and the N.C. Museum of Natural Sciences Foundation, and I was for a time a Trustee of St. Mary's College.

### 33. ROLAND MASSEY

*Senior---5'8"---155---fine speed---Pass receiver---Can play several positions---Good all around athlete.*

Roland was a multi-talented back on our Championship team. He could play in the defensive secondary, offensive backfield and wide receiver. Due to his drive and determination, I felt like he could help more in the backfield. He did not mind hitting you either so we used him also as a blocker. Roland was a "fire ball" and really pushed himself to be the best he could be. I admired his fighting spirit, and it carried him throughout his life.

I remember one thing Roland taught me and helped me so often in my future coaching days was to be sensitive to every player. Toward the end of the season, when we were rolling along with several victories, Roland scored a touchdown. A few minutes later one of the coaches came to me and said that Roland was upset and in tears. It turned out that I had not acknowledged Roland in any way after the score. I usually was all over the guys giving pats on the shoulders and hugs with plenty of enthusiasm and excitement. For some reason I failed to show Roland any of that, and it made him think, "What is wrong with me that Coach Riggs would be excited when others scored, but did not say anything to me when I scored?" From then on in my coaching career, I made a specific point to go to the person who scored and congratulate them. It really helped me to see that everyone needs praise and recognition for a job well done. I thank Roland for making me more aware and sensitive to the players I coached.

### Roland's Memories/Reflections:

Roland was not planning on playing football his senior year after playing for so many years growing up. He did not play much at all his junior year and had decided that it was not worth the time and effort to play as a senior. He shared that he changed his mind when at the first meeting with the new coach in the spring of 1970, I told them all that no one had a position on this team regardless of what they had done in the past. All positions were open for whoever proved they wanted them. He said he took me at my word and really believed what I said. He has often thought about what would have happened if he had not played football his senior year. Overall, as he looks back at his football and baseball playing days at Broughton, they were the best he could have hoped for.

One of Roland's biggest disappointments in football was his senior year when we played our rival Sanderson, and he desperately wanted to start at wingback. He and Eric Handy alternated in starting at the wingback position and they often carried plays in to the quarterback on offense. He did not start for that game and was very upset. However, due to the respect one was "supposed" to have for their coach, Roland said nothing.

Roland was very helpful to the black players at Broughton, especially his teammate Eric Handy. They both played the same position, and they could have been enemies due to competing for the same position. With Eric being black and Roland white, at that time it could even have been worse. However, the opposite occurred. Roland even let Eric use his car to travel back to his home between the morning and afternoon practices during some of the August two-a-day practices. Roland remembered years after high school when he was getting in shape to run and pass the physical in order to join the Marines, Eric helped him train and literally showed Roland how to run the mile, a part of the Marines physical exam, for the best time he could.

Roland also believed that doing the little things helped us win. Fumbling drill, 4th qtr. drills, and one big thing that made an impression on him and others was the way the coaches ran the film back and forth, to show the "swarming" defense and the importance of everyone hustling. He remembers me showing key blocks by players and making a big deal out of it, proving that football could not be played with just a few stars, but it would take everyone doing his job on every play together.

**Roland's Bio:**

Roland went to North Carolina State University after graduating from Broughton. He joined the KA fraternity at State and really got involved in drinking too much and partying, which hurt his grades. He ended up majoring in English, thinking he may want to coach and teach, but really went down a bad path with some bad people. He actually helped open up one of the first disco clubs in Raleigh when he was 22 years old but came to the conclusion that he had to make something more out of his life. All this time he was dating his future wife and girlfriend from Broughton, Teeny Maughn. Finally, with the help of Teeny and knowing Preston Ruth, one of his best friends and teammates from high school who was in the Marine Corps, he decided to join the Marines. He saw that he could break away from some old ties he had that were not good for him, could travel and contribute to the service of others. He went to Officer Candidate's School in June of 1978, and then in 1979 he married Teeny with Preston as his best man. Roland, like Preston, got his pilot's license in the Marines and also became a Tactical Fleet pilot.

Roland and Teeny Massey at celebration of his life Nov. 2014

Roland was deployed to Beirut in the 1980's and spent time there in the War Zone before he came out and  became a Naval Aviator with his friend and teammate Preston Ruth from Broughton. For one four-year assignment each, Roland and Preston were part of Marine Helicopter Squadron One. The Squadron's primary mission was flying the President of the United States. They both became Presidential Command Pilots and were in the White House Aircraft Commanders under President Bush (I) and President Clinton.

Roland took an early retirement offer from the Marines in 1993. After returning to Raleigh, getting in a Bible Study helped turn his life around even more. He joined a Friday morning Bible Study in the spring of 1995 and tried to live the Christ-like life as well as he could. Jesus was important to him and he was not ashamed of that. He and Teeny had one son and one daughter and lived in Raleigh where he was employed by Wake Stone Quarry as the head of Safety and Health.

Roland had pancreatic cancer for several years until he died in 2014. I was fortunate to spend some quality time with him toward the end of his life. He fought the cancer like he did everything else in life and was a tremendous example for all of us in how to handle suffering and death. He was faithful to God to the very end. The following email I received from Roland a year or so before he died. It reveals his heart and mind, some of his memories of that Championship year, and the type of man he had become.

Coach,

I hope you don't mind, "Coach," because I can just as easily fill that with David, teacher, friend, inspiration, but I pick Coach just to remind me of the long ago and how little difference there was in age, yet how great an expanse there was in knowledge, knowledge of character, determination, perseverance, and focus on the right things. John Holding and I sat at his home this past week and went through tons of newspaper clippings that he had. My mother had not saved so many, but a few, but John noticed that in many of them that he was mentioned, so, too was I. Coach, we were kings, we ruled our world, and yet we knew so little about the world and the important things in life. You taught us a lot of football, but, more importantly, and thanks be to God, you wove us together with so many other things. It truly was a moment in time, but one that I look at so much differently now than I did then. To be at your house, share a meal, and laugh at old and new things, was wonderful. I can't imagine how many lives you and Marie have changed over the years simply by example and walking out the faith you knew needed to be the core of all of us. Teeny and I talked about the fact that we didn't even get to talk about your vocational ministry and really what you and Marie had done, but, as I have learned from you and others, such as Casper Holroyd, or Ed Bailey (both who were and still are spiritual mentors to me, like you) that is how we should live in focus on others and their lives, and ways that we may introduce the ways of our Lord in the right way and time.

I have had a rough weekend, sleeping about 4-5 hours Friday after treatment, then 12 hours Friday night, followed by 12 hours last night and this morning. I am somewhat ashamed that I didn't have the courage and strength to go to services and Sunday school this morning (it must have been one of those "4th Quarter" drills I missed), but I also know that God has been gracious beyond my measure in allowing me to rest on the weekends and work during the week, exercise, take in some activities like golf or ballgames, but He has also reminded me of how grateful I should be for each day that He gives. I truly believe in my heart that He has something for me. He has something for me today to do, and I just have to listen and look for where He wants me working. To be a servant to Him we must serve, not simply make it through the day, though some days that is how it feels.

Thanks so much for your encouragement. We have found out last week from our doctors that this infusion chemo, through the port, may be indefinite. We had hoped it would be over around August or so, but we have now made plans through November. That news turned me a little bit, and the confusion began to set in, along with the anger or distrust. As I began to feel that and express it, God did as He alone can do, reminding me to whom I had given this cancer some 2 years ago. He is in charge and wherever He leads, I must follow    and be thankful. Not only did He speak to me, but He felt He needed a little stronger message, so last Thursday He sent me to the bedside of my niece's 16-year-old son at UNC Children's Hospital, where Blake, the son laid asleep from the pain killers and strapped to multiple chemo bags fighting his testicular cancer that had moved to his stomach, into his bones, and cracked 3 vertebrae. As I sat and talked and prayed with his mother and over him, I knew I would have more moments of doubt and confusion, but God is in charge; God is the one with all of the answers.

Again, too long, I know, but things start to come out of me and I don't want to hold back if Christ has shared part of His glory with me. I know that He   has in meeting and holding on to you and Marie. May He bless your house. I pray for you, Marie, and little Maylin in my daily prayers. May they always be answered to His glory and honor.

Roland

### 34. CHRIS MORGAN

*Senior---6'2"---270---Very hard worker---Good, strong boy.*

Chris and Jay Morgan were the only brothers on the football team. Chris was our biggest lineman. He was a key role player on our goal line defense and helped stop several crucial plays on our goal line in our championship run. Many of the players remember how valuable he was to our goal line defense. I remember Chris having a dry sense of humor and he has kept that throughout his life. Chris and Jay's mother, Mary Morgan, was a wonderful supporter of her children and of Broughton football. Chris and Jay's brother Roger played for me at Athens in 1980, and was a good wrestler also.

Chris remembers the mentality of players was tough. He recalls how great it was playing at Carter Stadium against Enloe during the regular season, and how proud he felt to be able to come back and play his final game in the State Championship at Carter Stadium also. One of the things he feels that overflowed into his life from his football season was perseverance. He learned he could do some things that he did not think he could do, and that certainly carried over to his successful career as a detective.

### Chris' Memories/Reflections:

The thing I remember most often about 1970 is Labor Day. In case you don't remember, it was hot; not warm and muggy, not uncomfortable, just HOT. It was the longest practice I ever remember. I have vague memories of some of the coach's cars being used to light the field. After practice I managed to crawl into the locker room, as most of us did. I took a nice long shower, got dressed and was ready to go. Then it happened; no brother, not at his locker, not in the shower, not in the training room, he was nowhere I looked. I started asking around and someone said he'd been in the toilet. I looked and there he was, doubled over on the john, looking more dead than alive. He was breathing, but he was pale and clammy and not moving much. It took a while but I finally got him up and moving. A couple of the guys helped me walk him through the shower and I did what I could to help get him dressed. I drove him home in my ancient Chrysler and managed to get him in the house without drawing too much attention from Momma.

Over the coming years I often reflected back on that one day as a gauge of my tolerance for exhaustion. During my sophomore year at State I put myself on a strict diet and training regimen. I often thought I was working too hard, but compared to Labor Day 1970, running three miles while eating 1000 calories a day wasn't that hard.

Even later during my career on the police department I often compared long, uncomfortable assignments from working traffic assignments to sitting in the woods in 100 degree heat behind a drug house, waiting for a deal to go down, to Labor Day 1970. I would always decide whatever I was doing really wasn't that bad.

What I Learned From The Season:

In addition to the above, I think the most important thing I learned was to be prepared. Due to a lot of things that went on that year, particularly during the summer, I was not in shape mentally or physically for what I wanted to accomplish. I take full responsibility but I just wasn't ready, which led to not being able to contribute to the team as I had envisioned. I would always try to never make that mistake again.

I think the other big thing I learned from that year was about the supremacy of team work and how important it was for me, personally, to be part of a team. In the football season of my junior year, things were such a mess. A group of guys who had been a team once, degenerated into very much a group of individuals with no true common purpose or goal. It was not really anyone's fault, everyone wanted it to be like it was before, but as Mr. Wolfe wrote, "You can't go home again." I will always associate the re-birth of the team with the direct influence of Coach Riggs and the other coaches. They put together a package that transformed a group of individuals into a team. They sold it to us and we bought it like we were women at a Black Friday sale. That was the real difference in the two years, we had some good players, God knows we had a lot of luck; but the real difference was we went back to being a team.

I had been a team member since the eighth grade and by the time I left Broughton High School, I had learned the true value of this. I often put this knowledge to use in my later life, when I traded the purple and gold of Broughton for the French blue and gray of the Police Department. It was easy to see the parallels in my old team and the one I joined for my career. I often longed for better coaching in my time on the Police team; sometimes it was there, sometimes not, but it was always better when we had great coaches.

**Chris' Bio:**

After graduating from Broughton I went off to college; first to beautiful Pembroke State in scenic Robeson County, then after nine long months I transferred to N.C. State. I graduated from State in 1975 with a B.A. in Politics (concentration in Criminal Justice). During my senior year I met my wife Kay; we celebrated our 41$^{st}$ anniversary this year.

In August 1975 I joined the Raleigh Police Department. I took the job as a way to support my wife (pregnant) and myself, with a plan to build up some experience and move on to bigger and better things. I shortly realized I would never leave that job. For many reasons, not the least of which being the "team" aspect I mentioned above, I knew I found where I was supposed to be. Police work in a town like Raleigh back then was often long periods of the mundane with brief bursts of intense activity. I enjoyed the mundane, which mostly involved telling people what to do, where to go and how to make it better. But, I lived for those bursts of activity, from fight calls, to car chases, to stuff you read about on the front page of the newspaper.

I served as a patrolman, detective, sergeant and lieutenant during my twenty nine years. I worked assignments in Field Operations (patrol), Special Operations (community policing) and Investigations (detective division). During my last eight years I was given the opportunity to serve as a supervisor, first as a sergeant, later as lieutenant, of the Major Crimes Task Force (homicide). This was the most simultaneously challenging, frustrating and rewarding job I can imagine. I loved every minute of it. I retired in 1994.

During my career and since I appeared on several television shows and helped with the writing of one book. These included:

The Deadly Dose by Amanda Lamb

"48 Hours Mystery" (twice) (CBS News)

"Forensic Files" (Cable)

"Deadly Women" (Investigation Discovery)

"Nightmare Next Door" (Investigation Discovery)

"Snapped" (Cable)

There were a couple more shows but I don't remember the titles. I also did a lot of local television news for a while after I retired. I guess I was something of a colorful character. I just wish it had paid better; meaning paid at all.

Chris Morgan

## 35. JAY MORGAN

*Junior---6' 2"---195---hustler and good worker---Has shown improvement during summer.*

Jay played offensive tackle on our Championship team. Jay was one of our bigger offensive lineman. He was always anxious to learn how he could improve and play smarter. He played well in his back-up role on our line and contributed many good plays for our offense. Jay worked hard and gave all he had in everything he did for us. He had a very quiet demeanor, but when put one-on-one with another player, could get charged up. He, like other linemen we had, was very smart and a thinker on the field. Jay was another player who loved and understood the game of football. He and I have kept up with each other and he has served with me as an assistant coach at several schools where I have coached. He is a good communicator and a caring individual which makes an outstanding coach. Jay and I have become close friends over the years and I appreciate so much his loyalty and his love for me, my family, and high school coaching.

**Jay's Memories/Reflections:**

Junior High School:

A couple things concerning the guys from Daniels Jr High. We were undefeated our 9th grade year (fall of 1968) and even then Coach Ketcham frequently mentioned to us that we would have State Championship potential when we got to Broughton. I think a lot of what he said was because of Jim Bass. Even then you could tell he was something really special and he did everything for us at Daniels - running back, punter, kickoff, and we employed a special 6-1 defense with Bass as the middle linebacker roaming from sideline to sideline. I know that I never went into a game not expecting to win when we had Jimbo on our side. He just inspired that type of confidence in you. Plus when you had to play against him in practice, you knew how good he was and I never played against anybody in a game that year or our JV year at Broughton that could come close to Bass (granted, I never actually played against Willie Burden or Charles Young, the 2 running backs at Enloe that both got scholarships to NCSU or Carlester Crumpler when he was at Wilson Fike). Coach Gealy at Daniels also told me once that he was amazed at the level of talent at Daniels when he started there. That was his first year of coaching after playing basketball at State and he said that he thought he was lucky to start his coaching career with athletes like us and would not have many groups like us.

I only mention this because I think it did have an effect on the Championship year. The guys who came through Daniels with me and then played on the JV team at NBHS did not lose a game for 2 years by the time we started our junior year. I even remember after our last JV game at Broughton, they had a big cake in the locker room that was

decorated with, "JV CHAMPIONS 1969 - STATE CHAMPIONS 1971."
When David Reynolds (who had gone to Martin Jr. High) saw it, he said,
"You Daniels guys still don't know what it feels like to lose!" and that
was true. We expected to win!! Even though Jim was on the Varsity for
most of our JV season, the confidence was contagious. Wells, Bass,
Turner, Paul Cauthen, Rick Hunter and I plus the others from
Daniels always expected to win. The guys in the class ahead of us, I
think, had started to accept defeat more casually, but I know that I
was shocked when we lost that first game to Grimsley. It was a new,
unpleasant experience. I think the expectations of winning by those
Daniels juniors was a part of the reason we were able to overcome the
hangover of losing that was experienced by the older guys during their
first 2 years at Broughton, where the Varsity had gone 3-7 both
years. But there was a lot of pride in the tradition at Broughton
and most of the guys in every class had a good overall work ethic.

BHS Practices:

Both Jay and Chris thought a lot of Coach Evans who coached the
line and also was their wrestling coach at Broughton.

The benches (don't know how we survived them)...running the mile
in 6:30, I had worked hard that summer but still didn't make it on the
first try because I was afraid I would run out of gas if I started out too
fast or tried to carry too much of a pace. Made it the second time just
because I understood more how to run it. Chris had to run it several more
times before he was cleared. I don't think he ever made the time but he
didn't complain and after six or seven times, you passed him on it.

The broom...still remember the time the coach who was helping you
run the agility station (I think it was Coach Kral) had to go in right
before our group had to do the crabbing. You threw some old broom
about twice as far as Coach Kral had done and said, "Crab to that
broom." It was funny afterwards but I don't think anybody was laughing
while we were crabbing about 50 yards.

Doug Murray having heat episode...Doug fell out during Coach
Evans' station, was laying on his back as white as a sheet. We gave him
some water and moved him to a shady spot. Robbie was pretty shook up
about it but Murray came around pretty quickly and was okay.

The chute…that was new to us for sure and everybody wondered what it was at first. It was not as sophisticated as what we used at Sanderson or anywhere since - just some 2X6's attached to some wood posts y'all stuck in the ground - but accomplished the same purpose. After a couple of guys hit it with their helmets, you knew that wasn't something you wanted to do.

"4th Quarters"…something else new. At first it was painful and we dreaded it, but after a while we understood the value of them and really used them to motivate us.

"Play Polishing"…this was later in the year but still remember running the same plays what seemed like dozens of times. Since we were platooning, there weren't that many guys to switch off with. We got pretty good at 44, 46 power and 18 pass.

The geese…late in the season there seemed to be a flock of migrating geese that flew overhead at least one day a week. We started to look at them as our good luck charm.

Labor Day 1970, 4 hr. practice…I had just been moved onto the starting o-line. (I had not played a single down against Grimsley; Murray Howell started that game.) Even though I was feeling the need to use the bathroom after about the first 2 hours of practice, I didn't want to ask to go in. I was on the toilet for about 30 minutes once we finished; Charles Banks saw me sitting back there and was worried about me and went out to get Chris, who was waiting in his car, the 1955 Chrysler. I eventually recovered.

Games:

Grimsley: I remember the loss 8-7 and not a lot else about the game itself but remember the film session on Monday (before the 4 hour practice). Coach Riggs commenting about 2 dozen times that Rich Eudy was "diggin' for worms again" because he had lost his feet on his block and was down to his hands and knees and not moving. Alan Parnell lining up on the wrong side on their extra point play. Our first exposure to the Morganton drawl of the phrase, "I just can't understand this!", something we all began to hope we wouldn't have directed at something we did.

Record 0-1.

PLAY WITH YOUR HEARTS

W-S Reynolds: Biggest memory is what Coach Riggs said in the locker room at Devereux Meadow right before we went out for the kickoff, about how cold the opposing coach had greeted him before the game and how arrogant they were. Then he talked to us about the girl student at Broughton with the underdeveloped arms wishing him luck during that week at school. Let's just say we left the locker room well motivated. David Dupree running towards our sideline when Wells Edmundson got hurt on the other side of the field saying, "Somebody get the doctor." Doug Murray saying on the bus back to school after the win, "We sent those demons (WSR mascot) right back to hell." (1-1)

<u>Enloe</u>: Remember the thrill of playing as a part of the doubleheader in Carter Stadium and the really long offensive drive we had, 19 plays I think, to seal the deal against Enloe. (2-1)

<u>Rocky Mount</u>: Biggest plays were Bass running back the opening kickoff for a touchdown and my guy George Jones blocking a punt to help them win the game. He made a great play and was a pre-season High School All American the next year but I still thought it was my fault. (2-2)

<u>Hillside</u>: Just remember the weather was a lot cooler and we got to play in Durham County Stadium which was a really great place to play. (3-2)

<u>Wilson Fike</u>: Very close loss and biggest memory for me was a screen play that we had just put in that week. Coach Evans preached all week about not going downfield too early and when Bass caught the ball, I hesitated because I thought I may have committed a penalty and the Fike player ran by me and tackled Jim. It did look bad and we got to see it replayed 8 times during the film session on Monday. Don't know how many times I heard the "I just can't understand this!" phrase but it was a bunch. (I remember many long film sessions during the season which were quite embarrassing at times, especially when Coach would rewind the film time after time after time.) Charles King, I think was trying to make me feel better after the film, came up and said, "What happened on that play, Jay? A mental lapse, it looked like a mental lapse..." (3-3)

<u>Sanderson</u>: Bass's two incredible runs in the second half and my recovering an onside kick are what I remember most. This was the last game I started and/or played in very much. Steve Brewbaker started

playing both ways the next week against Terry Sanford and I don't think I was in on more than 5-6 plays in any game the rest of the year. Only got in on one punt in the State Championship game. Brewbaker was better than me but I thought I had played well enough to get a little more time during the ensuing games than I did. We won them all after the T-S game so that's what's important though. (4-3)

Terry Sanford: How big they looked during warmups and how huge Brewbaker's guy was defensively (6'2", 275 lbs., Spiros Poulos) but Steve did a pretty job on him. I asked him at half time if he wanted to come out for some offensive plays in the second half to get some rest and he said he would stay in until they told me to spell him. I think he played every single play of that game including the kicking game. I remember Gary Neal's finger dangling as he came out of this game. Coach Thomas put his finger back in place there on the sideline; when Dave Dupree saw it, he almost puked on the spot. Of course, remember how upset everyone was in the locker room after the game; Brew not as much as some, he was too exhausted. (4-4) The first time I heard anyone suggest we should stop shaving and having haircuts until we won State Championship was when David Turner suggested it to Wells and me in Ms. Greiner's Chemistry class on the Monday after the Terry Sanford game; don't know if David had heard someone else mention it that day or not.

Ligon: For some reason don't remember much about this one. I know it was a muddy field and I think we played on a Saturday night at Chavis Park over in south Raleigh. (5-4)

Durham: A great game at home to finish the conference season undefeated and Durham was a pretty big rival back then. Brewbaker had a really good game with a couple of highlight film pancakes and the defense was really starting to take over. (6-4)

Dudley: A great road win at Grimsley's stadium to start the playoffs. Think we put in a wheel route for Bass in this game and we had a couple of big plays on it. Also Sandy Goodwin had a couple of big catches and defense played great again. Remember being in the restaurant we ate at after the game in Greensboro when we heard about Goldsboro upsetting Terry Sanford. Guys were really disappointed, wanted another shot at the Bulldogs. (7-4)

Goldsboro: The infield at Devereux Meadow making a couple of "tackles" for us when Bobby Myrick looked like he was about to get loose. How odd the single wing offense they used looked. Bass's great run (not as good as the second one against Sanderson, but close) and Coach Whisenhunt's remarks in The Raleigh Times article on the game the next day. (8-4)

Olympic: What a great day it turned out to be weather wise. Coach Thomas warning the defense all week about Randy Rhino. How open Charles King was on the first touchdown pass. The goal line stand the defense made near the end of the first half. Your halftime speech when you said, "This team doesn't know how to lose since that Terry Sanford game." Tackled Rhino on their sideline on a punt he almost took all the way (my mom actually got a picture of it from the News and Observer, framed it and gave it to me for Christmas) but I think Bass was right behind me and would have gotten him if I missed. Great bus ride back to the school after the game. One of the articles in the News and Observer where they quoted Shaner as saying, "Coach Riggs led us to the water and we decided to drink!"

Other random memories from the season:

* The locker room joke Chris and I played on Bernard with Brewbaker when we told Bernard to ask Brew about his sister being in the ballet and Steve responding straight faced and acting upset. "That's real funny, man, my sister's crippled!!" Bernard saying, "That's cold, man! Why you make me do that?"

* Shaner getting so emotional after it was announced that Ronnie King was ineligible to play because of his grades.

* Seeing Jim Lumsden in his hip to toe cast after the Terry Sanford game and realizing how much of the game he had played with that injury.

* Half the guys on the team imitating Coach Thomas just by saying basically anything but adding the word "stinkin'" after every other word. (i.e. "stinkin' hit," "the stinkin' guy," "stinkin' Shaner")

* The pregame meals in the school cafeteria, nothing fancy but they always had great toast and real butter you could get. The road game restaurant meals we had after the Terry Sanford and Dudley games.

* The cheerleaders decorating our school lockers during Homecoming Week.

* The families of the players were close to each other and supported each other all the time.

* The voluntary Sunday night film sessions in the coaches' office and how more and more guys started coming to them as the season went on.

* The Championship Banquet in the big ballroom over at the old Hotel Sir Walter and having Baked Alaska for dessert.

* Mr. Goodwin (BHS history teacher) actually taking part of his class time to talk about Greensboro Dudley on the Monday after the game. He said that the first half of that game was the most impressive that he had seen since he was at Broughton! I didn't even know that he went to our games! Guess I figured he would rather spend his time reading another book. When he said that in class, it just hit me that our season meant a lot to all kinds of people, even those you might not expect and the fact that a person as intellectually inclined as Mr. Goodwin cared about it, just seemed to make it even more special.

* Both my brother Chris and I thought a lot of Coach Evans who coached the line and also was our wrestling coach at Broughton.

* I guess the last thing would just be our friend <u>Jimbo Bass</u>. Random memories of the incredible things he could do on a football field...going back to Daniels when he effortlessly dropped a cut block on Chris Dameron one day in practice and it launched Chris about 5 yards down the field. Chris turned back laughing and said, "Bass, that was a heck of a block," laughing about it...The way Bass took charge in the Carnage game when we were about to blow our undefeated 9th grade season. I believe he actually willed us to win that one...The time he launched himself it seemed like about 7 feet in the air, as he was being tackled in the Enloe game at Carter Stadium just to get a couple of extra yards and maintain that long drive we had in that game...The 2 runs he had against Sanderson that you really can't even adequately describe to people who didn't see them, especially the second one where he went the last 5 yards backwards and with his body almost parallel to the ground...The run against Goldsboro where it looked like the guy had the perfect angle on him and Jim did one of those hesitation moves of his and just shrugged the guy off his outside shoulder...The way I just always felt we would

win because we had the best player on any field on our side…Jim and I were friends from seventh grade on and I really was in awe of him as a football player; it motivated me just to not let him down…He just could produce magic…Literally cried myself to sleep the night we found out that he had to go to Enloe his senior year because of busing. Still wonder what kind of senior season we would have had if we had still had Jimbo, Otto, Buddy Hudson, Dickie but especially Bass…the magic was gone.

Jay Morgan and Nephew Kyle

**Jay's Bio:**

1976 Graduated from UNC-Chapel Hill with BA/Physical Education; was on UNC wrestling team

1977-1980 In sales and management at Sportsman's Cove in Crabtree Valley Mall and in newly opened Cary Village Mall

June 1980 Worked for Pepsi Cola and also part time as night auditor for Downtowner Motor Inn on Hillsborough Street in Raleigh

1990-1992 UNC Teacher Certification Program at UNC-CH to acquire NC Teaching License.

1993 Full time volunteer assistant football coach on Coach Riggs' staff and assistant wrestling coach with Ron Crawford at Sanderson High School

1999 Moved to Marion, NC to become full time teacher and coach with David Riggs in McDowell County Schools

2004-2007 Worked at Johnson Lambe Sporting Goods and joined David Riggs' football staff at Fuquay Varina HS as full time volunteer assistant football coach

May 11, 2005 Saddest day of my life: my mom passed away from kidney cancer. She was a superior human being with incredible faith.

2007-2015 Telecommunicator at Raleigh-Wake 911 Center. Transitioned to part time volunteer football coach at FVHS

June 2015 to present: Telecommunicator with NC Highway Patrol

### 36. GRIGG MULLEN

*Junior---5'6"---189---No experience at all---Needs to pick up speed---Always has good hustle and trying to improve.*

Grigg did not play very much in the games, but was certainly a key man in helping us win the championship by his unselfish dedication. He played on the scout team weekly and helped us get better by practicing hard against our starters every single day. Football was completely new to him and he understood that he would have to use this season to learn about the game. Grigg is another one of those "unsung heroes" for our 1970 team. If I am not mistaken, he played quite a bit his senior year and really spent a lot of time in the weight room and gained strength and weight. I believe Grigg attended VMI after Broughton and "walked on" the football team his first year.

I have not been able to locate Grigg during the writing of this book.

### 37. DOUG MURRAY

*Senior---5'10"---180---One of the top defensive players---Strives for perfection---Great contributor---Hustler.*

Doug was a man in the midst of boys in many ways in 1970. He had a mustache and long hair and looked like he was 25 years old. He was a hard hitter and a go-getter. He may have delivered some of the hardest hits during the season on the game field as well as during practices. I remember Doug being very likeable, and he still is today. He was one of our stronger linebackers, and because of his size and hitting ability, he played more of our inside linebacker.

**Doug's Memories/Reflections:**

Several guys remembered that "Paco" (Doug) got caught by Coach Evans one game day after the pre-game meal. All the players were supposed to be in the wrestling room resting before the game that night. Coach Evans heard a bunch of noise and it was Doug Murray doing some kind of "chicken dance" entertaining all the guys. When Coach Evans walked in, Doug almost melted right on the spot. Some of the players still give Doug a hard time about that. Doug remembers playing cards at Charles King's in between two-a-day practices. He also has memories of the boards under the chute and definitely 4th quarter drills. "Back on the ball, run it again," he definitely remembers. Repetition, repetition, repetition was big in practices.

Doug commented about how fiery I was in our practices. I guess I was pretty high strung in my younger days as a coach. I always felt a coach must be energetic and excited about football. Football is a highly emotional sport, and I thought one could raise his level of ability through his being more emotionally involved. I felt like I have always played and coached from my heart, so I could not change that part of my personality. I never felt like I faked anything in my coaching, but instead it came from deep down inside of me. I would always say what I felt in coaching, and in that way I would wear my feelings on my sleeve. I also thought that players and people in general could be motivated if you could find their "hot buttons," and I certainly would try to do that. People play better and live better when they do it with their feelings and heart.

Doug remembers our coaches being fair, but tough. We would not think twice about chewing their butts out. "Get it right until…"And of course he remembers running the mile for time the first day, and he knew he had to run with someone who would make it; he thought he tried to keep up with Jim Bass.

In regards to race, he said he had been together with blacks in Jr. High and did not think a lot about it at that time. He did not think it was an issue on our team due to his being used to it and playing with blacks who were from his Oberlin neighborhood as he was growing up in Raleigh.

Once they all came together at Broughton, the rivalry of Daniels and Martin went away completely. It was one big team, and they were glad to be on the same team.

He remembers Robbie Jones, one of our managers in 1970, being fiery and getting a penalty in one of the ball games. Doug also pointed out that Coach Evans had played at NCSU and was one of Doug's heroes when he was growing up and then he loved it when Evans became his line coach.

Doug praised our secondary a lot and commented how smart they were football-wise. He also talked a lot about growing up together and playing with and against each other in Pop Warner. Families knew each other and were very close. JV's had been successful also, so they knew they were very good. Players played several sports and never quit any sport. They just loved to play the games.

**Doug's Memories/Reflections:**

Thoughts of '70 football: I really didn't know what to expect going into my senior year. First, there was talk of busing that would include the area where many of us lived (Five Points to old Wake Forest Road) going to Enloe. It wasn't until the end of June before the busing issue was delayed until the next year. Second, this was going to be the 3rd head coach and new assistant coaches in 3 years. Once I found out that I was still going to Broughton and met the coaches, I felt a little more comfortable. Until I found out we had to run the mile in a certain time and learn this new playbook!!! It was like going to English class which I dreaded! To make sure I ran the mile under the allotted time (lineman time), I ran with the backs with the push from Jim Bass. (Should have run with the linemen.) It nearly killed me but I made it.

August 15, football season was here. New head coach, a fiery but motivating young man (UNC grad) - forgave him on that. Coach Evans (NC STATE) huge and a former Cap grad, and Coach Thomas (APP ST.) both of these assistants who I really loved and respected. The new staff was hard on us but installed a breath of fresh air. The preseason grind, 2-a-days, 4th quarter drills, August was a killer! I remember the fact that the coaches wanted to platoon, kickoff, kickoff return, punt, punt return etc. to try to get as many players involved as possible and that made a lot of guys happy to get on the field. We lost our 1st game to Grimsley 8-7 despite Jim's unbelievable run down the sideline. Next week, we recovered with a win at WS Reynolds, despite our bus running late, hitting a car making a turn into Cameron Village that put us further behind. Third game of the season was exciting. Playing our cross town rival Enloe, which I had a lot of friends playing for them, at Carter Stadium, home of the Wolfpack in an event which also included Sanderson and Ligon. We lost close games to Rocky Mt., Wilson Fike, and then got blown out by Terry Sanford. We were 4 and 4, but 3-0 in conference play.

Coach Thomas and Coach Evans got the defense to watch game films after practice to help us understand opponent's offense better. RESULT: Shut out, no points, nada, our last 5 games, 2 regular season games and 3 state playoff games which included the State Championship game against Charlotte Olympic 14-0, which was played at Carter Stadium.

The 1st playoff game was in Greensboro against Dudley. They were huge and a 21 point favorite. The field had no grass, muddy and smelled like fish. It was awful. I remember Shaner and myself leading warm-ups and a News and Observer reporter came up to Coach Riggs and asked him what he was doing in the playoffs with a 6-4 record and how he felt about it. Enough said, fuel for the fire and the pregame talk to us could have sent us to the moon. Watching game film on Dudley helped so much. We had animal names for each formation they had. One particular was Elephant. We kept calling animal names out and they didn't know what was going on. End result: we won 21-0.

Next opponent was winner of Goldsboro vs. Terry Sanford. Goldsboro and the single wing came to town. It was the toughest, hardest hitting game that I played in that year. They had a player Danny Kepley who NEVER left the field, was a monster at running back and LB on defense. Great game 6-0.

State Championship week was freezing cold. Daily practice was tough but exciting. Game day on Saturday. We dressed like we had all week for practice. Wrapped from head to toe for cold weather, got to the stadium, hot as blue blazes. I remember we all had to strip down to play; it was hot!! 14-0 win!! It took me several weeks for winning a State Championship to sink in. I've got CRS now. Sorry, Coach.

**Doug's Bio:**

After graduation from Broughton, Doug went to Chowan to play football, but the school and program did not meet his needs. He transferred to Sandhills for two years where he attended school and played baseball. After two years, Doug transferred to ECU where he finished his major in P.E. and Health and his education degree.

After graduating from ECU, he coached and taught at Garner High School for two years. Then he worked for teammate David Reynolds for about three years before he decided that he wanted to return to coaching and teaching. He accepted a position at Zebulon High School in 1984. Zebulon High was consolidated into East Wake High School where Doug coached and taught until 2009.

Doug married his wife Sheila in 1992 and they live in Raleigh. Doug is now retired, works part time on a golf course and loves playing golf.

Doug and Sheila Murray

## 38. GARY NEAL

*Junior---6' 1"---180---good size---Fine prospect.*

Gary was a tough defensive tackle and played a lot for being a junior. I remember Gary being a mean, not dirty, player. He was tough and rough, and I do not remember him backing down from anyone in practice or games. We needed players like Gary, and he helped us become better week by week.

**Gary's Memories/Reflections:**

The 1970 Championship was a great highlight in my early life journey. Wow, 46 years have gone by. I played with many of our teammates in organized sports since little league baseball and football. Wow guys, what a fantastic journey we all had to the championship!

I tell you what, David Riggs that was just a great job! To all the young coaches, John Thomas, Robbie Evans and Mac Caldwell our hats are off to you for a job well done!

To the fine citizens of the beautiful city of Raleigh and the student body of Needham B Broughton High School...thank you! I personally felt 15 feet tall running out of the field house at Carter Stadium and seeing that massive cloud of bodies cheering us on to victory. Your support over the season and at the championship game was outstanding!!

Wishing you all the best and thank you for our beautiful life experience!

What a ride!

What I Learned From The Season:

The key to victory is digging deep into your soul and stepping up! Many times in my life journey, I was dogged tire and sometimes I could not just step up. Then I would hear those coaches' whistles of the 1970 season and hear those great coaches screaming "4th Quarter"!!!...dig deep and with any tough challenge, you can move through any obstacle in your way and achieve your victories.

It's been 46 years since the TEAM rocked Raleigh N.C., and we still hold that triumph in the record book. Those three young guys, fresh out of college put a plan in motion, and the stars aligned for the 1970 N.C. State 4-A Champions. I remember at the banquet, you promised us we would walk with what we accomplished for the rest of our lives......Coach you were so right...we all do and thank you!

**Gary's Bio:**

I moved from Carolina to Houston, Texas back in 1974. I started my insurance claims career with Allstate Insurance in 1976. I worked with several insurance carriers and also an independent adjuster for the last 38 years.

Two years ago I elected to move into public insurance adjusting. Now, opposed to working for the insurance carriers, I step into the home owner's or business owners shoes and become their claims advocate. My friends call me "little Nader." Some of that tenacious winning spirit from the miracle 1970 championship is still in my bones. Thanks to you, John, Robbie and Mac. What a beautiful memory! David Riggs that was a great job!!!

I live out in the country about 35 miles northwest of College Station, Bryan Texas. In a small town called Gause. If ya blink you will miss it....no stop lights and there are only cries of the coyotes in the evenings. It's peaceful. Traveled a bit over the years, lived a spell in Wyoming, San Francisco, Atlanta and Houston. Now I am finding simple pleasure in tending to my crystal garden. I have been a student of indigenous cultures for the past 18 years and been very privileged with association to several medicine elders from various tribes over the years. My heart guides me to the ways of the "old ones" and the harmony that is of their way. There is great importance for all of us to find the pathway to our true heart in these times.

Gary Neal

### 39. LARRY OTTO

Larry was one of the few sophomores we moved from the junior varsity team to the varsity during the 1970 season. He was a very capable player, and he played on defense for us during the playoff run. Larry filled in for Jim Lumsden after Jim was hurt in the Terry Sanford game. He played at linebacker as well as at monster back. Even though Larry was a sophomore, he played like an upperclassman. He was a sure tackler and very football-savvy. I remember he moved so good laterally on the field and was another one of our more versatile players.

### Larry's Memories/Reflections:

I went to Carroll Junior High in the 7th grade, Daniels Junior High in the 8th, 9th grade, Broughton High School in the 10th grade, Enloe High School in the 11th and 12th grade…and never moved. I made a lot of friends during those transfers from school to school but built very few deep relationships. I came to Broughton my sophomore year from a successful Daniels Jr. High football program. I started out playing JV ball and was called up to the Varsity when a defensive starter was injured during the final game of the regular season. I remember the Varsity barely made into the playoffs so I had few expectations of advancing too far into the playoffs. I was more concerned, and worried, about competing at this higher level. Mark Shaner, our nose guard/middle linebacker, scared me to death. He looked like a grown man in pads.

The only vivid memory I have during the playoff games was during the Championship game in Carter Finley Stadium against Charlotte Olympic. I was playing outside linebacker and Olympic was on about the five yard line, about to score. The quarterback threw a little quick pass out in the flat on my side and we stopped them from scoring. The game ended 14-0. That Broughton defensive team did not give a point during the playoffs, a record that I believe still stands to this day. We were a true Cinderella team and I was thankful to be a part of that team.

What I Learned From The Season:

That timing and providence are very important.

A State Football Championship helped define me as a man.

### Larry's Bio:

After our championship year I was transferred to Enloe for my final two years of high school. I then attended the University of South Carolina on a football scholarship. After a coaching change at USC, I transferred to Appalachian State University and graduated from there in 1977. In 1978 I began a career in the produce industry and married my high school sweetheart, Jean McNeill. Jean and I have 3 sons and 2 grandsons.

Larry and Jean Otto

**40. ALLAN PARNELL**    *Junior---6'---165---Wants to play badly--- Is a fast learner.*

Allan played our monster back and was another hard worker who was ready to do anything our coaches wanted him to do. I remember him wearing thick glasses under his helmet and it amazes me that he never broke them. Allan was another player who did not possess a lot of raw football talent, but made up for it with his intelligence and love for the game. I could count on Allan to do his assignment once it was given to him. He said he still remembers lining up on the wrong side of the field on the extra point in our first game against Grimsley. That was such an unusual mistake by Allan because he was one of the most reliable players we had. Of course, our coaches, including me, did not see that they were going for two either until it was too late. Allan contributed on defense during the rest of the season.

**Allan's Memories/Reflections:**

First, I don't know if this is an "outstanding" memory, but I remember being in the wrong place for Grimsley's 2 point conversion, a game we lost by 1. I remember the growing confidence we got playing in the rain and mud at Ligon. I distinctly remember the Dudley team singing, "Hey Hey Hey Goodbye" before the game. Then Jim Bass slashed through them and our defense shut down their offense. They were quiet after the game. I remember getting Herr Watts to attend the Goldboro game. That may be the only Broughton football game he ever attended. The thing I've told so many people is that by the time we got to the playoffs, there was an incredible confidence that we were going to win. No one said it. But we knew. I distinctly remember the confident smile on George Lattimore's face at one of the last practices. I had never experienced anything like that group confidence before, and I have never experienced it since.

What I Learned From The Season:

I learned the importance of perseverance. When we were 4 and 4, we could have played out the string, but with great leadership from coaches and players, we were able to come together for that incredible run. You just have to keep doing what you know will make you better. The final result isn't always a championship, but you can still achieve great things.

**Allan's Bio:**

Following Coach Riggs's footsteps, I went to UNC, graduating in 1976. I then spent two years in exile at Penn State, learning how not to go to graduate school (but making a great friend now at Bucknell who I still work with). I kept my goal of a Ph.D. after returning to Chapel Hill in 1978, working in a restaurant, taking a graduate course, and finding a mentor (the main lesson I learned at Penn State). (I got very lucky soon after returning south and met Ann Moss Joyner—more on her later). I became a full time graduate student in Sociology at UNC, with funding at the Carolina Population Center. I received my MA and Ph.D. from UNC.

My first job was a one-semester visiting appointment at the University of Hawaii. I was then on the staff of the Committee on Population at the National Academy of Sciences for 15 months, coming home every weekend from Washington. For eight years I was on the sociology faculty at Duke. I returned to UNC part time with one of the NIH grants I received, while also starting consulting. While at UNC, I accidentally became involved in civil rights analysis and advocacy, working with Ann. This was totally a leap of faith, not a well-thought out career path, but we persevered and it has worked out. We conduct research in support of advocates in fair housing and public schools, and I serve as an expert witness in civil rights cases across the country, most notably *Texans Department of Housing and Community Affairs v Inclusive Communities Project*, heard before the U.S. Supreme Court. In June, 2015, the court decided in our favor, allowing disparate impact evidence to be used in fair housing cases. I also work on public policy issues with Jim Johnson at UNC's Kenan Institute.

I married Ann Moss Joyner on October 17, 1981. We have one daughter, Hannah, who graduated from UNC-Asheville in 2014. She is in charge of the main horse barn (70 horses) and the barn/riding staff at Frost Valley, a 6,000-acre YMCA camp in the Catskills. Ann and I live on 43 acres in northwest Orange County. Ann moved an abandoned Primitive Baptist Church building 8 miles to our property and restored it for our office. We have horses, a donkey, dogs, chickens and a cat. I'm a member of St. Matthew's Episcopal Church in Hillsborough, and on the board of the Alamance-Orange Prison Ministry.

Allan Parnell and wife Ann

Like all of us, heartbreak and challenges have been part of living. My mother died on Labor Day 1981, just six weeks before our wedding. My

1970 teammate, Dickie Thompson, came to express his condolences. Our house burned to the ground on February 5, 2000, and we lost almost all of our material possessions. We learned the importance of friends and family, and learned to accept their care and love. My father died on September 5, 2005. Both of my parents are buried in Raleigh.

## 41. DOUG PERRY

*Junior---6' 1"---160---Has good hands---needs speed but should be able to play some at tight end.*

Doug was a lean and tough young player. He had a good understanding of what he needed to do to carry out his responsibility as a player. He played tight-end for us and had good hands in catching the football. His playing time was limited due to seniors playing ahead of him this year, but that did not take away from his positive attitude as far as I was concerned.

### Doug's Memories/Reflections

I can remember my thoughts when I showed up for Broughton football try-outs that first, hot summer practice. I kid you not, I thought there were more people trying out for that football team than were in the whole school I attended the year before. The year before had been the first year I played football at school. I loved being a part of that team and I had learned so much from my coach, Bobby Collins! But this Broughton school was 4 or 5 times larger! I felt my chances for making that team were slim!

Quick Flashback: My 9th grade year was my first taste of playing football. A couple years previously, Dad got fired from a little country church that "couldn't handle the truth," as Jack Nicholas would say. Seemed it was OK to preach about "loving your neighbor" as long as you didn't include Black Folks as being your neighbors! So we had to leave the little church parsonage they built for us! Fed up with church political BS, Dad moved us to Creedmoor, N.C. so he could pursue his doctorate degree from Duke University. I attended South Granville High School where I decided to try out for football.

The coach was Bobby Collins. I was scared of him! He walked around with a growl on his face. He introduced me to the concept that coaches try to kill you in the summer just a few weeks before school starts. After Coach Collins told me I made the JV Team, he said, "We are going to practice 2 times a day 'til school starts!" The very 1st day I thought, "What have I gotten myself into?" By the 3rd day, I was asking my Dad's advice about quitting! I told him I thought I would literally die from the heat and exhaustion, hoping he would feel sorry for me. His next words, though not appreciated at the time, set a course for my thought process for the rest of my life! He said, "Son, you do what you want to do. But, I feel, if you quit this team, it will be easier to quit the next hard thing that comes along, and thus, you will be setting up that pattern for your life!" Not what I wanted to hear, but I really respected my Dad, so I decided right then that I might die, but I would not quit! This was the beginning of learning a much cherished trait, reinforced by Coach Riggs the following year! Never, never, never quit! This would soon become a natural part of my thinking. Heeding Dad's advice, I showed up for practice the next day.

The school was so small that the JV team had to practice with the Varsity Team! The Varsity Team used the JV guys for tackling dummies, with Coach Collins' approval so we would be tough if we lived to make Varsity! Now, my older sister, she was so pretty and she was a good girl, and I never saw it coming! She had been on a few dates with some of the senior football players. She told me how they tried to "make out" with her but she wouldn't do it! I guess they assumed she told me, knowing I was her brother. I begged her to go kiss those guys after they, so obviously, started trying to kill me during football practice. They would triple team me and watch me fly even when the ball was nowhere around! But, in spite of all that, I loved the team aspect of playing football that first year! That positive experience deepened my desire to try and play football in Raleigh the next year where my Dad was starting his new job as Academic Dean at Peace College.

So here I am trying out for the Needham B. Broughton football team! So many people here trying out for this team! Such a big school! So hot! I was pretty intimidated by it all!

I started sizing up that Coach Riggs guy, comparing him to Coach Collins! I wasn't going to play for any sissy coach guy! No sir! Not after Coach Collins! By the end of that first practice, I knew I had to be on Coach Riggs' football team! He was just like Coach Collins except he didn't have that growl like he was gonna kill you if you messed up! So I started hustling! I just wanted to be on that team and contribute whatever I could. I knew Coach had a limit on the number of guys he would choose, so I was determined to give it all I had during those summer practices.

Fortunately, I had been running all summer, trying to get ready. At least here, I didn't have those three dumb-ass country boys trying to kill me on every play! I remember we were pushing so hard in those summer try-outs and practices that guys were puking over the fence at times. We were pushing so hard that when we would spit, it would be like cotton and float up with the wind. I remember thinking, I would give my birthright to get a cup of that salty Gatorade!

I can still remember, as if it were yesterday, how elated and grateful I was when I realized I made the Varsity team! That Coach Riggs had allowed this skinny, new kid, at this huge school, to be on his team!

I remember that the Team became like family to me. Because I had just moved to Raleigh during that summer, I had no friends and didn't know anyone in Raleigh when I showed up for those Broughton football summer try-outs! I remember how good that old salty Gatorade was during those two-a-day August practices! How I got so dry, when I tried to spit, that the wind would carry it up like it was cotton. Memories of driving that blocking sled with Coach Evans standing on it, screaming at us. Suicide drills and extra laps after practice. Wishing Bernard Williams would break a leg, or something, so I could get more playing time!

That football season was like a fairy tale season! There were so many times that things had to go just right. So many things that could have gone wrong! Yet, we kept winning! We were continually viewed as the underdogs! Coach Riggs didn't view us as the underdogs! He made us believe that we could win! We could see that he believed we could win! In fact, we became proud to be viewed as the small underdog team. We believed we could beat any team in the conference, if we would just play the football, on game day, that we had been so well coached during practice! As we neared the end of the season, it seemed we were playing better. Our belief was growing. We kept winning! I think it was God's gift to each member on our team. I feel football teaches men to be tough warriors. The parallel lessons of football to life on all planes are endless.

It's up to each man how many of those lessons he is open to. Then, eventually, it's up to each man to choose which team he will join and serve.

I hold special memories of every single member on the team! But, in particular, I remember thinking that as long as we could keep David Turner and Jim Bass healthy, put them with a couple big blocking guys, we would have a shot. I had so much confidence in David Turner as quarterback! Watching Jim Bass run and fake those defensive guys right out of their shorts was a thing of beauty! He made it look so easy!

Several times during those last few games and especially the Championship game, I thought we might be in for a big Gang Fight...or Fan Fight...Or Football Team Lynching! It was actually a little unsettling! I was not ready to be killed just because we kicked those Giant Football Players' butts in the Championship Game! It wasn't my fault that Jim Bass wanted to be on my team!

I didn't get much playing time in the games. As badly as I longed to play in all those games, I trusted Coach. I determined in my mind not to give in to the selfishness of making it all about me. I felt my role on this team was to give all I had in practice and be there if, and when, Coach needed me! Honestly, I was just so grateful to be on the team! I do believe that in my struggle to constantly keep team perspective over personal perspective, I was beginning to learn about submission, a very important thing to understand in this life! I should ask Coach if I ever petitioned him for more playing time. Actually, I can't remember if I did or not. But the point is, I did not see myself as a second class teammate. I just wanted to do what I could.

Little did I know when I started playing football at Broughton that this football team would go on to win the State Championship. Nor did I know that I would get to know so many great guys and develop a life-long bond that only comes from the highs and lows of doing "Combat" together. But even primary to all of that, I was not aware of the tremendous positive influence Coach Riggs would have on my life, and eventually, the lives of my 3 precious daughters, from being on his team and learning from him that Championship season! Conversely, I would also have the opportunity to be with Coach Riggs when we're losing. Not just losing...but losing badly. It was painful! Yet, I continued to glean lessons from Coach Riggs and his example, even more so, in the disappointing times! So, Coach, I thank you for investing yourself in my life and allowing me to be on your team and learn from you! You were one of the primary men in my life that set an example for me, who had traits that I so admired and wished to emulate.

**Doug's Bio:**

I went into the building business right out of high school. I built houses all around the Raleigh Area until about 2012 when I lost most everything monetarily, primarily, due to the prolonged housing recession.

Doug Perry with grandchildren

I married my wife Rita in 1976. We have three daughters who are the world to me, Amber, Tia and Heather. We are very close. Their husbands are my sons that I never had, Simon, Daniel and Sam. Tia has given us 2 grandchildren, Elliania and Hunter. Unfortunately, Rita and I were divorced in 2006. I have always been grateful for the lessons I learned from the coaches and for being a part of this football team. They have been helpful in dealing with the victories and the struggles that life deals each of us. Some of my most painful struggles have led to my most treasured understandings. I think the football experience was a microcosm shadow experience preparing each of us players for the life ahead of us.

## 42. WILLIS PRICE

*Junior---5' 8"---155---Utility man---Can play one of several positions---Learning fast---Should help.*

Willis played and lived in high school "marching to a different drummer," as I remember him. He was quick as a cat and probably could have played at wide receiver, but somehow he ended up playing in our offensive line. He was a very good athlete and played hard. He was very good as a pulling guard because of his quickness. He would hustle down the field to help out after his initial block. He and Mark Caudle were step brothers after his mother married Mark's dad.

Willis died in Atlanta several years ago of a brain tumor. He had been working in advertising in Georgia.

## 43. RANDY PROCTOR

*Junior---5' 8"---163---slow, but great attitude---Always hustling and trying.*

Randy played in our offensive line. He practiced hard and was another one of those guys who did not care about getting attention and being a starter because he realized he was not as capable as some senior players. He contributed as many others did by practicing hard and making the first team players better. He did a good job on the scout squad and was a loyal teammate.

### Randy's Memories/Reflections:

Besides all the obvious highlights, I remember Devereux Meadow was a dump but it was kind of cool we were one of the last to play there. It had a lot of history.

Seems like I remember Lumsden playing with a broken bone. Now that is sucking it up. I remember salt tablets and something new called Gatorade.

Previous to the year I remember Johnny Ford and myself lifting weights at the Y with some crazy looking guy named Rick Flare.

John Holding could throw a bullet but that ball was hard to catch.

I remember Jim Bass was covered in oil; you just could not get a solid hit on that guy.

What I Learned From The Season:

If you really worked at something, you could improve.

Believe!

**Randy's Bio:**

Graduated from UNC-CH in 1976. Primarily been in insurance business since 1978; earning CLU and ChFC. Used to play a lot of golf. I had some success and I think what I learned from that season helped. Currently when I have time I am obsessed with fishing, occasionally fishing with Rick Hunter. I have a 32 year old daughter in Asheville, a 28 year old son in Sydney, Australia and a 5 year old daughter who lives with my wife Jessica and me in Cameron Park, where I can see Broughton High School's clock tower.

Randy and Jessica Proctor

**44. DAVID REYNOLDS** *Junior---5' 11"---204---Good size --- Good hitter on offense---Should have a good year.*

We expected a lot from David as we entered the opening games of the 1970 season, and he did not disappoint us. He was another one of the talented juniors who had come off the undefeated season from the Junior Varsity team. He was a good and strong lineman and could have played several positions. He ended up starting at tackle and played a key role in our offense and opening up holes for our back.

David was one of the better athletic linemen who played on the 1970 team. He was selected to play in the East-West All Star Football Game after his senior year (1971) and won the Co-Defensive Player of the game. David received a football scholarship from N.C. State where he played for two years.

### David's Memories/Reflections:

I wrote things down at different times as they came to me:

- I guess to start off, nobody knew what to expect.

- 3 new coaches not much older than we were. It didn't take long to know how tough they were.

- The two-a-day practices moving to different stations with that dreaded whistle. Those days it was believed we didn't need to drink much water at practice. When we did get a short break, we had salted Gatorade.

- I remember all the running but the thing I remember the most was the "duck walk" and most of all, the "grass drill." Coaches would blow that whistle over and over until we could not even stand up. Of course, we hated all of that but I promise you there was no team in as good a shape as we were.

- The two-a-days were harder than my college summer practices. I cannot remember what game it was but when 4th quarter came and we crabbed up to the line of scrimmage, I remember seeing in the eyes of the other team that they could not believe it.

- Greensboro Grimsley game: I remember that guy running the kickoff for a touchdown. (Seeing you three coaches on the sideline wanting to get in that game and play yourselves.)

- As season progressed, totally changing defense mid-season - how smart that turned out to be for us.

- I remember the clicker when we watched game films and how we dreaded when we did something wrong and that clicker going back and forth. I can still hear it now as I think about it.

- After the Terry Sanford game when we were tied up 7-7 going into 2nd half; at that time they were ranked #1 and after the game, even though we lost, you made us believe we could play with anyone and, boy, as you know, we did.

- Thinking back of our home field being an old baseball field where a lot of it was dirt. It was our home field and we loved it.

- I remember the practices that lasted until dark. Blowing that whistle to hop inside to block after we had a punt blocked the previous week.

- Remember the song in the locker room, "Green Eyed Lady," being played every day.

- The geese that flew over the last several weeks of the season in a V form which we all knew meant victory.

- The Goldsboro game that, when we came onto the field, had all those buses and more fans than we did. I believe they were the toughest team we played all year. I remember firing off the ball to block the guy in front of me and he did not move an inch. I knew it was going to be a long tough night.

- I remember visiting the different churches of team members. I will never forget Charles Banks' church when everybody got up and danced and sang.

As I know you know, we did not have a lot of superstars on this team. You coaches taught us so much and got the best out of us. But, Coach Riggs, with your passion, heart, and hard work which most people have no idea were the reason we succeeded. We were made to believe and were so united as a team. Those locker room speeches before the games. That word HEART that was brought up at Jim Bass's memorial service after his death; well, you put that in all of us, Coach.

The tradition of a school that in the past dominated sports was brought back to life. That sports year - #1 Football - #1 Tennis - #1 Golf - and even finished #2 in Basketball and even could have won that except for a bad call on Phil Spence. Winning the State Football Championship in the way we did installed in all our minds something we are so proud of and will never be forgotten. First championship game played in a major college stadium. The people on the bridges cheering as we drove back to Broughton after winning.

Personally for me, you made my parents and my two brothers and sister so very proud of their son. I was the youngest and all my family went to Broughton. There is no way how much I could thank you for that football season and guiding me in the right direction for the future.

Then there was the next season…our team was split up. As great as my junior year was my senior year was that bad except for dating Cambey Pickard all year and how she kept me straight due to her faith in Jesus.

In closing, I remember at the end of my senior year, you called me into your office and told me I had been selected to play in the East-West All Star Game. You then told me you thought Charles Banks deserved it more which at the time hurt a lot. Well it gave me something to prove to you and myself. I probably had the best game of my career - Co-MVP on defense in that game. Somehow I need to thank you for that.

Thank you and the coaches so much for helping us have that successful season which changed our lives forever.

David Reynolds

**David's Bio:**

Received football scholarship from N.C. State where I played for two years. I had a very successful commercial landscaping Company—90 employees for 37 years in that business. I retired at the age of 58 and am living on a farm with 40 acres outside of Zebulon. I did not get married until I was 57 and then married a lovely lady, Mary Crumpler who is also from Raleigh.

## 45. PRESTON RUTH

*Senior---6'---165---Bad knee, but still is a hustler---Looks good at quarterback and safety.*

Preston was the glue that held our secondary together throughout the Championship season. He played safety and made a lot of the defensive secondary calls for us. He was not very fast at all for a safety who had to cover a lot of ground in our cover 3 zone defense. However, he made up for any lack of speed with his knowledge of the game and being prepared for each team we played. He was so good at watching the quarterback, gathering clues as to what was going to happen or happening. He moved quickly in the middle of the field, but just as important, he got everyone else in the secondary in the proper position on each play.

Preston had torn his ACL his junior year playing football and was still recovering in some ways from that previous year's injury. He rehabbed enough to start for us at our safety position on defense and was a good, reliable, consistent player.

Preston remembers that "social clubs" had been part of the student body at Broughton for many years, but they were losing importance at the end of the 1960's. These clubs were essentially made up of people from a similar social class. There were initiations and each member had a small pin that identified which club they were in. Preston and some others were part of the "Cavaliers" social club, but he did not think the clubs were any longer the "faddish" thing to be part of in 1970.

He has great memories from his high school days and really feels that a great deal of the success he and others have had in life was due to friendships growing up and his friends' parents knowing them all as they shared their lives together on the athletic fields and school. He recalls growing up as a junior high school student-athlete who looked up to the Broughton High School athletes with great respect for the program that had been established by people who came before him. They all seemed to know where they came from and almost revered the Broughton football program. He did not expect to play as a sophomore but instead knew he had to earn the right to be part of such a wonderful program.

Preston remembers that Coach John Thomas worked for Hal Thompson during the summers; even though he was looked up to as a teacher and coach, John worked in the summers to make his family money. This drew a lot of respect from Preston, and Preston saw that people needed to do what they had to do to make things work.

**Preston's Memories/Reflections:**

If I were to try and discuss outstanding memories about Broughton High School football, they would have to originate in 1967. That's when Jr. High football players, like me, from Daniels and Martin were watching high school championship football at Riddick Stadium on the NCSU campus.

All the 8$^{th}$ and 9$^{th}$ grade football players were there watching Al Godwin, Jimmy King, Sonny Leach and the names keep coming back to me; Brown, Coleman, Bradford, Ellington, and more, win championships. We learned the meaning of wearing a Broughton High School uniform and representing NBHS by observing these players display championship caliber play.

The following year as a Junior Varsity player, I was moved up to the Varsity team's final game. It was a great experience for me, as I ran back kick-offs and played quarterback for a few plays. What I remember most after we lost the game against Goldsboro that night was the tears and remorse of the senior players upon completing a rather disappointing 3-7 season. The tears were not because they lost the game or were ending their final season, but from believing they had let their coaches, school and community down. But for me, and other Junior Varsity players, their sincerity in the locker room after the game became a lasting memory that instilled in us the true essence of what it means to be a "team player" for Broughton High School. These players set the stage for the future 1970 State Championship High School Football team. Players like Todd Turner, Sonny Bass, Robbie Gorrell, Mike Carter and Dillon, Aiken and Anderson, to name a few, left lasting impressions on those of us who followed behind. We knew the value of "knowing where you came from, to know where you were going," a key ingredient to success.

Although we seemed to be in a good position at the beginning of the following season, we were unable to make it happen and ended the season again with a 3-7 record. Although the season never came together, we were still determined to sacrifice more and work harder the next season as we all knew that the "win" comes with hard work and sacrifice - you can't expect to win by just showing up.

On a more personal note, I remember from an otherwise tumultuous season, an encounter with Todd Turner who, as we now know, is a respected collegiate athletic director. After losing the game against Enloe, I spoke with Todd Turner at the Holiday Gym and he made a point to tell me I played well and I was one of the few guys "hitting." That, as you can tell, meant a great deal to me because, unfortunately, in the next game against Wilson Fike, I injured my right knee and that injury subsequently changed the way I could play football and baseball as a Broughton Cap.

In retrospect, I think the experiences we endured by the number of losses and disappointments leading up to the Championship game in 1970 have now become bittersweet as we now realize that the prior seasons made us all stronger and ready to play and give 100% as a team, not as an individual. Winning the Championship as a "team" effort, from that point on, created a lasting bond between us as players and throughout our adult lives that has lasted for decades. For me, it gave the meaning of winning a championship game a new meaning, as it was not about each of us as individuals, but about "us" as players working together for a common goal.

In the years prior to Coach Riggs, the football team practiced and trained under a more authoritative regime and a coach-athlete relationship was almost non-existent. So you can imagine my surprise when Roland Massey and I were invited over to the home of Coach Riggs and his wife Marie for dinner. And even more surprising was they asked us to bring our dates! Apparently the head coach, David Riggs and his wife Marie, wanted to get to know the seniors as more than just players. Imagine that! They wanted to impact our lives on and off the field.

Not only Coach Riggs, but the entire coaching staff, understood us, encouraged us and respected us as players, and in return, they earned our respect. Coach Riggs and the staff did not dictate and rule us through fear, but challenged us, talked to us, involved us and led us by example. They truly inspired us and empowered us as a football team.

In my opinion, the qualities that were captured in the making of a successful football team, made us unique as adults. The quality of the lives we've led through faith, success and failure, commitment and friendship, became apparent to me when we honored the passing of our friends and teammates, Roland Massey and Jim Bass. We as a team developed and implemented the Roland Massey Scholarship Fund and within two years we have awarded $15,000 to Broughton High School graduating athletes. The main contributors to the scholarship fund are the members of the 1970 Broughton Football Team, classmates and friends of Roland. We, as a collaborative effort, continue to provide support and funding in order to recognize the character displayed by Roland Massey throughout his life and career. Again, as a team, we came together to honor Jim Bass upon his recent passing. The number of teammates present at the memorial was inspirational. David Riggs, Rob Evans and John Thomas attended as members of the coaching staff in 1970. Jim Bass was a gifted athlete, a remarkable man who we admired as a high school and collegiate football player. We as teammates and classmates were again reunited in life and in memory of who we once were and what we once shared. Every handshake with a former player or friend became yet another reflection of our past, another story and now, a glimpse of where the future has taken us.

The most remarkable event with a teammate comes later in life with Roland Massey. In 1976, I was commissioned into the United States Marine Corps. I had become interested in a future in aviation while attending Elon College. After returning to Raleigh, prior to attending Naval Aviation Flight Training, I talked with Roland Massey about the potential, the challenges in becoming a Marine Officer and Naval Aviator. I distinctly remember describing Officer Candidate School as being similar to our high school football experiences. The physical demands, commitment to goals, the team work, character and self-sacrifice were key ingredients to success in a platoon, just like a football team. You rise or fall as a team and have to elevate the lowest common denominator to achieve success as a unit. Like coaches, the military was grooming leaders, not followers.

Believe it or not, approximately 1½ years or so later, I had completed flight school and Roland Massey had recently completed 12 weeks of Officer Candidate School and 9 months of The Basic School and was heading to Pensacola, Florida for naval flight training. But before Roland left on his assignment, he was heading to the altar to marry his high school sweetheart, Teeny Maughan. It was a military wedding with Marines in dress blue uniforms, sword arches and a joyful occasion for all, as again, we were reunited with the former teammates and friends from Broughton High School.

After completing approximately 6 years of flying in the Fleet Marine Corps, accumulating around 3,000 accident free flight hours each, I applied and was accepted to Marine Helicopter Squadron One. Roland soon followed and was accepted as we had similar careers, credentials as weapons and tactic instructors, fleet experience and our reputation qualified us for acceptance in the HMX-1 Squadron. The HMX-1 Squadron is stationed in Quantico, Virginia and tasked with Worldwide Helicopter Transportation for the President of the United States.

I served from 1985-1989 under President Reagan and President Bush and Roland served President Bush and President Clinton from 1989-1993. The squadron is tasked with many responsibilities, with Presidential service as the main goal. In the final year of a 4 year tour each pilot aspires to be selected as a Presidential Command Pilot, and both Roland and I departed the squadron as Presidential Command Pilots. For eight years, a member of our 1970 State Football Championship team served the President of the United States. We were both awarded the Presidential Service Badge. The odds of that being duplicated: infinitesimal! Roland and I both attributed our success in that environment to the experiences and friendships we had with our coaches and teammates at Broughton.

I continued my flying career with American Airlines, and Roland became an integral part of Wake Stone Corporation as the Safety Officer.

We both loved serving our country as United States Marines and we both wore the uniform of a Marine Officer with the utmost respect and pride. It was truly an honor representing the United States of America worldwide. We never took for granted the responsibility we had to represent and serve our state, our country and our families, teammates, classmates and friends from Broughton High School. It is amazing to reflect back on all the memories, friends and relationships that I have had over the years and realize that the coaches and members of a high school football team could have such an impact on my life. My life has truly been enriched because of the friendships and lessons I learned at such a young and impressionable age. It seemed that many of the players from the Broughton High School 1970 State Football Championship team were cut from the same cloth. Many distinguished men were molded from that Broughton High School Championship team. In addition, Roland, Doug Murray, Jim Bass, John Holding, Johnny Ford and I played on back to back Conference Championship baseball teams. I am thankful to have been a part of the victory, but more importantly a part of the team.

Preston, Kristin, and Kenan Ruth

In 1992, I married a Kansas farm girl I met while flying for American Airlines. I have lived in New Hill, just south of Raleigh on a horse farm since 1992. My wife, Kristin was a distinguished District Court Judge in Wake County and now she is in private practice with Smith Debnam Narron Drake Saintsing & Meyers, LLP in Raleigh. We have one son, Kenan, who is attending UNC Charlotte earning a criminal justice degree.

In closing, I would like to articulate an excerpt from the Roland Massey Scholarship Annual Senior Award Ceremony at Broughton High School: "The Roland Massey Scholarship Fund was forged from Broughton High School friendships and athletic endeavors that originated in the Holiday Gymnasium, 1968-1971. The fund is an example that Broughton High School friendships remain steadfast throughout life."

IN MEMORIAM: I would like to acknowledge Robbie Jones, Willis Price, Rick Eudy, and Sandy Goodwin who were part of the depth and character of the team.

### 46. MARK SHANER

*Senior---5' 9"---207---May be one of the best linemen in the area--- always hustling---good leader.*

Mark Shaner walked and played to a different drummer. He had long hair and a beard and did not look much like a football player to me. He was stocky and looked strong, which he was, but I would not have thought he was very good. However, you put him on that field, you better watch out. He was a very quick defensive nose guard for us. He got off the ball as fast as anyone we had and played with power. I am sure he put fear in a number of centers that he played against as well as a few of his own teammates - just ask Charles Banks.

Even though he looked like a hippie (uncommon for football players in 1970), he could play the game. He was one of the strongest players on the team, and he really had fun playing football. One of the great honors he received from his teammates was that they elected him and Jim Durham as captains as we began the season. I remember I would talk a lot to Mark to find out how the team was feeling and where the boys' heads were. He was a joy to coach and interesting to get to know as a person.

**Mark's Memories/Reflections:**

The entire thing was outstanding - the good, the bad, the ugly, the pain and heart break, and then the joy. We did what only we knew we could do. We did what seemed to some the impossible.

I will start this with a bit of history prior to the season of 1970. While in class one day, I got a call from Joel Long, the boys' counselor, who could have a book written about him all by itself. He was a great man and an excellent boys' counselor. I had been kicked off the Broughton football team with 3 games to go in 1969 as a junior, and it was for good reason. For reasons I thought were right at the time. In reality I was a victim of a bad attitude and wrong thinking and, as far as I was concerned, I was done with football at Broughton. It took some time and great people to help me extract my head from out of my rectum. However, a man like Joel Long has the ability to see something else in a person, and for some reason, he saw that in me. He called me into his office late in my junior year to ask me if I would be open to meeting with the new head football coach for Broughton for the coming fall 1970. We had that exchange where Joel Long gave me space and time to whine and tell him I had no interest in playing again, and he acted like he listened but did not really hear one word. He just said, "For me, will you just meet with him?" Because of my love and respect for Joel Long (of course which I never expressed to him), I said yes.

Mr. Long arranged that appointment a few days later and called me to his office to meet David Riggs. When I went to his office, I thought, *Where is the new coach? There is only a small young man in here.* Naturally that was David Riggs and I was as usual, trying to extract my foot from my mouth. Coach Riggs said a lot of things to me, but this was something I did remember. "I have looked at films - you can play the game and you are fast with regards to running but what were you eating last year? 'Cause near the end of the season you had gotten fat." Man, I loved that…someone no matter if they pissed you off, tells the truth.

Somewhere in that meeting, I decided to give it a try again and I asked Coach one simple question, "Coach Riggs, do you care if I come to practice next year with long hair and a beard?" His reply, which I wonder if he might have regretted later was, "I do not care if you wear a dress to practice, as long as you give me always 100%." In my mind at that moment, I decided to test this man and see if he was true to his word.

I also decided that if I was going to play again, that I was coming to the field in August in great shape ready to play. I had promised him 100% and he had promised me the freedom to be stupid. I was good with that.

Coach Riggs gave all those who might attend practice the next year a set of guidelines and what he expected. One of those was that linemen had to run the mile in a certain time before they could play; running and d-backs had to qualify at a harder level. I decided that I would run my time and be able to do that as a back and not as a lineman. I worked two jobs all that summer. One from 7:00 am to 3:30 pm (Thompson Construction). Then I would come home, change my clothes and go to the Broughton practice field every Monday – Friday, work out and run the mile from 4:00 pm to 6:00 pm and then go to my janitors job at 6:30 pm to 10:00 pm each day. When we finally had tryouts, I remember this and it was so funny: I was running the mile and Coach Evans was calling out times. As I went past him finishing my third lap, he called out, "You are way ahead - relax." I was running beside or near George Lattimore and I did not know he ran the mile in track but I remember thinking in my ignorance, *I am going to waste this guy.* So I keep the pace and started picking it up as we were rounding the third turn; George was with me at every step and would not let me pull away. Then I thought, *I have a good kick and I will blow him out in the last 100 yards,* so when I got there, I kicked it in and guess what? George kicked in with me and blew my socks off. I was disappointed. I did not care if I had a great time from Coach Evans. I just got beat. However George said to me after we had finished, "Man, I did not know you could run like that. You need to come out for track and run the mile because you gave me all I wanted and I have run the mile for years." Just like me to pick out someone like that to compete with. However after many life-long years, I finally figured out that I was one twisted type A personality…so I have adjusted and I live with it and I like it. My children say that my often used line with them when they were growing up was, "What the hell were you thinking when you…?"

So here I was with long hair that I had not cut in 4-5 months and a beard (no dress) but if I had it to do over again, I would have worn the dress to try to get to Coach. But he did stick to his word as practice started. My first shock came when we voted for team captains. I had no idea on this earth that I might be voted by my teammates to be a captain. Hell, I did not even vote for me. I was sure based on the past that this would never happen, but for some crazy reason that only GOD knows, I was voted as a team captain with Jimmy Durham. I think what saved me was that I was in great shape and was totally out front that entire first two weeks, and my teammates saw that, respected it and had trust and faith in me that I am not sure I had in myself. I think this might have really been the start of the "magic" - it was a magical season for we did what some thought was impossible.

My next memory was this: we would have these 4 station 15 minutes drills of constant movement and then break for rest and water. When I was going to get water, Coach Riggs called me over and said, "I want to ask you something. How does the team and you feel about our chances this year?" I did not hesitate and I do not know why but I said, "Coach, we are going to win it all." His reply was, "Mark, I am serious about this." I repeated myself. I know why he asked me again because I was so full of it most of the time and playing around so much that he thought I did not take his question seriously, but I very much did. I remember thinking (but never would I say this to the new coach - we did not have this relationship yet), *If you don't believe it then you should pack up and leave now.* I was a bit of a twisted type A personality.

Coach Riggs was such a different man than I was used to as a coach in the past. He was a religious man, loved his faith and did not try to hide that. When Coach was really pissed off, he would start to say "dang it" and "darn it" and beat his fist into his open hand and you knew for him to get to that point, he was a bit warm. Coach instilled in us that whoever was in the best shape physically and mentally when the fourth quarter of the game started would win the game. We bought into that thinking, hook, line and sinker. At the end of practice we had 4th quarter drills of constant movement. However some of us got a taste of 5th quarter. This was the Riggs' quarter of punishment for anything against the rules: being late for practice or whatever, but for me, it was mostly for cussing which he hated.

One day during the season I was with Coach Thomas who was the defensive coach and we were going over some drills and the offense of the next team we were to play and we were not getting it done. I was a defensive player and defensive captain and when it was not going good for us in practice, I would take it a bit personally. So on this particular hot day, I looked around to see where Coach Riggs was since he was the offensive and d-back coach. I knew that if we kept screwing this up, I was going to blow a fuse and Coach Thomas might let me get away with that but not Coach Riggs. I saw that he was down at the other end of the field about 100 yards away so I felt safe. (5$^{th}$ quarter was hell.) We continued to screw up the defensive assignment and I came undone and started the colorful language and expressions of a sick twisted A personality when I heard these words, "Well, Shaner, you have 5$^{th}$ quarter. Do you want to try for the 6$^{th}$ quarter?" I was so freaked out as to how he knew that I was about to explode and had walked up behind our practice with his little black book that your name went into when you earned the extra love and the 5$^{th}$ quarter. I almost started to cuss about that until I caught myself and just said, "No, Coach." But when he left, I just looked at Coach Thomas and said, "How the hell did he know when to come here? Is my helmet tapped for sound?"... However, I was also a bit impressed...

THE SEASON STARTS:

In my honest opinion, we should have either been undefeated for the year or, at the worst, one loss. 9-1 before the playoffs.

We started with Greensboro Grimsley and we had total control of that game. We were up 7-0 with seconds left and all we had to do was punt the ball. I knew we could hold them on defense as we had done that all night. However the punt was blocked and carried into the end zone and then we blew the 2 point conversion assignment and lost 8-7. That was due to a lineman blocking to the outside and not the inside on punt formation. We had practice the next week and on Monday Coach sent everyone in but the punt team and they started another practice on punt blocking assignments. When I came out of the locker room after showering and dressing, it had become dark and Coach had moved the punt team to the high school parking lot and I remember thinking, *That will never happen again - he is not too fond of mistakes.* We are 0-1.

Next week we played Winston Salem Reynolds. We beat them and punished them for the failure we had the week before. After the game I got to visit with their quarterback as he wanted to talk about my beard…yes, I still had the long hair and beard (I was really testing poor Coach Riggs. I was a butthead.). Their QB and I talked a few times over the year and he was recruited to Duke. He said to me, "That was a tough game for us. Our coach said you guys were average but you pushed us around the field all night long and I was pressured in the backfield all night long. You have a good team and you gave us a butt kicking." So I had some hope for the future. We are now 1-1.

The 4th game we play Rocky Mount and for some reason Coach moved me to tackle in that game. I had a terrible game and we lost that game in the last seconds. It was a strange game with not much defense and high scoring offense and we took the lead with only a minute and seconds to go with a field goal. Then we allowed them to get a touchdown due to a defensive letdown in the last seconds and we lost. I was miserable.

The Monday after that game and going into the new week, Coach Riggs stopped me in the area outside his office after practice and said he wanted to talk to me. To set this up, you have to realize by now that I had developed a deep love for Coach Riggs and a deep respect for him. I would do anything for him. He was a hero to me and my father figure that I did not have the luxury of enjoying. He said to me, "Mark, you are not doing your job." You could have cut me with a knife and I would not have hurt as much as it did right then. They had this All Metro Team Pick each week and I think I had made that team each week. I said, "Coach, what more do you want me to do? I am playing my ass off." I might not have said "ass" because that would have been 5$^{th}$ quarter, but I was in shock. Coach said to me, "That is not your job to lead the team in stats. You are not here to be great and have great stats. As captain, your job is to see that all other people who play, especially on defense, play better than they are, even if you have to turn it down a notch." I was so confused as a 17 year old kid who only wanted to win. I thought I was doing what I needed to do. I sulked a day or two and decided he was right. I totally changed my approach to the game and with my teammates and it started to jell for us after the Wilson game that was that very week. I was introduced to the concept of sacrifice. Coach taught me a very valuable life lesson that I have never forgotten to this day and I am so glad he had the balls to tell me the truth and to care about me. It is not about you, it is about us. From that point on, I was really his to direct in whatever way he chose. He probably does not remember this, but I believe it was truly inspired from someone other than him.

During the early part of that same week at practice, Coach Evans said to me, "After our coaches' meeting today, you will be moved back to inside linebacker and nose guard depending on the defense used because you like to roam too much and you don't stay at home which you have to do as a tackle." He said to me, "You are just a head hunter." I remember thinking, *Yes, I am looking for something to kill.*

When we played Hillside I was so sick. I had a temperature of around 102 to 103 but I told Coach I was going to play but if we got up, then to take me out. We were beating them, so late in the third or early in the 4$^{th}$ quarter, Coach pulled me out of the game and told me to take a seat. We then had an offensive series and back to defense. After a few plays for the defense, Coach comes up to me and says, "You have to go back into the game. We are too thin - the defensive alignment is not right and you are the glue so you have to go back in." I just said, "Ok." I remember thinking, *One more score here and I can just stay on the bench. Coach will not care.* So I did a stunt and when I entered the backfield, I saw the quarterback handing off the ball to the halfback. So I decided to just go between them and steal the handoff which I did. I took the handoff and I was gone - it was clean and I had gone about 15 yards towards their goal when you hear that whistle that stops all plays. I turn around and start to head back to the referee who again are not my most loved people and he said to me, "I am not going to give you that….it was too easy…you guys have been handling this team all night long. I will give you the loss at the point of contact but not the ball." If I had not been sick, I think I would have gotten thrown out of that game but I just started laughing and the referee did also and so that was the end of that. Coach asked me later when that defensive series ended what happened and I just said, "I do not know." I finished the entire game but that was funny.

Our 6th game we played Wilson Fike and I hated Wilson Fike. They had been the king on the block for a while and my relatives lived in that area. (Most of all, I knew we should have been 3-0 when we played them, not 1-2.) We controlled that entire game and scored first. They tied us at 7-7. I had hit their quarterback as hard as humanly possible for me earlier in the game and he left the game. Late in the game when his team started to drive the ball, he had a miraculous healing and came back into the game when they were on about the 30 yard line. With all diplomacy I called him a "puss" and said, "If I get to you again, you will not come back into this game." I had a bead on him and hit him damn good but he still released the ball before the hit and it was a touchdown...we lose again...we are 3-3. This is probably the only team that legitimately beat us the entire season.

I was now physically, spiritually and emotionally sick. I remember the feelings still to this day. My stomach actually hurt. I think I cried for about 2 hours that night and I do not think I got over it for days. I do remember that Coach Riggs tried to console me but I could not be consoled and I just told him this, "Coach, only good is going to come out of this," and it did.

The only game we lost after that was to Fayetteville Terry Sanford at their home. We changed our offense and defense because we gave them way too much respect. At half time it was 7-7 but in the second half with guys playing a new offense and defense that we had not done all season and had to learn in 4 days, the wheels just came off with multiple mistakes and we lost 28-7. We were by then 4-4, playing 500 ball as we had some other wins and there were two conference games left on the schedule.

Coach Riggs was about a perfect coach all year but that game was his only mistake. After that Wilson game loss, we came together in a way we did not know about until later. You can only recognize magic and blessings after they happen. We were ready to beat anyone and Coach did not know that and we might not have known that either. But it was so. We never lost again all the way to the 4-A State Championship.

Jim Lumsden got his knee torn up in the Sanford game which was a big loss because you could always depend on him to be where he was supposed to be and that made it easier for me as a roaming idiot. It was a big loss and I hated to be without him.

However this final road was not going to be easy. We had conference games at the end of the regular season. We had to win them all to win our conference. At that time only the conference winner went into the playoffs and everyone else went home. We played Ligon at home and

PLAY WITH YOUR HEARTS 303

shut them out defensively. We are 4-0 in the conference and we play Durham the next week at home. We beat them 14-0, shut them out and now we were 6-4 overall and 5-0 in the conference.

There is a funny story about Steve Brewbaker in the Durham game. He was responsible for a lot of our success and never really got the praise from the media he deserved. He played both ways offense and defense and was always productive. Durham was undefeated in the conference before we played them so it was us or them who would make the playoffs. Near the end of the third quarter, the referee calls a timeout on his own, comes to me and says, "I want to talk with you." He says, "I need you to do me a favor. I want you to ask your defensive tackle to ease up on the guy in front of him for the rest of the night." I was a bit shocked and so I basically gave his words back to him, "You want me to go into our huddle and ask one of our players to take it easy on the guy in front of him, is that right?" He said, "Come with me." He took me to the offensive huddle of the Durham team and told the guy who was playing offensive tackle in front of Steve Brewbaker to lift up his jersey. This kid's stomach was purple from the forearm that Steve was punishing him with all night long. I asked the referee, "Is our player doing anything illegal?" He said, "No." "Well, I will tell him and let you know how he feels." I was almost cracking up inside to go back to the huddle and tell Brewbaker about this because I already knew the response. So I told Steve and he kind of turned to me with this look of total disbelief and basically said, "You tell those - - - - if they cannot play the game to put someone else in front of me who can." "Ok, Brew, I will be right back." I delivered the message from Brew to the referee which, due to my twisted A personality, I so loved and he said, "OK." There was one more play and that guy was gone to the bench. A new guy came into face the BREW and I never heard any more about that. I felt sorry for that guy. We win, we are 6-4 but 5-0 in our conference, having beaten Enloe, Sanderson, Hillside, Ligon and finally Durham in the conference.

We are in the first round of the playoff against Greensboro Dudley. We start practice for the week and Coach Thomas brings out their plays after we watched films and says they run something we are going to call "the elephant." Who knows why, but it was an uneven back field to the strong side. So during the week we are going over their plays and making sure we have our defensive assignments. After looking at this thing for about 2 days, I said, "Coach Thomas, every time they do this shift and uneven back field, they run to that side." He said, "You cannot say that because they can easily run to the other side," and he was correct in that but after two more days, when none of their plays went to the other side, I brought it up again. He corrected me again and looked a bit frustrated with me. I know now that he wanted me to play this straight up, not play averages and take chances and that is 100% true in college but this team had a bad tendency.

I decide that at game time I was going to test slanting towards the strength and cheat. It was like shooting fish in a barrel. We were up 22-0 at halftime. Our offense was clicking on all fours. We had their defensive number and it was over.

Another funny thing happened in the second half when the team started to run all pass plays with trips and we went into a spread defense which put me in pass coverage. Well, a guy like me in pass coverage - even if I could catch, I had so much tape and pads on my arms and hands that it was almost impossible. Well, there I was in pass coverage and no one was open, so the receivers had gone deeper and deeper, the line was pressing the quarterback and he let it go right at me about 25-30 yards deep downfield. I went to intercept and lost the ball as it hit my hands. Well, right behind me was Preston Ruth set up to make the interception (I could not see that) and he proceeded to give me hell about that and why I had gotten in the way of his interception. Remember: an interception to a d-back is like a hard sack on the blind side of a quarterback to a lineman.

Preston Ruth was the very best. I saw him do something one night; I think it was the Goldsboro play-off game but it might have been Durham but it has been 45 years. It was a passing down, third down and long, and we had pressure on. I got blocked and could only get a hand on the QB. Just as he released the ball, I looked upfield and the receiver had button hooked back towards the sidelines and the ball was coming into him just above belt high. Preston was filling extremely fast and the referee was right beside the receiver at the sidelines and I remember thinking, *This is going to be interference.* Just at that moment Preston Ruth jumped completely over the receiver with his legs pointed forward so as not to hit him and, as he was going over the top of the receiver, he bent down or bent forward and intercepted the ball. The referee could not believe what he had just seen nor could I. It was one of those special amazing moments. He was a real athlete and played with full heart. Preston Ruth almost did not play that year. He had a bad knee from baseball and he was told if he injured it again, he would not be able to play baseball, and that was his love. So we talked and he told me he had decided to quit and he was telling the team the next day. However he could not live with that decision, changed his mind and decided to hell with the knee. "I am in!" and that was a blessing.

After our first playoff game, we had had 3 shut out games in a row. Ligon, Durham, Greensboro Dudley and now it is time to face the "Beast of the East" Goldsboro which had only lost one game. They came to our town and dressed at our school for our game at Devereux Meadow. They were in the gym after they dressed and we were we on the opposite side of the gym - they were talking about us and laughing at us. I remember thinking, *These turds are ripe for the picking and we are going to do that to them.* We win 6-0 and are headed to the Finals at Carter Finley Stadium.

That game with Goldsboro was like a war. One time in that game as I was running down their quarterback who went out of bounds on their sideline, before I had the joy or opportunity of breaking him, the Goldsboro head coach yelled at me (he was only about 10 feet from me), "Hell, Shaner, why don't you hit somebody?" I was shocked that he even knew my name and wondered, *what the hell does he mean by that?* and so I decide to fulfill all his dreams with the hope that I might get another sideline shot near him but that never happened.

If you play defense, you live for the hit and you love any hit, no matter where it comes from, offense or defense. That night in the second half, I was on the sidelines near mid-field watching the offense when I saw a blitzing linebacker coming through the line. I saw who I thought was John Clarke who did not have a man on him. We were passing the ball and our quarterback David was in the pocket; John had peeled back with his back towards our sidelines and the linebacker never saw him sitting in that frog position. John exploded into this linebacker's ribs and

DAVID RIGGS

hit him so hard that it lifted him off the ground. I got so excited about that awesome hit, I almost ran on the field. I wanted our offense to bog down so that the defense could get back on the field and hit like that and do some spanking. Is that nuts or what? We needed points.

We played our ass off in that game and the coaches saved the game. They had discerned that a 25 dive to Jim bass on the left side of the offensive line broken to the outside would go all the way. I call it a 25 dive (it probably had another name) but it was Jim Bass over the tackle, broken immediately to the side lines. When the second half started, it was 0-0 and it was a defensive war. I remember thinking if this does not work, Jim Bass is going to be dead as Goldsboro had one hell of a large defensive line. The first time we got the ball, we ran that play according to Coach Riggs' directions each time on the first series until it worked. I remember it did not work the first time but on $2^{nd}$ or $3^{rd}$ down, I saw Jim Bass disappear and I could not see him for a second as the offensive was on the 20 yard line or so on the Goldsboro side of the field. But then I saw fans on the Goldsboro side stand up and shouting. I knew then it was a race and no one could catch Jim. He went the distance for 6 points, compliments of the offensive line, Jim Bass and the coaches' plan.

Later in that game late in the $4^{th}$ quarter, Goldsboro started a drive. We had missed the extra point when we scored and I knew if they scored, we would lose. It was their only real sustained drive for the night. They finally drove the ball down to around the 30 yard line and we stopped them short on third down. They had to go for it as it was very late now in the $4^{th}$ quarter. (Coach will not like hearing this and I have never told it but to a few.) They called a time out and then after that, lined up in the offensive formation to run the play for the first down.

Have you ever had one of those experiences that seems to take minutes but only lasts a few seconds? We were in a 4-4 defense and I was an inside up linebacker. I looked at the running back who lined up on the right side, facing the defense and he was staring at the left side of the defensive line and I wondered why...then it came to me like lightening...this guy looks where he is going to run...I made a crazy, instant decision. If I was wrong, it could have cost us the game. I abandon my responsibility when the ball was snapped and move immediately around my guys to the left side of the line, leaving a hole where I should have been. When I made the turn into the backfield, there was my sweet little man with the ball and I gave him a big, loving hug about 2 yards deep in the backfield. End of game. We took over on offense and ran the clock out. Hello, Finals and Carter Finley Stadium in Raleigh, NC and, hello, Charlotte, who we played.

The Finals were won before we ever took the field. I remember watching our guys getting dressed at the stadium at NCSU and I remember seeing Jim Little and Kent Kistler putting on slings when they were getting dressed. I said, "What the hell are you guys wearing?" They took that opportunity to tell me about how defense got all the glory and they did all the work with no mention and that they had both separated their shoulders so many times during the season that if they lifted their arms too high that they would come out of joint. The harnesses were there to keep them from lifting their arms during the game and to stop them from automatically being dislocated. They are my kind of hero. I love that story and these guys were often outweighed by 50 or more pounds but they always did the job. Their hearts were way too big for their bodies.

Coach Evans had come up to me that day before the game in the locker room and asked me what I thought and I told him this game was over. The job had been done and we were here just to finish. He confirmed that to me and said he had only seen a locker room like this a few times in the past - it was the attitude that "this game is done and over and we lose to no one." Coach Evans was so right. All week long at practice all we heard about was Cook and Rhino from Charlotte and how good they were. I got so sick of hearing their names that I told our defensive coach that they put their pants on like everyone else and that the end results would be the same.

The first time we got the ball in the first half, the offensive team took the ball down the field again and scored. I watched from the sidelines and they looked like a well-oiled machine. It was amazing. When the defense took the field after the kickoff, Coach Riggs got hit in the throat by a kicking tee thrown off the field by George Lattimore (actually, it was thrown off by the referee). He was down on the sidelines and I did not know. First play for us on defense, I was a down nose guard and we were in a 5-3. I on purpose jumped through the right gap expecting a run to one of the great ones. It was absolutely right and I picked him up, slammed him to the ground as hard as possible and told him, "All day long, big boy." It cost us 5 yards. I looked to the sidelines to get the defensive signs and to see if coach was looking in my direction about the offside. I could not find him because he was on the ground hurt from the kicking tee that I still did not know about. Next play from scrimmage it was 2$^{nd}$ and five and with these two hot dog running backs, I figured it will be a running play. Jumped the ball again to the strong side like last time and, yes, there was the other running back with the ball. I hit him hard but could not slam him down as the referee was quick on that whistle after my last fun event. Well, that was another offside penalty, 5 more yards and a first down. I had the audacity to go to the line referee and ask him, "Am I lining up offsides or am I jumping the snap?" He said, "You are jumping the snap." I said, "Well, make sure, Referee, because I am pretty fast." What a bunch of BS...I was doing it to send the message. However, my great teammate Steve Brewbaker gave me hell about jumping offsides twice and asked me if I was going to personally escort them to the end zone, so that had to be the last time for that.

At half time it was 7-0. The first time our offense took the ball in the second half, they marched down the field like a well-oiled machine and scored again. It was 14-0 and that is how the game ended. We shut out the last two regular season conference teams we had to beat and all 3 teams we played in the playoffs for 5 shutouts in a row. Hard to lose when you give up no points. We peaked and matured as a team at the perfect time.

The game is over and everyone is happy yet what I remember most that struck me deeply was the look of loss and disappointment and sadness on the faces of the team we had beaten. Over the years since, I have coached a lot but mostly baseball because my one year in the local high school where we lived when I helped coach a 9$^{th}$ grade team that was 9-1, it was decided by the school board (not the head coach or the team) that I was a bit too aggressive.

I have won many playoffs games as a coach and a State Title for Babe Ruth baseball but when we were not successful, I took every loss home with me. Many times I experienced the feelings I saw that day on the field of the team we beat for the 4-A State Championship. I then also knew how our coaches felt and especially Coach Riggs when we lost. When we were struggling in the early part of the season, Coach got a few letters from older fans who had gone to Broughton and they were not very supportive, to say the least. He read all of those to us which was probably around the Rocky Mount or Wilson Fike game. It was a blessing to get the criticism.

I never told Coach this and I wish I had. I got a letter of intent from Duke University. It was a bit intimidating for me and I did not respond. I had the SAT grades to attend, 1150, but I also felt that it was too close to home. I got another letter when I did not answer the first one and later after that, a call from the quarterback from Winston Salem Reynolds who told me he was going there and wanted to know why I had not responded. I just told him I was thinking about it. I was not the brightest light on the porch and these type things were not up for discussion in my home. I should have gone to Coach. I went to Western Carolina University as a walk-on where 53 people tried out; they took 3 of us and I was one. I played one year, got offered a scholarship at the end of the year, turned that down, went home and never went back to college again. My experience in college and why I left is another whole book.

What I Learned From The Season:

Never to stop, never to give up, never to quit. To keep the goal in front of you and focus on that, not things along the way towards that goal which try to take the momentum away from you. I sometimes hate the word "love" because it is abused so much in our society today, but I learned to love my teammates. The definition of love is simple: you want the very best for someone, you want to assist them to accomplish their goals and dreams, you do not want them to get hurt or sidetracked in any way. You want them to have joy and happiness and success. You do all that you can to support them and not to get in the way. You learn to SACRIFICE yourself to help others achieve. I learned to lay it on the line and to go for it and not hold anything back and not to worry about the consequences or failure, as that will take care of itself. You cannot feel too bad, even if you fail, when you give it everything you got.

I also learned that I loved my Coach and why. Because he first loved me and wanted all the things above for me. Coach Riggs was our success; he was not much older than us and he understood us. He always stuck to his guns and his rules and I liked that. He was a good man, an honest man, and he did what he said he would do. He was a faithful man and a righteous man and it had a big impact on me later in life. I have thought about him often over the last 45 years. I learned to be obedient and to follow the plan…that is hard for a twisted type A personality.

He never did ask me to cut my hair or beard. He only told me one time that it would hurt my chances to get a scholarship to play because those type of things scared coaches. I finally did trim the hair and shave, not because of any scholarship pressure because that made me want to keep it longer, but because Coach won. I could not break him or make him go against his word in Mr. Long's Boys' Counselor office. When I realized that, then I was done with all of that. Coach is my hero and he will always be my hero. He also has a great wife Marie and I always love her as well and their commitment to their marriage and each other.

**Mark's Bio:**

My life after my first year in college has been one large "4$^{th}$ quarter." I decided that I always wanted to work for myself as I am psychologically un-employable. So I became an entrepreneur and have had many businesses over the years. Some I made great money and success in and some I lost everything. My sons all said they were not going to do that, because it was always feast or famine. However as they have gotten older in life, all of them seem to have a desire to work for themselves. It is in the gene pool, I am afraid.

I met a great, young woman from Bailey, NC who was 5 years younger than me named Jane Elizabeth Finch and we got married on July 1st, 1978 when I was 25 years old in Raleigh, NC. We lived in the Raleigh area until I was around 35 and then we moved to Iowa, the heart of the Mid-West. I always tell everyone I had to go out of town to find someone who did not know me, to be able to get married.

We have been faithful to each other and have enjoyed this mortal, earthly journey together for 38 years, and it has been almost the best thing I have ever done. We have 4 boys and 4 girls and 10 grandchildren who have lived all over the world. They live in these states: Utah, Arizona, Colorado, Hawaii, and Missouri. It costs a fortune to visit them and we do not get to have them around as much as we want. They all call me the "mean granddad" because I always pick on them but they seem to love the attention.

Marriage and family have been a great blessing to me and that is because of my faith. One year after being married we had the opportunity to investigate the Church of Jesus Christ of Latter Day Saints (known as Mormons). We felt that what we were taught was the truth and so we joined early in our lives and early in our marriage. We have been faithful to that commitment for 37 years and it has enhanced our marriage and family. The children are all much better than their dad, and it is because of their great mother who has always sacrificed so much for them and put their needs way ahead of hers. She is truly a mother in Zion. I do not think I would trade my life's experience for anything. It was good for me.

Thank you, Coach Riggs, Coach Evans and Coach Thomas.

Thank you, teammates, who gave it everything and never quit or gave up. It was great to be part of that.

Thank you to the Broughton students and parents who always supported us and did not give up on us, even when it looked hopeless.

Finally, thanks to the team managers and trainers who made it all possible with their unselfish dedication to the cause. They were never given the praise they deserved.

Mark and Jane Shaner

## 47. ASHLEIGH SPAIN

*Senior---5'11"---175---Inexperienced---Has picked up some speed.*

Ashleigh played in our line for the 1970 team. He played sparingly, but did give good effort in all practices. Due to his work ethic and desire to help, he made us a better team by being so conscientious about doing his best in practice and on the scout team. He, like many others, served this team well and helped us become what we were—Champs.

### Ashleigh's Memories/Reflections:

Ashleigh did not play football until he was a sophomore. He loved baseball and played on the Broughton baseball team all three years. He actually went out for the football team on a dare by a friend and made the team as a lineman. He appreciates making good friends with several other players. He remembers playing in the State Championship game at Carter Finley Stadium and that still stands as quite a highlight of that season for him. Yet, one of the best memories he has was his role of always preparing himself and his teammates for games that year. Ashleigh feels he learned to always be his best and help others to do the same and that is what we saw he did in practice. He saw himself as one who helped the team to prepare for and be at their best for the Friday night games. He and his dad used to talk about this goal of "doing his best" in all he did and that served him well that particular year as well as into his future.

### Ashleigh's Bio:

After graduating from Broughton in 1971, Ashleigh joined the National Guard. He attended UNC-Wilmington for a year, then due to his love for metal work, started his own blacksmith business. After working with horses in his business for a couple years, he got a position with UPS in 1975 and worked with them until 2015 when he retired. Ashleigh married his wife Jo Ann in 1981 and has been happily married for 35 years. They have one daughter Kacy (30) and one son Justin (33) and both live nearby in Raleigh area. Ashleigh appreciates the friendships he gained from playing sports during his high school years. He did martial arts for over 15 years, but like most of us, his body cannot handle that now. He loves to fish and hike and being outdoors in his retirement years.

## 48. GARY STAINBACK
*Senior---6'---163---good hands at split end---Good kicker.*

Gary played wide receiver for us and was our extra point kicker and also served as our kick off person early in the season. Gary was a key man in our kicking game because he could often put the football in the end zone when he kicked off. That made a huge difference for us since it would make our opponent begin on the 20 yard-line and give us good field position to begin the game.

### Gary's Memories/Reflections:

Reflecting on that high school senior year, I recall initially the uncertainty among several of the players because of the change in the football coaching staff. However after the training began near the beginning of the school year, those concerns were put aside very quickly. As with each new season of a sport, there's always positioning where players are trying to fulfill their desire to play a particular position. This too took place, but the 4th Quarter drills were a real surprise. Here we are working our rear ends off, and then expecting the practice session to come to a close and you suddenly hear, "4th Quarter Drills.'" And the end of practice, drills start all over again. As hard as that was, it paid off in the end.

Players on the team played their best, and some suffered injury either during practice or a game. We lost games during the year, however peaked in our team performance when it really counted. I believe those 4th quarter drills were a big part of that late season peaking. We saw the players on the other team breathing more deeply, gasping for breath, and we believed we were in better shape physically such that we could overcome any odds, particularly in that 4th quarter.

The lessons I learned from that season have stayed with me since:

1. Put forth your best efforts and no one can fault you.

2. Prepare, prepare, prepare, and develop a plan.

3. Stay alert, particularly for the unexpected.

4. Enjoy the moment. After all, it's just a game.

I was very fortunate to be part of this team, and to have been taught by the coaching staff.

### Gary's Bio:

After graduating from Needham B. Broughton High School, I graduated from East Carolina University with a major in Psychology and minor in Mathematics. During my senior year at ECU I married Teresa Ann Owens. After graduating from ECU, I worked in a mental health center in eastern N. C. for a couple of years, then began working on a Master's Degree and Certificate of Advanced Study in School Psychology from East Carolina University. After completing that degree, I went on to obtain a Doctorate in School Psychology from N.C. State University. While completing my Master's Degree, I switched working from mental health to the public schools (New Bern City Schools), and finished the Doctorate while working for the Tarboro City Schools as their Exceptional Children's Program Director. I then moved to a job with East Carolina University, Brody School of Medicine, Department of Pediatrics as a Senior Psychologist (PhD position).

Stainback - Gary Stainback

I was an assistant director for the Greenville Developmental Evaluation Center, and performed evaluations on children and young adults who had suspected or known serious developmental delays. Some years later I became Director of the Center, when there was a merger of these centers with the Early Intervention Program in North Carolina. I retired from that organization (Greenville Center for Developmental Services Agency, or CDSA) with 36 years of state service. While retired, I still do some teaching for the ECU Psychology Department, typically teaching developmental psychology, introduction to psychological testing, and abnormal psychology.

While I was working on my doctorate in psychology, my wife Teresa and I had our first child Amanda who is now married and has two wonderful grandchildren for Teresa and I to indulge. Our second daughter Betsy is another joy in our life, and has two children as well. Altogether Teresa and I have two boys and two girls as grandchildren, which keep our lives fairly busy.

### 49. BILL "BILLY" STARLING

*Senior---6'2"---180—Letterman----Looks good at split end and safety----Has good speed and can catch the football.*

"Billy" was one of our wide receivers. He had good speed and was really our main deep threat along with Eric Handy. Because of his hands and speed he won the starting position at wide receiver. Billy ran very good routes in our passing game and could adjust to defenses we ran up against. He led Broughton in both 1969 and 1970 in receptions and he was an outstanding blocker from his wide receiver position. Billy had more than his share of struggles and challenges in his youth and growing up in Raleigh. However, in many times has worked and persevered through life and has been very successful in all he has done. Billy has a very friendly personality and that has carried him through his high school, college, and adult life.

I met Billy at the Hilton at RDU over 6 years ago for breakfast to catch up. He was one of the first interviews I had for this book and he gave me motivation and encouragement to write the story about the 1970 Champions. He was very open with his life and the stories he had from that season.

### Bill's Memoirs/Reflections:

Billy came from a tough and complex family background. His mother and father divorced when he was about 13 while attending Daniels Jr. High School. His father was an alcoholic and his mother was bipolar. He said when the divorce happened he was upset and in a way looked down on because most parents did not get divorced, especially parents who had children at Daniels and Broughton. They lived in North Hills and had to move from a large nice home to a small apartment in Cameron Village. It was embarrassing for a young teenager. As he went to Broughton, he escaped all "bad" family happenings by pouring himself into athletics. He played football, basketball, and track in high school and was a "super jock" in many ways. He had several girlfriends and was popular.

Bill does not remember there being any racial problems at Broughton, especially among his teammates. He remembers having Butch Rochelle, who was a black teammate from their basketball team, over to his apartment at Cameron Village to spend the night, and when his mother was out of town he would allow Butch to bring his white girlfriend to his apartment.

A couple things stand out to Bill about the Championship team. One Friday night early in the season when we were 1-3, he had several other players over to his apartment and they were all partying and drinking. They were not celebrating the losses, but they were just having a party. He says he will never forget that Preston Ruth, who was our safety, came in and told all of them they should be ashamed of themselves drinking and partying in football season. Preston insisted that this was not going to help "us" be winners. That night Bill said it helped him to focus on the right things and improving the football team. Preston and his actions that night had a lasting impact on him.

Bill told me the story how he got his chipped tooth, which he still has, by trying to tackle Jim Bass in an early two-a-day one on one tackling drill. Robbie Evans, one of our assistant coaches, had babysat Billy and his brother when Robbie was 17 or 18 and Billy was 11 or 12. They lived in the same neighborhood as they were growing up, and who would have ever thought that a few years later that "Coach" Evans would be coaching Billy at Broughton?

Bill feels like he learned a lot about life in that football season. He remembers the story I told about my playing days at Carolina and how I felt like I had cost UNC the game with Wake Forest my senior year. I was playing defensive back and a Wake Forest back was carrying the ball on the other side of the field from me, and I figured that someone else was surely going to make the tackle. However, the tackle was missed and

I had slowed down and practically quit running, thinking that someone else would make the play. Bill says that I really emphasized that we at Broughton could not have my attitude on that play if we were going to be winners and hustlers.

The Goldsboro game was the semifinal game of the 1970 state playoffs. Bill remembers me talking to the team about not having any "mouthing" going on and to play with respect toward Goldsboro and their All-State running back Bobby Myrick. On the opening kickoff, Bill was covering down the field and was clipped in the back of the legs by Myrick, but the penalty was not called. Bill recalls being really angry and was tempted to go and try to knock Myrick's head off. However, instead Billy got up and hit him on his shoulder pads and said, "Good block."

I remember the great catch Billy made in the Championship game at Carter Stadium against Olympic High School. Roland Massey was our wingback and was left-handed. In the middle of the game, I had called a halfback pass from Roland to Billy, and it was a crucial play because it set up our second and last touchdown that game. Billy lined up wrong on the left side of the formation instead of the right side. When he realized this and that Roland was coming toward his side, he was alert and football savvy enough to run a route that would put him where he needed to be for the pass, and he did. He made a great catch on our 14-yard line, and two plays later we were in the end zone.

The highlight of his high school life was athletics, especially the State Championship season his senior year.

He had wanted to go to the University of North Carolina after high school, but did not get in, and he was crushed. He went to East Carolina for two years and finally did transfer to North Carolina where he graduated with a business degree. He married his high school girlfriend and left North Carolina and went to California to start life anew, in many ways wanting to get away from his family life.

He got his Masters at Stanford University in Palo Alto, California. Not long after this he and his wife divorced. He met Dana, his present wife, and she is "the love of his life." They have two amazing, bright and loving sons, Greg and Tyler. Sadly, Tyler unexpectedly and tragically died in 2015.

Bill is a creative brilliant thinker and instrumental in a think tank that has focused on heart transplants, defibrillators, and research for heart diseases. His dad died in the early 1990's and his mother committed suicide in 1998. Chris Morgan, who played on the State Championship team with Bill, was the investigating officer and detective in his mother's suicide. Bill mentioned that Chris had written him a note explaining the death of his mother and how she did not suffer. That meant a lot to Bill and he was appreciative of Chris's sensitivity, even though they had not seen each other in years.

In 1996, Bill was flying all over the world with his business and work and was in London, England for the wedding of his friend and former teammate David Dupree. Preston Ruth and Jim Lumsden, other teammates from that 1970 team, were also in attendance at the wedding. It is amazing to me that all these men were busy with their own lives but had kept up with one another enough to be part of David's wedding in England. David and Bill both have been extremely successful in the business world and have spoken on the same program to the UNC Business School.

A few years ago, Bill served on the UNC Business School Board of Directors with a man from Greensboro. They got to talking and found out they were playing high school sports in 1970. Billy asked him if he played football and he said yes, he had played for Dudley High School in Greensboro. Billy asked him if he remembered the quarterfinal game of the state finals that year; he grimaced and said he was shocked that Broughton had won and it still hurt over 40 years later.

**Bill's Bio:**

Bill received his BSBA degree from the University of North Carolina at Chapel Hill and his MBA degree from the University of Southern California. He began his 39-year career in the medical technology device industry at American Edwards Laboratories. He was subsequently part of the founding management team and Director of Marketing for Advanced Cardiovascular Systems, Inc. and was cofounder, Vice President and Board member of Ventritex, Inc. (acquired by St. Jude Medical in 1997). He was cofounder and Chairman of the Board of Directors and President/CEO of Cardiac Pathways Corporation (acquired by Boston Scientific Corporation in 2001).

Bill has has made outstanding contributions in the medical device technology industry over his professional career. Bill is CEO of Synecor Company, a business generator of new Life Science companies based in the Research Triangle Park. As CEO of Synecor, Mr. Starling is a cofounder of and continues to play integral roles in the initial eight companies founded and incubated by Synecor: BaroSense, Inc., Bioerodible Vascular Solutions, Inc., InnerPulse, Inc., TransEnterix, Inc. (a surgery company developing the world's first patient-side robotic surgical system for single incision surgery), Interventional Autonomics Corporation, NeuroTronik Limited, and Aegis Surgical Limited and Atrius Limited ( two Irish-based companies in the structural heart field). The start-up companies Bill has co-founded today represent over $4 billion in annual revenues and he is responsible for raising over $250M in private and public capital for these development stage companies.

Bill and Dana Starling

Bill serves on the Stanford Stroke Center's Board of Advisors at the Stanford University Medical Center. He also serves on the Kenan-Flagler Business School Board of Visitors (Chairman 2009-2014), Chairman of the UNC/NCSU Department of Biomedical Engineering Industry Advisory Board and the Chancellor's Innovation Circle at the University of North Carolina at Chapel Hill where he frequently guest lectures to undergraduate and graduate students on entrepreneurism. He is the recipient of the 2016 UNC Kenan-Flagler Leadership Award, awarded annually to an alumnus for exceptional achievement in a career field, personal endeavor or service to UNC Kenan-Flagler.

## 50. JIM STONEHAM
*Senior---5'10"---175---Has been hampered with a bad ankle.*

Jim played defensive end for us in 1970. He was a worker and always was trying to improve as a player. Jim wanted to contribute to our team and make it better as well as wanting to play himself. He had a very tough first two years since he was so small, but his senior year, he was 6' tall and weighed 175 pounds. Jim had hurt his ankle about two weeks prior to the beginning of football practice, and that hampered him all season. He played for us as a substitute especially when we ran into a lot of injuries as we progressed through the season.

**Jim's Memories/Reflections:**

He remembers the tradition of Broughton football as he grew up in Raleigh. He did not play until his sophomore year at Broughton; he thought he would have a chance to make the team since Sanderson High School had opened up that year and many players from the previous year were going to Sanderson. At the beginning of summer practice, he missed running the mile in time by just a few seconds. The new day he came back and ran it in 6:26, making it just in time; he was very proud of that since his ankle was bothering him quite a bit. Jim started the 2nd game of the season as a defensive end against Winston-Salem Reynolds. He played well and recovered a fumble, but remembers allowing one of the Reynolds runners to get outside of him on a couple plays. The next game Jim was replaced by Wells Edmundson, but did play in games the rest of the season. He said his vision was bad and he wore glasses, but did not wear them in ball games. "I was blind as a bat and could hardly follow the action on the field from the sidelines. I wish I had had contacts."

Some of the specific things he remembers are:

- Senior leadership: Mark Shaner, Jimmy Durham, George Lattimore, Doug Murray, Preston Ruth, David Dupree, Phil Ficklin, Roland Massey, Jim Little, Kent Kistler, Steve Brewbaker, John Clark, John Holding,

Charles King, Billy Starling.

- 4$^{th}$ quarter drills, enough said.

- Losing Jim Lumsden in the Fayetteville game; he was having a great year.

- The loss to Fayetteville was very disheartening, but I believe our determination to succeed grew out of that game.

- Changing to the 4-4 defense, great move mid-season, carried us to the playoffs.

- John Holding's punting was a great asset to our field position.

- Team chemistry, we really came together and fought as a unit.

- The Goldsboro game, hardest hitting game I have ever seen at the high school level.

- Underdogs, we were the only ones that thought we could do it. Our team reminds me of the 1983 NCSU Basketball team that won the National Championship.

- The coaching staff did an outstanding job, fresh, energetic, and inspirational...the year was a perfect conversion of the intangibles required to make an improbable run at a championship. I really believed that you would make another run the next year with the base of talent returning, until busing scrambled the magic of 1970.

- The 1970 Broughton football team was a special unit. It set the tone for the school year, one I refer to as the last great year of Broughton High School. I know that is not true, but it was an incredible year.

**Jim's Bio:**

Jim is in business development in logistics in Raleigh. He has two children.


### 51. DICKIE THOMPSON

*Junior---5 8"---150---Good desire all the time---Looks good at defensive back.*

Dickie played in our defensive backfield. He was a lot like our other backs and players in that he was a hustler. He played behind the senior defensive backs who were good. He certainly made his contribution in the secondary as we had several injuries during the season. Dickie was very dependable and reliable, so he was first to go in when we were hurt by injuries. Dickie's father, Hal Thompson hired a lot of Broughton people to work for his construction company during the summer. Several players on the championship team along with Coach John Thomas worked for Thompson Construction Company. Dickie and his brother took over the company several years ago.

### Dickie's Memories/Reflections:

1. I remember that season got started off to a bad start for me, beginning with the very first day of practice. We had to run on the track for a certain amount of time to see how far we could go. I had always trained the opposite way by running a certain distance and then seeing how long it took me. We all had to do the running test to check our fitness and I was concerned that if I went out too fast I would "run out of gas." So I held back and ended up with "too much left in the tank" and did not pass the running test. Coach Riggs came up to me afterwards and said he was surprised that I wasn't in better shape. I was so embarrassed because I really had worked out hard all summer and had done a lot of distance running. Everyone that didn't pass the test had to do it again the next day after practice. I ran the test again and easily made it making sure that I went all out that time. I caught a lot of good natured grief from teammates!

2. I knew that we had the makings of good team but certainly didn't have any idea that the season would turn out as it did. The players like me who came from Daniels Jr. High played on 2 undefeated teams there during our 8th and 9th grade years. When we got to Broughton in the 10th grade, we had new teammates from Martin Jr. High who was our big junior high rival. Instead of them being our opponents, they were now going to be our teammates which took some time to accept. We were competing for starting positions and had some pretty tough scrimmages. We went undefeated that 10th grade season. Being at Broughton which was such a big school was a big adjustment and being on both the football and track teams gave me a sense of place which helped me make the transition from junior high to high school.

3. I was a defensive back and played backup to the senior starters, Jimmy Durham, Preston Ruth, David Dupree, and John Holding who were all really good players. However, I did get quite a bit of playing time when one of them got injured or needed a break. I also

played on special teams. I always was thankful for my playing time and felt the coaches tried hard to let everyone play a role in the success of the team. I also felt we had a "team" feeling with the n o n starters treated no differently than the starters. I remember one of the home games we played at Devereux Meadow, I hit my left hand on the top of someone's helmet breaking my thumb. I didn't tell anyone about it because I was worried that I would have to come out of the game and miss my playing time. I have a big knot on my thumb joint as a reminder. I don't regret that decision.

4. I remember that bus ride back after we lost to Fayetteville. We pretty much got roughed up down there and Jim Corter got knocked so hard that he had a concussion. It seemed like a very long bus ride back which was mostly very quiet. I remember Coach Riggs talking to us on the bus on the way home. He didn't scream and tell us how sorry we played that night. He told us how much talent we had on the team and that if we would play as a team and not individuals, we could accomplish great things. How true! I truly believe that was the best coaching he did all year. He was such a motivator and knew how to reach us. We knew he cared for us and the players (me included) loved him for caring about us. Even when we didn't live up to our potential. I think that game was our last loss.

5. I remember how shocked I was coming out on the field during the Championship game at Carter Finley to see how many people were in the stands. Wow! The citizens of Raleigh really got behind the team.

6. I remember the football banquet after the season at the Sir Walter Hotel on Fayetteville Street. Very fancy and nicely done. It was my first introduction to Baked Alaska which we had for dessert. I still have my trophy on the shelf in my study at home.

7. I remember how disappointed I was to learn after my junior year that I was being transferred to Sanderson High School due to the forced busing policy of the school system. I personally went before the School Board (pretty intimidating for a 17 year old at the time) and asked them to let me stay at Broughton for my senior year. I was turned down and assigned to Sanderson, which looking back really rocked my world. New school, new coaches, new teammates, and I

think I only knew about 5 people in the entire school. I was thinking about not going out for football until one night when Sanderson football coach Jim Brown called me and said he really wanted me on his team which really lifted my spirits. I worked out extremely hard that summer because I knew I would have to prove myself all over again. On top of all that, Ligon High School was being closed and being split up into thirds with the students going to Broughton, Sanderson, and Enloe. Very difficult times to say the least. Fights in the hallways, fights at football practice mostly between black and white players and black and white coaches not getting along at times. I guess I was lucky in that I wasn't from Sanderson or Ligon and wasn't really looked at as being on one side or the other. I really liked Coach Brown as a person and knew he was going through a very difficult time, just as all the other schools at the time. I think I had a good year playing at Sanderson which went to the State playoffs. A very talented team but too fragmented and no sense of team to be a champion.

8. While at Sanderson we had to play against my old teammates at Broughton and Enloe during the season. When we played Broughton I was fortunate enough to intercept one of David Turner's passes and ran it back for a touchdown helping to win the game. Playing against my good friends on the Broughton team was strange because I felt like I was still a part of them but I was still competitive enough that I really wanted to beat them. When we played Enloe, I remember having to key on my friend Jim Bass who was Enloe's best player. He was quick and shifty and he got by me more than once. A great player.

9. Lastly, Coach Riggs, I just want you to know how blessed I was to have had you for a coach. You made a lasting impact on my life. You weren't afraid to show us your love for Christ and your love for us. Even us non-stars. I think being a part of that team helped prepare me for the rest of life, both good and bad. And thank you for letting us know your beautiful wife, Marie. We all thought she was gorgeous! Also thank you for that coaching staff you put together that year. Robby Evans and Coach Thomas were great coaches and so approachable.

**Dickie's Bio:**

Dickie is a lifelong resident of Raleigh whose family has a long history in Raleigh dating back over 100 years. After being educated in the Raleigh City School system, Dickie attended NC State University where he received a BS degree in civil engineering. While at State, he served as president of Theta Chi Fraternity. Professionally, he has worked for over 38 years in his family's general contracting company, J.M. Thompson Co. which constructs commercial building projects in Raleigh and throughout the state of North Carolina.

Although new to the City Council (elected to Raleigh City Council in 2016), he certainly isn't new to community involvement. Dickie is currently the chairman of the Raleigh Durham Airport Authority and is the past chairman of the Raleigh Planning Commission. He is the council's liaison to the Raleigh Little Theatre, Raleigh Convention Center & Performing Arts Complex Commission, and the Parks Recreation and Greenway Advisory Board. He has formerly served on the Raleigh YMCA Board of Directors, Hayes Barton United Methodist Church Board of Trustees, and the Board of the Raleigh Rescue Mission.

Dickie and Angie Thompson

Dickie has spent many enjoyable years coaching youth teams in Raleigh Little league baseball, CASL soccer, and YMCA & Salvation Army basketball leagues.

He has a special passion for mission outreach with his church and has gone on many Appalachian Service Project (ASP} trips with high school students. He has also made multiple mission trips to Central America and Haiti to aid with the earthquake relief effort.

His hobbies include cycling, golf, hiking, yard work, and time with family and friends at Emerald Isle.

Dickie and his wife, Angie, have been married for 37 years and were blessed with a daughter Lauren, son Travis and his wife Elizabeth.

## 52. DAVID TURNER

*Junior---5' 10"---145---Good athlete---Quarterback on undefeated Junior varsity team last year.*

David Turner was the perfect quarterback for this team. He was a good solid runner. He threw the football with a lot of zip on it and could throw the long ball if necessary. He knew the game well and could control the team and the game itself. I allowed David to call his own plays, at times, in the huddle because I trusted him and he knew the players in the huddle as well as I did or even better. As I have said before, coaches can take the game away from players if they are not careful, but with David Turner I wanted him to be able to take control. David knew his limitations at the quarterback position and did an outstanding job at playing within himself.

The other thing I remember was that this team had great respect for David and trusted him with the game. David was patient and very seldom got rattled due to mistakes he or we made. He was a fiery leader and knew when to talk firmly and hard with his teammates, and he knew when he needed to encourage them.

David talked a lot about the toughness of the senior class and how he thought that was a major part of the success for the 1970 team. David remembers that many of the players on the team were very smart. Jim Corter made 1600 on the SAT if he remembers correctly and Jim Corter is now a professor at Columbia University.

Mrs. Jean Turner, David's mother, remembers the friends of David. She was shocked one day when she came home and found David making sandwiches for lunch and she saw two long big black legs in the kitchen. She went in and met Phil Spence, who was a basketball teammate of

David's at Broughton. She was shocked to find a black person in her home, but certainly accepted Phil. It was just a sign of the times.

David went on to South Carolina on a football scholarship. He gave up football, but he did the pole vault on USC's track team for a season. After a couple years at South Carolina, he transferred to Appalachian State University in Boone along with his good friend, Jim Bass.

David was in a bad automobile accident later when he was working in Virginia. The doctors did not know whether he would live or die for a while. He stayed in the hospital in Virginia for several weeks, and then his family had him moved to Rex Hospital in Raleigh. I remember visiting him in the hospital, and he was injured pretty badly. He has recovered now, but still has some bone and muscle problems, but is playing a lot of golf. He has fought back from this accident and injuries and lives in Wilmington, N.C.

**David's Memories/Recollections:**

(David's written memories and reflections are in the Introduction. He was kind enough to allow me to use many of his thoughts and memories in the Introduction to this book. You can tell he is quite a writer.)

**David's Bio:**

Many years have gone by since our 1970 Championship season, but, rest assured, it was one of and possibly the best year of my life and I'm sure for many others who were a part of it all. Occupation and jobs history to me is non-essential. I have made a comfortable life from the jobs I have had and I have been able to help support my family. For that, I am proud. That is about all I have to say about that. The biggest and most influential happenings can be summarized into 4 events. I will give them to you in chronological order, not necessarily in order of importance. I have also taken the liberty to provide a sort of "life lesson learned" comment on each. At least that's the way I look at it…This may be a little more or maybe a little less than what a "bio" is supposed to be but it's what I have:

1) In 1977 I was in a bad automobile accident which from which I was lucky to survive. It left me with greatly diminished physical capacities from what I had been accustomed to and frankly had taken for granted. The moral here is to be thankful for everything you have. Never take your health for granted and no matter how bad you may believe you

have been circumstantially compromised, there are many who have it much worse than yourself yet do much more with it than many ever accomplish. And always give thanks for those who help you through any time of need for they are God's angels.

2) I was extremely lucky to find a woman who I love and who loves me. We got married in 1988. That is a blessing that cannot be understated. We are way too fragile and needy to traverse this world alone. It may be a family member or the person you love and share your life with, but I would think it is a lonely and difficult life without someone to share it with on a day to day basis. Her name now is Cindy Turner.

David Turner

3) My wife blessed us with a son Taylor who has no idea how much I really love him and I am not so sure he needs to know. At times, it becomes overwhelming to me and I am not sure that is such a good thing. All he really needs to do is live a good and honest life, treat others well and follow his heart while putting others ahead of himself as much as possible. What more can a parent ask?

4) My dad Craven Turner died in 1997. I miss him every day. I can only hope he knows. There is so much I wish I could share with him today and let him see again all those he loved and those who loved him. Sadly, my son doesn't really remember him. My mom is still with us and is doing great at 93 years. She is everything you could ever want your mother to be. We are all blessed to have her.

I would be remiss not to add how much it means to have had that "once in a lifetime" experience with so many people who are still some of my best friends to this day. We shared something that we are all so lucky to have been a part of together. We may not even realize how much. That year bonds us all in a way that almost defies explanation. Many of that group are no longer with us but so many still are. I personally want to thank all of you for being part of a most important and unique time that will bond us together for the rest of our lives.

## 53. PAUL USSERY

*Junior--- 5' 11"---180---Inexperienced, but is a hustler---Wants to learn.*

Paul played in the offensive line for us. He was not a starter, but gave his all in practice for this team. Like several juniors on this team, he had very good and talented people playing in front of him who were seniors. This did not hinder him in any way from being the very best teammate he could be.

### Paul's Memories/Reflections:

What I remember most about the special 1970 team is the closeness and many friendships of the team. I also remember you and all of the coaches preaching that we were ALL links in the chain and no one person can break the chain.

I truly believe the closeness of the team and striving to play as a TEAM and not as a bunch of individuals led to our success! I learned like so many others from that team that if you strive toward goals, work harder than anyone, play as a team, by the rules and move forward you will succeed. The best athletes always do not win and we certainly were not the most talented.

### Paul's Bio:

After graduation from Broughton, I attended NCSU and majored in Business Administration. I worked in New York and the DC area for Department of Defense, Technology, and Software companies in senior financial and business management positions.

I have been married to my best friend and the love of my life Louise for over 35 years, (February 14, 1981). She worked for a major Department of Defense contractor in senior Human Resources positions.

We have a daughter Lisa who is 30 years old and has worked as a veterinarian technician for 10 years. Lisa recently moved to Palm Coast, Florida and just purchased a home about ten miles from us.

Louise and I both retired at the end of December 2014 and moved from Fairfax, Virginia to Palm Coast, Florida in April 2015.

Our favorite vacation has probably been going to Cancun. Now that we are retired and settled in Florida we will be planning some special vacations and getaways.

Paul and Louise Ussery

## 54. TOM WAGONER

Tom was the Sports Information Director for Broughton football and worked closely with the Broughton Athletic Department. He and his staff worked hard to compile as accurate and complete information as possible about the 1970 Broughton football season and published all in a pre-season brochure. Its purpose was to give the students and fans a better understanding of the BHS football team and to provide the members of the press, radio, and television information for their coverage. I was so impressed that Tom had done such an excellent job on the pre-season comments and organization. It was done with a lot of class and excellence.

### 55. HARRISON WARD

Harrison was one of the managers on our team. Harrison was always very involved in everything we did on the football field. He did his job as a manager plus more, as I remember. Harrison and Robbie Jones made sure we had all the shields, footballs, tees, towels, and pads ready for all our practices. He and all the managers were also responsible for having water ready and available for the players during our practices and games. He and Robbie were totally involved in their jobs as managers but were also rabid fans of their team. If I am not mistaken, I think both Harrison and Robbie had flags thrown against them during the season. Of course, I was not happy with that since our team was penalized, but that shows you their love for the Caps.

#### Harrison's Memories/Reflections:

Robbie Jones and I had known each other since the 7th grade at Martin Jr. High School. We had both been equipment managers the year before; that was a big help going into the '70 season. The all-new coaching staff and their work ethic made for a better environment, and Robbie and I really felt like we as managers contributed to the team.

Team Memories:

- Mark Shaner and Phil Ficklin showing up for 2-a-days with full beards.

- Charles Banks would come home with me to eat lunch between practices. My parents were in Europe and my mother had left my brother and I enough food for an army.

- Bob Womble would help us load out for game nights and we would help him with all the tape jobs. Trading out jobs helped a lot.

- Bob, Robbie and I would get into the coaches' locker room and would "borrow" their purple knit shirts to wear for the games. I guess they eventually figured it out!

- Learning that a flock of geese flying overhead in their V is a sign of good luck. Back then Canada geese were not a common sight, but that happened every week at practice at least the last half of the season and to cheers from everyone.

- Driving my mom's car onto the field at Devereux Meadow to unload and load all the equipment for games.

- Buying game and bus tickets for my parents during lunch at the cafeteria.

- Watching Charles King run right in front of me along the sideline after catching his TD pass in the Championship game. He later told me at Jim Bass' Wake that was the only pass he caught all year.

- I also felt that there was never a sense of urgency during that season. Even though we lost some early games we probably should not have, everybody still seemed to know that we were winners. Unscored on in the last 5 games proved that point.

Those are some of my memories, but what does EVERYBODY remember EVERY TIME WE GET TOGETHER? The unsportsmanlike conduct penalty that I got at Fayetteville Terry Sanford. Even managers can get that call I guess. Unfortunately Robbie Jones passed away about 2004. We were kind of a Mutt and Jeff duo, but David Reynolds later said it was as if we really loved it and we did.

**Harrison's Bio:**

In 1975 I eventually started my college career at Atlantic Christian College in Wilson, N.C. I graduated in 1980 and moved back to Raleigh to work for WATCO Corporation, a Raleigh based mechanical contracting business where I still work. My main duty is estimating, but I wear many hats including selling our sheet metal shop fabrication.

While I was at Atlantic Christian, I met Kathy Marcom from Garner who was in nursing school there and we married in 1981. Our oldest son Cameron was born in 1985 and our youngest Robert was born in 1990. Cameron is a Project Manager for Sullivan Eastern Contracting in Morrisville and Robert lives in Wilson and works for BB&T in their offices.

In 2006 we moved to the southern part of Wake County near Willow Springs and I still live there. Sadly Kathy passed away in 2010 with cancer. I enjoy working in my yard, fishing, hunting, anything outdoors. I hope to work just a couple of more years and retire. That part is still up in the air, but I look forward to it.

Harrison Ward

## 56. BERNARD WILLIAMS

*Junior---6'---152---Looks good at offensive and defensive end---Good desire.*

Bernard was a wonderful asset to our State Championship team due to his fun-loving attitude and spirit. He contributed a lot by being willing to serve on the scout team and making his teammates better as he improved himself at the same time. Bernard played on special teams and always was hustling to make plays. He played offensive and defensive end and was always eager and ready when he was called upon.

### Bernard's Memories/Reflections:

Bernard grew up in the Oberlin Road neighborhood, which was a black neighborhood near Broughton High School. Bernard, as other black players, had experienced quite a bit of discrimination and racial prejudice by white teachers, students and people in general.

Bernard attended Daniels Middle School in 7th - 9th grades, where he was called out by a white coach to fight him if he wouldn't do exactly as the coach said. Bernard said he was just a kid and here this coach wanted to fight him.

His mother and father had split up early in his life, and he was living with his father. Bernard played baseball, football, and basketball as he was growing up, but neither of his parents ever saw him play a game in any organized sport at school. That disappointed him a lot, as you can imagine. His mother did come to the State Championship banquet held at the Sir Walter Raleigh Hotel after the season, and that made him very happy and proud.

When he came to Broughton as a tenth grader, he had a lot of respect for Broughton and the former players who were ahead of him. Bernard credits sports for keeping him out of trouble all through his middle school and high school years. He was influenced by Eric Handy's father, who was a teacher and coach at the all-black Ligon High School. He was good friends with Eric and Mr. Handy was a good role model for him as a father and citizen.

Bernard remembers me pulling him over one day in practice and saying, "You have been smoking, haven't you, Bernard?" He admitted it, and I told him he did not need to be smoking, that it was not healthy, and if he did it again, he would be kicked off the team.

Bernard, overall, has fond memories from pre-game meals in the cafeteria where we had roast beef or hamburger, salad, potatoes, and iced tea. He said Larry Height always was asking for anyone's potato peel to eat. Ligon and Hillside were both all-black high schools in 1970, but were both in the same 4-A Football Conference with Broughton, Enloe, and Sanderson. In 1971, when Ligon High School was closed due to integration, Bernard was called "nigger" by some white people and "Uncle Tom" by some of the black players from Ligon. He and some of the black athletes who had been attending Broughton before that time, were caught between a rock and a hard place in many ways. He said it was tough to live in "both worlds" and get along with everyone. However, Bernard was never one to back down from anyone and tried to stand up for what he believed, but it was a difficult time to be doing that in the 1970's.

Bernard was the player who shared his football cleats with Eric Handy during the Dudley playoff game in Greensboro. Eric had forgotten one of his cleats in the rush to get on the bus and good old Bernard came through by sharing his football cleats. They would swap off as Bernard came off the field from special teams and Eric would go on for offense. True Teammates.

**Bernard's Bio:**

Bernard felt like the disciplining from the mile, fourth quarter drills, and football in general prepared him for the Navy, which he joined after graduating from Broughton in 1972. Bernard was able to travel in the Navy and was with the 7th Fleet out of Norfolk, Virginia. After the Navy, Bernard attended Wake Tech and got his machinist degree and used that to work his way up in several companies in the Cary and Raleigh area. He worked for Bristol-Myers for 23 years. Bernard has two daughters who he is close to, and they all live in Raleigh.

Bernard Williams

## 57. BOB WOMBLE

Bob was trainer for the Broughton High School football team in 1970. He was very serious about his job of being student trainer, was very organized and loved his work. I remember Bob being strict with guys with what he expected from them. We only had a whirlpool and two hydrocollator pads for injuries, but Bob did a great job in spite of this. He did almost all of the taping of players with the assistance sometimes of our managers. He kept a neat training room and was very serious about his responsibility. As I remember, Bob worked well with our managers, players and coaches. He must have been a good trainer to put up with me in my first year of being a head coach. The only teaching and instruction in becoming a high school trainer was a clinic in Greensboro run by Al Proctor, who was the NCSU trainer in 1970. So a lot of what Bob knew he learned on his own.

**Bob's Memories/Reflections:**

While this may seem strange to you, my most vivid memories of the 1970 football team are of the music in the locker room and training room. Songs that stand out are "Joy to the World" by Three Dog Night (which, as a lover of Beach Music, I can't stand), and "Girl Watcher" by the O' Kaysions (much more my style). Any time I hear that Three Dog Night song it immediately reminds me of the locker room. The other thing that strikes me about the 1970 football team is how our regular season games were all over the state, when now the team barely leaves Wake County.

Finally, in retrospect I cannot believe how young you and Coach Evans were. I recall the first time I met you, in mid-summer 1970, when you and Coach Evans gave me a ride home from the NCHSAA annual meeting in Greensboro. I had been attending a clinic for student trainers held in conjunction with the meeting and the annual All-Star games. Looking back, the two of you were just a few months removed from college!

**Bob's Bio:**

After graduating from Broughton, I graduated from Wake Forest University, where I majored in Economics, from the School of Law at Washington and Lee University, and from the School of Law at Georgetown University, where I obtained a Master of Laws in Taxation. I practice corporate and tax law in the Raleigh office of K&L Gates, a large international law firm. I enjoy taking a really complex situation, and working through all of the nuances to help my clients obtain their objectives. I have remained active at Broughton, and about 10 years ago organized the Broughton Capitol Foundation and later served as its President.

For 34 years I have been married to the former Lynn Brady, who grew up in Winston-Salem and graduated from UNC- Chapel Hill (where she was on the tennis team). My son Robert, who is 28, and my daughter Margaret, who is 25, both graduated from Broughton (where Robert was on a State Champion golf team, and where Margaret played soccer and was on the cross-country team), and from Washington and Lee University (where Robert was on the golf team). Both Robert and Margaret live in Atlanta, where they both work in finance. I have attached a picture of my family from late 2010, when we were lucky enough to have a private tour of the West Wing of the White House. The doors right behind us lead to the Oval Office.

Athletically, I enjoy playing golf, paddle boarding, and working out. Lynn and I used to play quite a bit more golf than we do now, but parenting and work cut into that! I try to run or work out in some other way just about every day, and thankfully have been able to avoid ruining my knees, hips, shoulders, etc.

Bob, Robert, Margaret, and Lynn Womble

**The Coaches**

## COACH ROBBIE EVANS

Coach Evans was such a key to our State Championship offense. He was a hard worker and devoted teacher and coach of young men. I regret he left coaching after a couple years because many young people lost out on having him as a role model. However, I know countless others benefited from him entering the ministry and they had the privilege of his leading in various churches in Virginia and North Carolina. Robbie had the experience of playing football at Broughton and at NCSU which made him well-known to many of these players he coached in 1970. He was a demanding and fair coach.

**Coach Robbie Evans's Memories/Reflections:**

What I remember most about the 1970 team is not so much the specifics of games, plays, etc. We certainly had good talent on that team, but I'm not sure it was exceptional talent.

What was exceptional was heart, a belief in each other, and a spirit to persevere! If we coaches taught anything beyond x's & o's, it was the meaning of teamwork. The analogy of the "link in the chain" stands out in my mind. When everyone feels a part of something and puts his best effort forward to do his job unselfishly, good things happen. Football is the ultimate team game, and those young men of the 1970 team, in my mind, epitomized the meaning of teamwork. From starters to those who played sparingly, everyone contributed; everyone made a difference; everyone was a champion! We were fortunate to have that late run to the Championship, but to me, more than winning was our coming together, loving each other, and believing in each other! Though my coaching career was brief, I still remember and shall never forget those great young men and the experiences we had together. These young men blessed us coaches beyond measure; I just hope we blessed their lives to some small degree! I am forever grateful to have had this experience with everyone who was a part of that memorable season! GO CAPS!

**Coach Evans' Bio:**

- Assistant Football Coach, 1970 Raleigh Broughton State Championship Team

- Coached one more year at Broughton, 1971

- Left coaching and teaching and went into family business in Raleigh, 1972

- Married Lavinia Ruth Vann in 1972, one son Samuel Vann Evans, born 1975

- In 1973, followed call to Christian ministry and went to Union Theological Seminary in Richmond, VA
- Graduated from UTS in 1977, Doctor of Ministry
- Served 35 years as a pastor in the Presbyterian Church (USA), retired in 2012
- Officiated high school football for 25 years
- Currently living on small farm in Yadkin County, NC
- Enjoying being a grandfather

Coach Rob and Lavinia Evans

## COACH JOHN THOMAS

Coach Thomas was the leader of our defense in 1970. He helped lead us to the five straight shutouts. I realize the players got the job done, but Coach Thomas had put it together. He was so good in teaching the players what they needed to know. He always was emphasizing the basic fundamentals of the game and that is one of the reasons we had shutouts in the last five games. John was a pleasure to coach with and made such a difference in our team. He was disciplined in all that he did and that overflowed to the players. His humor at times kept me and others loose on the field. He was a "stinkin'" good coach and person. He was a successful head coach at several schools in North Carolina.

**Coach John Thomas' Memories/Reflections:**

I will attempt to give you a history of where I coached, and how long I was there. I will also write whatever memories my brain can formulate. I started at Wendell, starting a football program for grades 6, 7 and 8. I was the only coach, and I had a blast. After the season was over, I thought I knew stuff. I, of course, did not know what I did not know.

I honestly do not remember exactly how I got to Broughton. I don't remember talking to anyone in the Central Office. My only memory is talking to Joel Long a couple of times. That doesn't seem possible but that's all I can remember. I know I was very excited about being on the staff at Broughton.

The season was magical and extremely important to the rest of my career. I, of course, began learning what I knew and what I did not know. That process is still ongoing.

I have many memories of the season. The early practice and the earlier games of the season, I don't remember well. Devereux Meadow is a fuzzy memory. I can visualize the great Jim Bass's run against Sanderson, and a little bit of the playoff game against Goldsboro, but that's about it for the Meadow. I remember getting beat soundly at Terry Sanford and all of us feeling like we were going to win all the rest of our games. The rest of the regular season is not a clear picture at all. The playoffs are a little more focused in my memory. I remember the offense of Goldsboro, sort of a single wing thing, with Myrick at tailback. I don't remember details but I'm pretty sure we won fairly close with a couple great runs by Bass, some timely throws by Turner, and some good team defense.

Somehow we all (I think) scouted Greensboro Dudley the next week and they looked awfully good. I don't recall where we played in Greensboro, but I think the formula was about the same as above, except I remember the game not being as tense as the week before.

The State Championship game is the strongest of the actual game memories. The formula was much the same as the last three or so games. One part of the formula I hadn't mentioned at least for this game was Gary Stainback sticking all of the kick offs in the end zone.

If I tried to name all the starters I could not do it without a program. Part of that is due to so many household moves since that time (with loss of saved programs) and an erosion of my memory capacity. Sometimes names and stuff just come up easily, sometimes not. I believe this: we had some guys that could really play. On defense I would say the secondary was as a group, better than any that I ever had. They were smart, athletic, and knew how to make plays. There were quite a few guys who were playmakers that their size and times would not impress. Like Mark Shaner, Doug Murray, and Wells Edmondson. More contributed but I don't remember their names. I do believe it was your leadership that was the inspiration for so many to over-achieve.

I can't remember how big the o-line was, but I'm guessing less than just about all high school backfields today. You and Robby turned the offense into an efficient one, with only one big time playmaker.

I remember everybody watching for the geese during the playoffs.

And I still remember the thud of a heavy plastic object hitting a somewhat hollow flesh type object. That, of course, was the kick off tee being thrown off the field and hitting you in the throat. Thought that might be the end of you, very concerned, but my young dumb brain seemed stuck on getting the defense ready.

Coach John and Brenda Thomas

**Coach Thomas' Bio:**

1969-70  Wendell

1970-74 Broughton, 2 yr assistant with Dave Riggs, 2 yr assistant with Frank Roberts

1974-77 New Hanover, Head Coach

1977-84 Broughton, Head Coach

1984-87 Cary, Head Coach

1994 Retired from Wake County

## COACH MAC CALDWELL

Coach Caldwell was our Head JV coach in 1970 and he was a good one. Mac also helped coach the ends on the Varsity defense. Mac had more experience in coaching than anyone else on our staff.  I remember he was very steady and consistent in all he did. He certainly added to our Championship season and made a difference in many players' lives he coached over the many years. He helped me remain calm and cool in the midst of the battles.

**Coach Caldwell's Memories/Reflections:**

Coach Caldwell thinks that the youth of our coaching staff helped relate to many of the players in 1970.  He remembers the defense swarming to the ball in every game. Mac helped prepare our JV team for the Varsity. He remembers Wells Edmundson being knocked out in one of the later conference games and insisting on going back into the game. Coach Caldwell told him he could not re-enter because of the danger to him - insightful in 1970 - and refused to allow Wells to play any more that game.

**Mac's Bio:**

—Graduated from Christ School in Asheville

—Joined Navy

—Attended Mars Hill College

—Coached and taught at Ft. Belvoir, Va. for 3 years

—Married his wife Suzie

—Coached at Daniels and Carroll Jr. High School

—Came to Broughton in 1970 and coached football and basketball and tennis

—Retired in 1992

—Has 3 children and lives on Lake Norman in Charlotte, N.C.

## COACH MIKE KRAL

Coach Kral was the only coach that was already at Broughton before 1970 and was the only staff member from the previous coaching staff. He coached the backs on our JV team and helped out in scouting the Varsity's opponents during the season. He would be gone every Friday night to scout, so he did not see us play in live action until the final game of the season. Coach Kral also coached baseball for Broughton and therefore coached some of the players in baseball and football. His work and coaching were a valuable contribution to our program.

### Coach Kral's Memories/Reflections:

His fondest memory is the State Championship game and the uniqueness of it being played in a college stadium. He remembers how speedy Jim Bass and Roland Massey were in both football and baseball. Mike felt like John Holding's punting in several games made such a difference in field position during our run for the Championship.

### Mike's Bio:

- Coach Kral is from Oak Hill, N.C.
- Graduated from UNC-Chapel Hill in 1964.
- Taught and coached in Aberdeen, N.C. 1964-1965.
- Taught History at Broughton 1966-2002.
- Married to Charlotte Edwards Kral who taught at several high schools including Broughton. They have one son, Michael.
- Mike and Charlotte are retired and living in Raleigh.

## COACH DAVID RIGGS:

### Coach Riggs' Memories/Reflections:

This book tells it all for me. I was indeed fortunate to be on this ride with this team and experience the thrill of victory and the agony of defeat as we lived through the 1970 football season together. I learned a lot by coaching this team, but what has been extraordinarily special is reliving it through this book.

### Bio After Broughton:

- Attended Regent College (Vancouver, British Columbia) and Abilene Christian University 1972-73

- Head football coach and history teacher at Cary High School 1973-1979
- Head football coach and history teacher at Athens Drive High School 1979-81
- Minister at Brooks Avenue Church, Raleigh, NC 1981-85
- Minister at University Church in Fairfax, Va. 1985-89
- Head football coach and history teacher at Sanderson High School 1989-99
- Head football coach and history teacher at McDowell High School 1999-2004
- Head football coach and history teacher at Fuquay Varina High School 2004-08
- Head football coach at Holly Springs High School 2010-11
- Retired 2011

Marie and I have been blessed with three children, Ashley (43), Kelly (41), and Gresham (35) whose families all live within 45 minutes of our home in Fuquay Varina. Our five grandchildren, Conner, Alaina, Zane, Maylin, and Landon have brought immense joy to us in our retirement. We still love to study, reflect on and grow in our spiritual lives and relationships with others, to travel in this amazingly beautiful and interesting world we live in, and to spend time with family, immediate and extended.

Marie and David Riggs Celebrating our 47th Anniversary

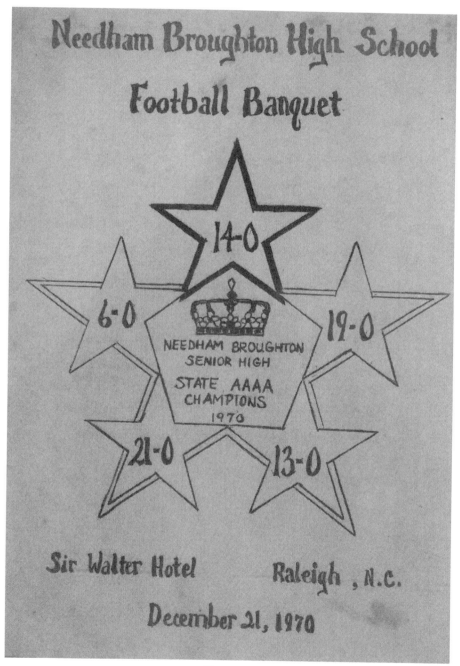

Banquet

## 1970 FOOTBALL RECORD

| | | | |
|---|---|---|---|
| 7 | Broughton | 8 | Grimsley |
| 19 | Broughton | 6 | Reynolds |
| 20 | Broughton | 6 | Enloe |
| 15 | Broughton | 19 | Rocky Mount |
| 21 | Broughton | 0 | Hillside |
| 7 | Broughton | 14 | Fike |
| 16 | Broughton | 7 | Sanderson |
| 7 | Broughton | 28 | Sanford |
| 19 | Broughton | 0 | Ligon |
| 13 | Broughton | 0 | Durham |
| 21 | Broughton | 0 | Dudley |
| 6 | Broughton | 0 | Goldsboro |
| 14 | Broughton | 0 | Olympic |

1970 Schedule

Jim Durham  Mark Shaner  Coach Riggs

CHAMPS!

## EPILOGUE

"Efforts and courage are not enough without purpose and direction."
- John F. Kennedy

That State Championship season is one that stays in a team's memory forever. I have always understood that athletics was much more than just winning a game or coming out on top when you play. Athletics truly is about relationships, competition, life lessons and purpose. But winning is important. If we had been beaten by Olympic in that 1970 Championship game, this book would probably not be written. Also, and even more important, many relationships that evolved through what this team experienced together may not have been as deep or may not even have been maintained like they have been over the years.

After our festive Championship Banquet, I will never forget one of the players coming up to me after receiving his trophy to ask, "Coach Riggs, is this trophy all we get after all of that work, running, playing and winning the State Championship?" That comment had a tremendous impact on me at that time. I went for weeks thinking about what a good question that was. We as coaches, players, parents, and families had put many hours into the football season, going all the way back to the spring of 1970. I thought of all the 16mm films I had watched over the summer in preparation for the season. I thought about all the sacrifices players, parents, coaches, and families had made over the summer and pre-season practices - routines disrupted getting the players to and from practices and games, late meals, untold hours devoted to this season, etc. As I thought about all the sprints, calisthenics, weight lifting, time put into football, and all the planning that went on for months, I became tired myself just thinking about it all. Then the question, "Is this trophy all we get?"

That got me thinking about life and what its purpose is. After these many years, the trophy (and I still have mine) is rusted, broken, and scarred quite a bit. The trophy itself is not worth all the many sacrifices, time spent, hard work, pain, blood and bruised bodies, but it is a symbol and represents all of the above. But much more - what I think we all got out of that season was learning to never give up. We learned how to encourage one another, which is one of the greatest gifts people can give to each other. We learned that when one teammate gets hurt and suffers, we all do, discovering in our hearts that love runs deeper than race, economics, losses, disappointments, athletic abilities, and much more. That trophy represents all the funny stories, heartaches, victories, and camaraderie we were able to experience together. I realize that experiencing that football season and all that came with it by myself would have been so empty and unfulfilling. But experiencing that season with other people who committed themselves and participated on that team was exceptionally fulfilling and worthwhile.

I was 24 years old, fresh out of graduate school, in my first job as a young inexperienced coach and school teacher, and I am not sure if I ever had given much thought to, "What is life all about?" I remember the song, "What's It All About, Alfie?" But after that Championship season, the question asked to me, "Is that all we get?" and the fact that as a first year coach, I had been blessed to have been a part of a team who "won it all," a goal that probably all coaches dream of, I found myself asking the deeper question, "What is life all about?" This truly began a life-long journey of trying to discover the answer to that question. We seem to mess life up in all kinds of ways with our self-centeredness, greed, working our way to the top, trying to get to be #1 regardless of how we get there and stepping on others to win out. This question of, "Is this all there is?" launched me on a journey to answer that deeper question, trying to find the purpose of life, and to live it.

The following spring after the State Championship, the Raleigh School System decided to close Ligon High School for the 1971-72 school year and follow through with the forced busing in order to get full integration. The 1954 Brown vs. Board of Education Supreme Court decision had declared that segregation was no longer legal, but complete integration of black and white students in schools did not take place until the 1970's in most places in the South.

That is a different story, another story perhaps for another time. Things would radically change, and many friends and relationships were affected due to the fact that students were assigned to different schools based on where they lived. We lost a good number of players from the Championship team to Enloe and Sanderson.

I decided to leave Broughton after my 2nd year there, not because of the changes in the school system but because there was a void in my life. Even though I had helped lead a team to the N.C. State Football Championship, there were questions resonating in my mind like:

Who is God?

What is God's purpose in my life?

Where did the Bible come from and why should I believe it?

What am I supposed to be doing with the rest of my life?

I left coaching and teaching to seriously pursue answers to some of these questions I had about life, God, and my purpose, questions that had surged in my mind after the 1970 Championship. Marie and I decided to take at least a year off from teaching, and I resigned from Broughton in the spring of 1972. We had come in contact with Regent College in Vancouver, British Columbia in Canada through a former Broughton and UNC football player, Bill Brafford. I had coached Bill when I was on the UNC Freshman football staff and we had stayed in touch when I went to Broughton to coach. Bill had attended Regent one summer and was excited about it. Regent was a trans-denominational school started by an Oxford University professor, Dr. James Houston, for people who already were in a profession, but wanted to study the Bible, God, and religion and seek to better integrate them into their daily lives. That sounded good to me, so Marie and I rented our house in Raleigh, packed up our clothes and a little camping equipment in our new station wagon (the only new car we have ever bought), and began the journey camping across the U.S. on our way to Vancouver, British Columbia.

After spending the year studying the Bible and pursuing the question of what is life all about, I found enough answers to satisfy myself. I did find some answers after studying, discussing, and reflecting on the Bible and on Jesus. The funny thing is the answers were demonstrated in that 1970 season in so many ways. What I mean by that is that life is all about relationships, loving and caring for others and enjoying these relationships, about living each day fully and being the best you can be in every phase of life, no matter what life hands you. If I (we) would devote myself to doing these things, this world would definitely be a better place. I decided to return to coaching and teaching and was offered the Cary High School head football job in 1973. I knew I could impact others by coaching and teaching in high school. Over the years, Marie and I began asking players to our home, which we had barely done at Broughton, about four or five players every Wednesday evening for her spaghetti, homemade bread and brownies during football season, a tradition that our entire family came to love.

As I have been writing this book, I have come to realize how much this team has meant to me and to each other. This special season laid the foundation for much of my coaching philosophy from 1970 until I retired in 2011. As I look back at the seven different high schools where I coached, I realize I built on the foundation I learned from these young men in 1970. I always continued to learn from others and develop my own philosophy. In the 1990's I wrote an article that summarized my coaching philosophy that had started with that special Caps team:

### Football is More than a Game

There are a lot of things going on in our society today that concern me. The enemy of American growth, as I see it, is the potential within ourselves to become lazy, to slow down, to get discouraged, to quit, to fail in self-discipline, and to lack creativity and commitment to working together.

With many discouraging things happening in our society, I see the game of football as a great avenue to teach much about life. There are many valuable lessons to be gained from participating in football on the high school level. In the right perspective, I believe that football can be one of the most wholesome, exciting, and valuable activities in which any young man can participate. It teaches boys to work hard, to have control of themselves, to gain self-respect, to give forth great effort, and at the same time to learn to follow the rules of the game, and to respect the rights of others, and to stay within the bounds dictated by decency and sportsmanship.

Football teaches people how to "win." I am not talking about just winning a ball game, but winning the battle over "self." Sure, winning the game is important, but learning to develop poise, confidence, and pride in oneself and one's undertakings is the real objective of "winning" football. We need to remember that being a winner does not mean that you always win the game, but it has to do with striving to do one's best.

I feel that high school football is a great way to build any young man's overall character and therefore his life. Character develops from hard work, from never giving up, from helping each other to be one's best, from striving for unity in working with each other, and from being proud of doing one's best. Playing football is great, but we must never lose sight of the fact that it is just a game, that it is a means to an end. We should encourage the boys to work hard and enjoy it, but never forget that you cannot play football all your life.

I really believe football is one of the greatest games in the world. I have played and coached both on the high school and college level. Football has taught me how to work hard and play hard with my fellow man in the true spirit of sportsmanship. If you let it, and with the right kind of leadership, football will give you some permanent values that will make you a better citizen and a better human being. I would like to encourage any young man to join our football program.

Much of what I learned about coaching AND LIFE is from that miraculous season of 1970 made up of a group of young men who loved to play the game unselfishly. Even though I have had similar teams, none quite was so special as The Caps and their 1970 Championship Team.

"When you can do the common things of life in an uncommon way,
you will command the attention of the world."
- George Washington Carver

1970 Champions

Is this all we get?

## ACKNOWLEDGEMENTS

Tim Stevens, sports writer for the Raleigh-based News and Observer, wrote an article in 2004 about the 1970 Broughton State Championship football team. In response, several players across the country and locally sent him emails about that season. Tim was kind enough to send them to me when I was coaching at Fuquay Varina. All of that renewed my thinking about how special this team was, and it was the beginning of the journey of writing this book. In 2010 soon after retiring from coaching, I had the opportunity to be with several former Broughton players, and we had a tremendous time recalling memories and events of that Championship season. Then this book truly began and I began to relive it.

I have always believed, and still do, that a head football coach gets far too much credit for having success with a team. The players on this team have given me too much credit for our Championship season. I would love to say that I deserve it, but I know better. It truly was a TEAM Championship and <u>everybody</u> - from the players and the coaching staff to the administration, parents and families, cheerleaders and students  - contributed to the magic and success of that season.

Often one person writes a book and this book was written primarily by me, but I do not think of myself as a writer. I am a coach and teacher. This book comes alive only because of the many insightful, caring, unique, and brilliant people who have contributed to it. In fact, it does come alive and is so meaningful because it was lived out.

I would like to acknowledge my gratitude to many people who have helped make this book a possibility. First of all, Stuart Albright, who was the first person I called several years ago when I was writing my first book for my grandchildren. He has been very encouraging in the years I have known him and I deeply appreciate his wisdom, guidance, and experience in helping me complete this task. Stuart has written several books about high school football and students he has taught and coached. He has taught Creative Writing at Jordan High School for 15 years and coached football there also. He has had a tremendous impact on so many young people.

I am also so thankful to Roland Massey who encouraged me and motivated me to write this book. Roland, who played wingback for this 1970 team, was diagnosed with cancer about 6 years ago. Every time he and I met for coffee or lunch he would say, "Coach, you need to write that book." I regret that he is not here (along with several others from this team) to read it, but his spirit is throughout the pages of this book. He is a big part of it being completed.

I am grateful that Jane Holroyd and other cheerleaders had enough foresight to make an incredible scrapbook of the Championship season and present it to me and Marie for Christmas in 1970. This was long before "scrapbooking" became popular, but their work of putting together each game's paper clippings from the News and Observer were a tremendous part of this book. There are other photographs, keepsakes and special football articles in this scrapbook which make it truly one of a kind.

Obviously, the players and coaches on this team are the primary contributors to the story of the season in 1970. Over the past five years I have been able to spend time with many of the players and all of the coaches to catch up and share, and have been able to track down almost, but sadly not all, of the players to renew contact with them. Through emails, phone calls and times spent with them, they have shared where and who they are now, their memories of 1970 and their reflections about what we experienced together and learned during that unforgettable football season. Their stories are the true treasure in this book.

I cannot thank my wife enough for her continued enthusiasm, interest in and encouragement to me for writing this book. No one will enjoy this book more than she will. She has cried, laughed, cheered, and talked about this season and especially about the boys who made this all possible. She has served as my critic, editor, and encourager. Probably as much as anything, she has been a great listener. Thanks, my love, for being my assistant coach and my best friend all these years.

Made in the USA
Columbia, SC
28 April 2022